FOUNDATIONS OF THE AMERICAN ECONOMY

THE AMERICAN COLONIES FROM INCEPTION TO INDEPENDENCE

VOLUME V

FOUNDATIONS OF THE AMERICAN ECONOMY

THE AMERICAN COLONIES FROM INCEPTION TO INDEPENDENCE

Edited by
Marianne Johnson
Steven G. Medema
Warren J. Samuels

VOLUME V

Mercantilism and Colonialism, Part II

Routledge
Taylor & Francis Group

LONDON AND NEW YORK

First published 2003 by Pickering & Chatto (Publishers) Limited

Published 2016 by Routledge
2 Park Square, Milton Park, Abingdon, Oxon OX14 4RN
711 Third Avenue, New York, NY 10017, USA

Routledge is an imprint of the Taylor & Francis Group, an informa business

BRITISH LIBRARY CATALOGUING IN PUBLICATION DATA

Foundations of the American Economy: the American Colonies from Inception to Independence
  1. Economics – United States – Sources 2. United States – Economic conditions –
  Sources 3. United States – Economic policy – Sources
  I. Samuels, Warren J. (Warren Joseph), 1933- II. Johnson, Marianne III. Medema,
  Steven G. IV. From theocracy to secular, materialist commercial society V. Individu-
  alism and the structure of power VI. Colonial money, credit and debt VII. Mercantilism and colonialism, part I VIII. Mercantilism and colonialism, part II
  330.9'73

LIBRARY OF CONGRESS CATALOGING-IN-PUBLICATION DATA

Foundations of the American Economy. 1. The American Colonies from Inception to Independence / edited by Marianne Johnson, Warren J. Samuels, and Steven G. Medema
  p.cm
  Includes index.
  Contents: v.1. From theocracy to secular, materialist commercial society – v.2. Indi-
  vidualism and the structure of power – v.3. Colonial money, credit and debt – v.4.
  Mercantilism and colonialism, pt. 1 – v.5. Mercantilism and colonialism, pt.2.
  1. Economics – United States – History. 2. United States – Economic conditions – To
  1865. I. Johnson, Marianne. II. Samuels, Warren J., 1933- III. Medema, Steven G.

HB119 .E17 2001
330'.0973'09032-dc21

                                                                              2001036917

ISBN-13: 978-1-85196-727-8 (set)

New material typeset by
P&C

CONTENTS

AN ENQUIRY INTO THE RIGHTS OF THE BRITISH COLONIES

Richard Bland, *An Enquiry into the Rights of the British Colonies; Intended as an Answer to 'The Regulations lately made concerning the Colonies, and the Taxes imposed upon them considered.' in a Letter Addressed to the Author of that Pamphlet* (London, reprinted 1769), pp. 5–23.

Richard Bland (1719–76) was born in Virginia to a respectable family. He was educated at William and Mary College and later at the University of Edinburgh. Bland held a variety of positions in the legislatures and conventions leading up to the War of Independence, including a long-held seat in the Virginia House of Burgesses. Deeply involved in the first Continental Congress and movements against the Navigation and Stamp Acts, Bland was one of the first to sign Virginia's non-importation agreement.

In *An Enquiry into the Rights of the British Colonies*, Bland discusses the distinction between the 'power to tax' and the 'right of Parliament to impose taxes' based on the extent and legality of the representation of the colonies in Parliament. Bland argues in the tradition of John Locke that if citizens are deprived of their natural rights, they should be permitted to leave the society and form another one of their own organisation. Hence, as the Navigation and Stamp Acts violate the rights of the colonists under both the British constitution and the charters granted to the American colonies by Great Britain, Americans had the right to request the removal of the regulations. If the restraints and regulations were not removed, Bland argues, Americans then had the right to rebel. This is an argument that reappears later in this volume, in John Taylor's *Tyranny Unmasked*.

AN ENQUIRY
INTO THE
RIGHTS OF THE BRITISH
COLONIES;

Intended as an Answer to
"THE REGULATIONS LATELY MADE
CONCERNING THE COLONIES AND
THE TAXES IMPOSED UPON THEM
CONSIDERED"
In a Letter addressed to the Author
of that Pamphlet

BY
RICHARD BLAND
OF VIRGINIA

WILLIAMSBURG,
Printed by ALEXANDER PURDIE, and Co.

LONDON,
Re-printed for J. Almon, opposite Burlington-House,
Piccadilly

MDCCLXIX.

An Enquiry into the Rights of the BRITISH Colonies; intended as an Anſwer to " The Regulations lately made concerning the Colonies, and the Taxes impoſed upon them conſidered." In a Letter addreſſed to the Author of that Pamphlet. By RICHARD BLAND, of Virginia.

Dedit omnibus Deus pro virili portione ſapientiam, ut et inaudita inveſtigare poſſent et audita perpendere.

LACTANTIUS.

SIR,

I TAKE the liberty to addreſs you, as the author of " The Regulations lately made concerning the Colonies, " and the Taxes impoſed upon them, conſidered." It is not to the man, whoever you are, that I addreſs myſelf; but it is to the author of a pamphlet, which, according to the light I view it in, endeavours to fix ſhackles upon the *American* colonies: ſhackles which, however nicely poliſhed, can by no means ſit eaſy upon men, who have juſt ſentiments of their own rights and liberties.

You have, indeed, brought this trouble upon yourſelf ; for you ſay, that " many ſteps have been lately taken by the " miniſtry, to cement and perfect the neceſſary connection " between the colonies and the mother-kingdom, which " every man who is ſincerely intereſted in what is intereſting " to his country, will anxiouſly conſider the propriety of, " will enquire into the information, and canvaſs the princi- " ples upon which they have been adopted; and will be " ready to applaud what has been well done, condemn what " has been done amiſs, and ſuggeſt any emendations, im- " provements, or additions, which may be within his know- " ledge, and occur to his reflection."

Encouraged therefore by ſo candid an invitation, I have undertaken to examine, with an honeſt plainneſs and free- dom, whether the miniſtry, by impoſing taxes upon the co- lonies by authority of parliament, have purſued a wiſe and ſalutary plan of government, or whether they have exerted pernicious and deſtructive acts of power.

I pretend not to concern myſelf with the regulations lately made, to encourage population in the new acquiſitions: time

B

caɴ

can only determine, whether the reasons upon which they have been founded, are agreeable to the maxims of trade and found policy, or not. However, I will venture to observe, that if the most powerful inducement towards peopling those acquisitions, is to arise from the expectation of a constitution to be established in them, similar to the other royal government, in *America*, it must be a strong circumstance, in my opinion, against their being settled by *Englishmen*, or even by *foreigners*, who do not live under the most despotic government; since, upon your principles of colony-government, such a constitution will not be worth their acceptance.

The question is, whether the colonies are represented in the *British* parliament, or not? You affirm it to be an indubitable fact that they are represented, and from thence you infer a right in the parliament to impose taxes of every kind upon them. You do not insist upon the *power*, but upon the *right* of parliament, to impose taxes upon the colonies. This is certainly a very proper distinction; as *right* and *power* have very different meanings, and convey very different ideas : for had you told us that the parliament of *Great-Britain* have *power*, by the fleets and armies of the kingdom, to impose taxes, and to raise contributions upon the colonies, I should not have presumed to dispute the point with you ; but as you insist upon the *right* only, I must beg leave to differ from you in opinion, and shall give my reasons for it.

But I must first recapitulate your arguments in support of this right in the parliament. You say, " the inhabitants of the " colonies do not indeed choose members of parliament, nei- " ther are nine-tenths of the people of *Britain* electors ; for " the right of election is annexed to certain species of pro- " perty, to peculiar franchises, and to inhabitancy in some " particular places. But these descriptions comprehend only " a very small part of the lands, the property and people of " *Britain* ; all copyhold, all leasehold estates under the " crown, under the church, or under private persons, though " for terms ever so long; all landed property, in short, that " is not freehold, and all monied property whatsoever, are " excluded. The possessors of these have no votes in the " election of members of parliament; women, and persons " under age, be their property ever so large, and all of it " freehold, have none : the merchants of *London*, a nume- " rous and respectable body of men, whose opulence " exceeds all that *America* can collect; the proprietors of that " vast accumulation of wealth, the public funds ; the inha- " bitants of *Leeds*, of *Halifax*, of *Birmingham*, and of *Man- " chester*, towns that are each of them larger than the largest
" in

" in the plantations ; many of leſſer note, that are incorpo-
" rated ; and that great corporation, the *Eaſt-India* company,
" whoſe rights over the countries they poſſeſs, fall very little
" ſhort of ſovereignty, and whoſe trades and whoſe fleets are
" ſufficient to conſtitute them a maritime power, are all in
" the ſame circumſtances : and yet are they not repreſented
" in parliament ? Is their vaſt property ſubject to taxation
" without their conſent ? Are they all arbitrarily bound by
" laws to which they have not agreed ? The colonies are
" exactly in the ſame ſituation ; all *Britiſh* ſubjects are really
" in the ſame ; none are actually, all are virtually, repre-
" ſented in parliament : for every member of parliament ſits
" in the houſe, not as a repreſentative of his own conſtitu-
" ents, but as one of that auguſt aſſembly by which all the
" commons of *Great-Britain* are repreſented."

This is the ſum of what you advance, in all the pomp of
parliamentary declamation, to prove, that the colonies are repreſented in parliament, and therefore ſubject to their taxation ; but notwithſtanding this way of reaſoning, I cannot
comprehend, how men, who are excluded from voting at the
election of members of parliament, can be repreſented in that
aſſembly ; or how thoſe, who are elected, do not ſit in the
houſe as repreſentatives of their conſtituents. Theſe aſſer-
tions appear to me not only paradoxical, but contrary to the
fundamental principles of the *Engliſh* conſtitution.

To illuſtrate this important diſquiſition, I conceive we
muſt recur to the civil conſtitution of *England*, and from
thence deduce and aſcertain the rights and privileges of the
people, at the firſt eſtabliſhment of the government, and diſcover the alterations that have been made in them from time
to time ; and it is from the laws of the kingdom, founded
upon the principles of the law of nature, that we are to ſhow
the obligation every member of the ſtate is under, to pay
obedience to its inſtitutions. From theſe principles I ſhall
endeavour to prove, that the inhabitants of *Britain*, who have
no vote in the election of members of parliament, are not
repreſented in that aſſembly, and yet that they owe obedience
to the laws of parliament, which, as to them, are conſtitu-
tional, and not arbitrary. As to the colonies, I ſhall conſider them afterwards.

Now it is a fact, as certain as hiſtory can make it, that
the preſent civil conſtitution of *England* derives its original
from thoſe *Saxons*, who, coming over to the aſſiſtance of the
Britons, in the time of their king *Vortigern*, made themſelves
maſters of the kingdom, and eſtabliſhed a form of government in it, ſimilar to that they had been accuſtomed to live
under

under in their native country * ; as fimilar, at leaft; as the difference of their fituation and circumftances would permit. This government, like that from whence they came, was founded upon principles of the moft perfect liberty : the conquered lands were divided among the individuals, in proportion to the rank they held in the nation † ; and every freeman, that is, every freeholder, was a member of their wittinagemot, or parliament ‖. The other part of the nation, or the non-proprietors of land, were of little eftimation §. They, as in *Germany*, were either flaves, mere hewers of wood and drawers of water, or freedmen ; who, being of foreign extraction, had been manumitted by their mafters, and were excluded from the high privilege of having a fhare in the adminiftration of the commonwealth, unlefs they became proprietors of land (which they might obtain by purchafe or donation), and in that cafe they had a right to fit with the freemen in the parliament or fovereign legiflature of the ftate.

How long this right of being perfonally prefent in the parliament continued, or when the cuftom of fending reprefentatives to this great council of the nation, was firft introduced, cannot be determined with precifion ; but let the cuftom of reprefentation be introduced when it will, it is certain that every freeman, or, which was the fame thing in the eye of the conftitution, every freeholder ‡, had a right to vote at the election of members of parliament, and therefore might be faid, with great propriety, to be prefent in that affembly, either in his own perfon, or by reprefentation. This right of election in the freeholders, is evident from the ftatute 1ft *Hen.* 5. ch. 1ft, which limits the right of election to thofe freeholders only who are refident in the counties the day of the date of the writ of election ; but yet every refident freeholder indifcriminately, let his freehold be ever fo fmall, had a right to vote at the election of knights for his county, fo that they were actually reprefented : and this right of election continued until it was taken away by the ftatute 8th *Hen.* 6. ch. 7. from thofe freeholders who had not a clear freehold eftate of forty fhillings by the year at the leaft.

Now this ftatute was deprivative of the right of thofe freeholders who came within the defcription of it ; but of what did it deprive them, if they were reprefented, notwithftand-

* *Petyt's Rights of the Com. Brady's Comp. Hift. Rapin. Squire's Inquiry.*

† *Cæfar de Bell. Gall. Tacitus de Germ.* c. 28. *Temple's Mifc.*   ‖ *Tacitus de Germ.* c. 11.   § *Ibid.* c. 25.
‡ 2 *Inft.* 27. 4 *Inft.* 2.

ing

ing their right of election was taken from them? The mere act of voting was nothing, of no value, if they were reprefented as conftitutionally without it as with it : but when by the fundamental principles of the conftitution they were to be confidered as members of the legiflature, and as fuch had a right to be prefent in perfon, or to fend their procurators or attornies, and by them to give their fuffrage in the fupreme council of the nation, this ftatute deprived them of an effential right ; a right, without which, by the ancient conftitution of the ftate, all other liberties were but a fpecies of bondage.

As thefe freeholders then were deprived of their rights, to fubftitute delegates to parliament, they could not be reprefented, but were placed in the fame condition with the non-proprietors of land, who were excluded by the original conftitution from having any fhare in the legiflature, but who, notwithftanding fuch exclufion, are bound to pay obedience to the laws of parliament, even if they fhould confift of nine-tenths of the people of *Britain*; but then the obligation of thefe laws does not arife from their being virtually reprefented in parliament, but from a quite different reafon.

Men, in a ftate of nature, are abfolutely free and independent of one another, as to fovereign jurifdiction *; but when they enter into a fociety, and by their own confent become members of it, they muft fubmit to the laws of the fociety according to which they agree to be governed; for it is evident, by the very act of affociation, that each member fubjects himfelf to the authority of that body, in whom, by common confent, the legiflative power of the ftate is placed : but though they muft fubmit to the laws, fo long as they remain members of the fociety, yet they retain fo much of their natural freedom, as to have a right to retire from the fociety, to renounce the benefits of it, to enter into another fociety, and to fettle in another country; for their engagements to the fociety, and their fubmiffion to the public authority of the ftate, do not oblige them to continue in it longer than they find it will conduce to their happinefs, which they have a natural right to promote. This natural right remains with every man, and he cannot juftly be deprived of it by any civil authority. Every perfon, therefore, who is denied his fhare in the legiflature of the ftate to which he had an original right; and every perfon, who, from his particular circumftances, is excluded from this great privilege, and refufes to exercife his natural right of quitting the country, but re-

---

* *Vattel's Law of Nature, Locke on Civil Govern. Wollafton's Rel. of Nat.*

minas

mains in it, and continues to exercife the rights of a citizen in all other refpects, muft be fubject to the laws, which by thefe acts he *implicitly*, or, to ufe your own phrafe, *virtually* confents to: for men may fubject themfelves to laws, by confenting to them *implicitly*; that is, by conforming to them, by adhering to the fociety, and accepting the benefits of its conftitution, as well as *explicitly* and directly, in their own perfons, or by their reprefentatives fubftituted in their room *. Thus, if a man whofe property does not entitle him to be an elector of members of parliament, and therefore cannot be reprefented, or have any fhare in the legiflature, " inherits " or takes any thing by the laws of the country to which he " has no indubitable right in nature, or which, if he has a " right to it, he cannot tell how to get or keep, without the " aid of the laws, and the advantage of fociety; then, when " he takes this inheritance, or whatever it is, *with* it he " takes and owns the laws that gave it him.   And fince the " fecurity he has from the laws of the country, in refpect of " his perfon and rights, is the *equivalent* for his fubmiffion to " them, he cannot accept *that* fecurity without being obliged, " in equity, to pay *this* fubmiffion : nay, his very continuing " in the country, fhows, that he either likes the conftitution, " or likes it better, notwithftanding the alteration made in it " to his difadvantage, than any other; or at leaft thinks it " better, in his circumftances, to conform to it, than to feek " any other; that is, he is content to be comprehended in " it."

From hence it is evident, that the obligation of the laws of parliament upon the people of *Britain*, who have no right to be electors, does not arife from their being *virtually* reprefented, but from a quite different principle; a principle of the law of nature, true, certain, and univerfal, applicable to every fort of government, and not contrary to the common underftandings of mankind.

If what you fay is a real fact, that nine-tenths of the people of *Britain* are deprived of the high privilege of being electors, it fhows a great defect in the prefent conftitution, which has departed fo much from its original purity ; but never can prove, that thofe people are even *virtually* reprefented in parliament. And here give me leave to obferve, that it would be a work worthy of the beft patriotic fpirits in the nation, to effectuate an alteration in this putrid part of the conftitution ; and, by reftoring it to its priftine perfection, prevent any " order or rank of the fubjects from impofing upon

---

* *Wollafton's Rel. of Nat.*

" or

" or binding the reſt, without their conſent." But, I fear, the gangrene has taken too deep hold to be eradicated in theſe days of venality.

But if thoſe people of *Britain* who are excluded from being electors, are not repreſented in parliament, the concluſion is much ſtronger againſt the people of the colonies being repreſented, who are conſidered by the *Britiſh* government itſelf, in every inſtance of parliamentary legiſlation, as a diſtinct people. It has been determined by the lords of the privy council, that " acts of parliament made in *England*, without name-
" ing the foreign plantations, will not bind them *." Now what can be the reaſon of this determination, but that the lords of the privy council are of opinion, the colonies are a diſtinct people from the inhabitants of *Britain*, and are not repreſented in parliament ? If, as you contend, the colonies are *exactly in the ſame ſituation* with the ſubjects in *Britain*, the laws will in every inſtance be equally binding upon them, as upon thoſe ſubjects, unleſs you can diſcover two ſpecies of *virtual* repreſentation ; the one, to reſpect the ſubjects in *Britain*, and always exiſting in time of parliament ; the other, to reſpect the colonies, a mere non-entity, if I may be allowed the term, and never exiſting, but when the parliament thinks proper to produce it into being, by any particular act in which the colonies happen to be named. But I muſt examine the caſe of the colonies more diſtinctly.

It is in vain to ſearch into the civil conſtitution of *England* for directions in fixing the proper connection between the colonies and the mother-kingdom ; I mean, what their reciprocal duties to each other are, and what obedience is due from the children to the general parent. The planting colonies from *Britain*, is but of recent date, and nothing relative to ſuch plantation can be collected from the ancient laws of the kingdom; neither can we receive any better information, by extending our enquiry into the hiſtory of the colonies, eſtabliſhed by the ſeveral nations, in the more early ages of the world. All the colonies (except thoſe of *Georgia* and *Nova Scotia*) formed from the *Engliſh* nation in *North-America*, were planted in a manner, and under a dependance, of which there is not an inſtance in all the colonies of the ancients ; and therefore I conceive, it muſt afford a good degree of ſurprize, to find an *Engliſh* civilian † giving it as his ſentiment, that the *Engliſh* colonies ought to be governed by the *Roman* laws ; and for no better reaſon, than becauſe the *Spaniſh* colonies, as he ſays, are governed by thoſe laws. The *Romans*

---

* 2 *Pur. Williams.*   † *Strahan in his Preface to Domat.*

eſtabliſhed

eſtabliſhed their colonies, in the midſt of vanquiſhed nations, upon principles which beſt ſecured their conqueſts; the privileges granted to them were not always the ſame; their policy in the government of their colonies, and the conquered nations, being always directed by arbitrary principles to the end they aimed at, the ſubjecting the whole earth to their empire: but the colonies in *North-America*, except thoſe planted within the preſent century, were founded by *Engliſh-men*, who, becoming private adventurers, eſtabliſhed themſelves, without any expence to the nation, in this uncultivated and almoſt uninhabited country; ſo that their caſes is plainly diſtinguiſhable from that of the *Roman*, or any other colonies of the ancient world.

As then we can receive no light from the laws of the kingdom, or from ancient hiſtory, to direct us in our enquiry, we muſt have recourſe to the law of nature, and thoſe rights of mankind which flow from it.

I have obſerved before, that when ſubjects are deprived of their civil rights, or are diſſatisfied with the place they hold in the community, they have a natural right to quit the ſociety of which they are members, and to retire into another country. Now when men exerciſe this right, and withdraw themſelves from their country, they recover their natural freedom and independence: the juriſdiction and ſovereignty of the ſtate they have quitted, ceaſes; and if they unite, and by common conſent take poſſeſſion of a new country, and form themſelves into a political ſociety, they become a ſovereign ſtate, independent of the ſtate from which they ſeparated. If then the ſubjects of *England* have a natural right to relinquiſh their country; and by retiring from it, and aſſociating together, to form a new political ſociety and independent ſtate, they muſt have a right, by compact with the ſovereign of the nation, to remove into a new country, and to form a civil eſtabliſhment upon the terms of the compact. In ſuch a caſe, the terms of the compact muſt be obligatory and binding upon the parties; they muſt be the magna charta, the fundamental principles of government, to this new ſociety; and every infringement of them muſt be wrong, and may be oppoſed. It will be neceſſary, then, to examine, whether any ſuch compact was entered into between the ſovereign, and thoſe *Engliſh* ſubjects who eſtabliſhed themſelves in *America*.

You have told us, that " before the firſt and great act of " navigation, the inhabitants of *North-America* were but a " few unhappy fugitives, who had wandered thither to enjoy " their civil and religious liberties, which they were deprived
" of

" of at home." If this was true, it is evident, from what has been said upon the law of nature, that they have a right to a civil independent establishment of their own, and that *Great-Britain* has no *right* to interfere in it.   But you have been guilty of a gross anachronism in your chronology, and a great error in your account of the first settlement of the colonies in *North-America*; for it is a notorious fact that they were not settled by fugitives from their native country, but by men who came over voluntarily, at their own expence, and under charters from the crown, obtained for that purpose, long before the first and great act of navigation.

The first of these charters was granted to Sir *Walter Raleigh* by queen *Elizabeth*, under her great seal, and was confirmed by the parliament of *England* in the year 1684 *.   By this charter, the whole country to be possessed by Sir *Walter Raleigh* was granted to him, his heirs and assigns, in perpetual sovereignty, in as extensive a manner as the crown could grant, or had ever granted before to any person or persons, with full power of legislation, and to establish a civil government in it, as near as conveniently might be agreeable to the form of the *English* government and policy thereof.   The country was to be united to the realm of *England*, in perfect LEAGUE AND AMITY ; was to be within the allegiance of the crown of *England*, and to be held by homage, and the payment of one-fifth of all gold and silver ore, which was reserved for all services, duties, and demands.

Sir *Walter Raleigh*, under this charter, took possession of *North-America*, upon that part of the continent which gave him a right to the tract of country which lies between the twenty-fifth degree of latitude, and the gulf of *St. Laurence*; but a variety of accidents happening in the course of his exertions to establish a colony, and perhaps being overborn by the expence of so great a work, he made an assignment to divers gentlemen and merchants of *London*, in the 31st year of the queen's reign, for continuing his plantation in *America*. These assignees were not more successful in their attempts, than the proprietor himself had been ; but being animated with the expectation of mighty advantages from the accomplishment of their undertaking, they, with others, who associated with them, obtained new charters from king *James* the first, in whom all Sir *Walter Raleigh's* rights became vested upon his attainder ; containing the same extensive jurisdic-

---

* *This charter is printed at large in Hakluyt's Voyages, p.* 725, *folio edition, anno* 1589 ; *and the substance of it is in the* 3d *vol. of Salmon's Mod. Hist. p.* 424.

C

tions,

tions, royalties, privileges, franchifes, and pre-eminences, and the fame powers to eftablifh a civil government in the colony, as had been granted to Sir *W. Raleigh*, with an exprefs claufe of exemption, for ever, from all taxes or impofitions upon their import and export trade.

Under thefe charters the proprietors effectually profecuted, and happily fucceeded, in planting a colony upon that part of the continent which is now called *Virginia*. This colony, after ftruggling through immenfe difficulties, without receiving the leaft affiftance from the *Englifh* government, attained to fuch a degree of perfection, that in the year 1621, a general affembly, or legiflative authority, was eftablifhed in the governor, council, and houfe of burgeffes, who were elected by the freeholders as their reprefentatives; and they have continued, from that time, to exercife the power of legiflation over the colony.

But upon the 15th of *July*, 1624, king *James* diffolved the company by proclamation, and took the colony under his immediate dependence, which occafioned much confufion, and created mighty apprehenfions in the colony, left they fhould be deprived of the rights and privileges granted them by the company, according to the powers contained in their charters.

To put an end to this confufion, and to conciliate the colony to the new fyftem of government the crown intended to eftablifh among them, K. *Charles* the firft, upon the demife of his father, by proclamation the 13th of *May*, 1625, declared, " that *Virginia* fhould be immediately dependent upon " the crown; that the affairs of the colony fhould be vefted " in a council, confifting of a few perfons of underftanding " and quality, to be fubordinate and attendant to the privy- " council in *England*; that he was refolved to eftablifh ano- " ther council in *Virginia*, to be fubordinate to the council " in *England* for the colony; and that he would maintain the " neceffary officers, minifters, forces, ammunition, and for- " tifications thereof, at his own charge." But this proclamation had an effect quite different from what was intended; inftead of allaying, it encreafed the confufion of the colony; they now thought their regular conftitution was to be deftroyed, and a prerogative government eftablifhed over them; or, as they exprefs themfelves in their remonftrance, that " their " rights and privileges were to be affaulted." This general difquietude and diffatisfaction continued until they received a letter from the lords of the privy-council, dated *July* the 22d, 1634, containing the royal affurance and confirmation, that " all their eftates, trade, freedom, and privileges, fhould be " enjoyed

" enjoyed by them in as extenſive a manner, as they enjoyed
" them before the recalling the company's patent;" where-
upon they became reconciled, and began again to exert themſelves in the improvement of the colony.

Being now in full poſſeſſion of the rights and privileges of
Engliſhmen, which they eſteemed more than their lives, their
affection for the royal government grew almoſt to enthuſiaſm;
for upon an attempt to reſtore the company's charter, by authority of parliament, the general aſſembly, upon the 1ſt of
April, 1642, drew up a declaration or proteſtation, in the
form of an act, by which they declared, " they never would
" ſubmit to the government of any company or proprietor,
" or to ſo unnatural a diſtance as a company, or other per-
" ſon, to interpoſe between the crown and the ſubjects; that
" they were born under monarchy, and would never degene-
" rate from the condition of their births, by being ſubject to
" any other government; and every perſon who ſhould attempt
" to reduce them under any other government, was declared
" an enemy to the country, and his eſtate was to be forfeited."
This act, being preſented to the king at his court at *York*,
July 5th, 1644, drew from him a moſt gracious anſwer, under his royal ſignet, in which he gave them the fulleſt aſſu-
rances, that they ſhould be always immediately dependent
upon the crown, and that the form of government ſhould never be changed. But after the king's death, they gave a more
eminent inſtance of their attachment to royal government, in
their oppoſition to the parliament, and forcing the parliament
commiſſioners, who were ſent over with a ſquadron of ſhips
of war to take poſſeſſion of the country, into articles of ſur-
render, before they would ſubmit to their obedience. As theſe
articles reflect no ſmall honour upon this infant colony, and
as they are not commonly known, I will give an abſtract of
ſuch of them as relate to the preſent ſubject.

1. The plantation of *Virginia*, and all the inhabitants
thereof, ſhall be and remain in due ſubjection to the commonwealth of *England*, not as a conquered country, but as a
country ſubmitting by their own voluntary act, and ſhall enjoy ſuch freedoms and privileges as belong to the free people
of *England*.

2. The general aſſembly as formerly ſhall convene, and
tranſact the affairs of the colony.

3. The people of *Virginia* ſhall have a free trade, as the
people of *England*, to all places, and with all nations.

4. *Virginia* ſhall be free from all taxes, cuſtoms, and im-
poſitions whatſoever; and none ſhall be impoſed on them,
without conſent of the general aſſembly; and that neither

forts

forts nor castles be erected, or garrisons maintained, without their consent.

Upon this surrender of the colony to the parliament, Sir *W. Berkeley*, the royal governor, was removed, and three other governors were successively elected by the house of burgesses; but in *January*, 1659, Sir *William Berkeley* was replaced at the head of the government by the people, who unanimously renounced their obedience to the parliament, and restored the royal authority, by proclaiming *Charles* the second, king of *England, Scotland, France, Ireland*, and *Virginia*; so that he was king in *Virginia* some time before he had any certain assurance of being restored to his throne in *England*.

From this detail of the charters, and other acts of the crown, under which the first colony in *North-America* was established, it is evident, that " the colonists were not a few " unhappy fugitives who had wandered into a distant part of " the world to enjoy their civil and religious liberties, which " they were deprived of at home," but had a regular government long before the first act of navigation, and were respected as a distinct state, independent, as to their *internal* government, of the original kingdom, but united with her, as to their *external* polity, in the closest and most intimate ʟEAGUE AND AMITY, under the same allegiance, and enjoying the benefits of a reciprocal intercourse.

But allow me to make a reflection or two upon the preceding account of the first settlement of an *English* colony in *North-America*.

America was no part of the kingdom of *England*; it was possessed by a savage people, scattered through the country, who were not subject to the *English* dominion, nor owed obedience to its laws. This independent country was settled by *Englishmen* at their own expence, under particular stipulations with the crown: these stipulations, then, must be the sacred band of union between *England* and her colonies, and cannot be infringed without injustice. But you object, that " no " power can abridge the authority of parliament, which has " never exempted any from the submission they owe to it; " and no other power can grant such an exemption."

I will not dispute the authority of the parliament, which is, without doubt, supreme within the body of the kingdom, and cannot be abridged by any other power; but may not the king have prerogatives, which he has a right to exercise, without the consent of parliament? If he has, perhaps that of granting licence to his subjects to remove into a *new* country, and to settle therein upon particular conditions, may be one. If he has no such prerogative, I cannot discover how

the

the royal engagements can be made good, that " the freedom
" and other benefits of the *Britiſh* conſtitution" ſhall be ſecured to thoſe people who ſhall ſettle in a new country under
ſuch engagements ; the freedom, and other benefits of the
Britiſh conſtitution, cannot be ſecured to a people, without
they are exempted from being taxed by any authority, but
that of their repreſentatives, choſen by themſelves.   This is
an eſſential part of *Britiſh* freedom ; but if the king cannot
grant ſuch an exemption, in right of his prerogative, the
royal promiſes cannot be fulfilled ; and all charters which
have been granted by our former kings, for this purpoſe, muſt
be deceptions upon the ſubjects who accepted them, which to
ſay, would be a high reflection upon the honour of the crown.
But there was a time, when ſome parts of *England* itſelf were
exempt from the laws of parliament : the inhabitants of the
county palatine of *Cheſter* were not ſubject to ſuch laws * *ab
antiquo,* becauſe they did not ſend repreſentatives to parliament, but had their own *commune concilium* ; by whoſe authority, with the conſent of their earl, their laws were made. If
this exemption was not derived originally from the crown, it
muſt have ariſen from that great principle in the *Britiſh*
conſtitution, by which the freemen in the nation are not ſubject to any laws, but ſuch as are made by repreſentatives elected by themſelves to parliament; ſo that in either caſe, it is
an inſtance extremely applicable to the colonies, who contend
for no other right, but that of directing their *internal* government by laws made with their own conſent, which has been
preſerved to them by repeated acts and declarations of the
crown.

The conſtitution of the colonies, being eſtabliſhed upon
the principles of *Britiſh* liberty, has never been infringed by
the immediate act of the crown ; but the powers of government, agreeably to this conſtitution, have been conſtantly
declared in the king's commiſſions to their governors, which,
as often as they paſs the great ſeal, are *new* declarations and
confirmations of the rights of the colonies. Even in the reign
of *Charles* the ſecond, a time by no means favourable to
liberty, theſe rights of the colonies were maintained inviolate;
for when it was thought neceſſary to eſtabliſh a permanent
revenue for the ſupport of government in *Virginia,* the king
did not apply to the *Engliſh* parliament, but to the general
aſſembly ; and ſent over an act, under the great ſeal of *England,* by which it was enacted, " by the king's moſt excel-
" lent majeſty, by and with the conſent of the general aſſem-

---

* *Petyt's Rights of the Commons. King's Vale Royal of England.*
" bly,'"

" bly," that two fhillings per hogfhead upon all tobacco exported, one fhilling and three-pence per ton upon fhipping;
and fix-pence per poll for every perfon imported, not being
actually a mariner in pay, were to be paid for ever as a revenue, for the fupport of the government in the colony.

I have taken notice of this act, not only becaufe it fhows
the proper fountain from whence all fupplies to be raifed in
the colonies ought to flow, but alfo as it affords an inftance,
that royalty itfelf did not difdain formerly to be named as a
part of the legiflature of the colony ; though now, to ferve a
purpofe deftructive of their rights, and to introduce principles of defpotifm unknown to a free conftitution, the legiflature of the colonies are degraded even below the corporation
of a petty borough in *England*.

It muft be admitted, that after the reftoration, the colonies
loft that liberty of commerce with foreign nations, they had
enjoyed before that time.

As it became a fundamental law of the other ftates of *Europe*, to prohibit all foreign trade with their colonies, *England*
demanded fuch an exclufive trade with her colonies. This
was effected by the act of 25th *Charles* 2d, and fome other
fubfequent acts; which not only circumfcribed the trade of
the colonies with foreign nations within very narrow limits,
but impofed duties upon feveral articles of their own manufactory exported from one colony to another. Thefe acts,
which impofed feverer reftrictions upon the trade of the colonies, than were impofed upon the trade of *England*, deprived
the colonies, fo far as thefe reftrictions extended, of the privileges of *Englifh* fubjects, and conftituted an unnatural difference between men under the fame allegiance, born equally
free, and entitled to the fame civil rights. In this light did
the people of *Virginia* view the act of 25th *Charles* 2d, when
they fent agents to the *Englifh* court, to reprefent againft
" taxes and impofitions being laid on the colony by any au-
" thority but that of their general affembly." The right of
impofing *internal* duties upon their trade, by authority of parliament, was then difputed, though you fay it was never
called into queftion ; and the agents fent from *Virginia* upon
this occafion, obtained a declaration from *Charles* 2d, the
19th of *April*, 1676, under his privy feal, that impofitions or
" taxes ought not to be laid upon the inhabitants and pro-
" prietors of the colony, but by the common confent of the
" general affembly, except fuch impofitions as the parliament
" fhould lay on the commodities imported into *England* from
" the colony :" and he ordered a charter to be made out, and

to

to pafs the great feal, for fecuring this right, among others, to the colony.

But whether the act of 25th *Charles* 2d, or any of the other acts, have been complained of as infringements of the rights of the colonies or not, is immaterial; for if a man of fuperior ftrength takes my coat from me, that cannot give him a right to my cloak, nor am I obliged to fubmit to be deprived of all my eftate, becaufe I may have given up fome part of it without complaint. Befides, I have proved irrefragably, that the colonies are not reprefented in parliament, and confequently, upon your own pofition, that no new law can bind them, that is made without the concurrence of their reprefentatives; and if fo, then every act of parliament that impofes *internal* taxes upon the colonies, is an act of *power*, and not of *right*. I muft fpeak freely; I am confidering a queftion which affects the *rights* of above two millions of as loyal fubjects as belong to the *Britifh* crown, and muft ufe terms adequate to the importance of it; I fay, that *power*, abftracted from *right*, cannot give a juft title to dominion. If a man invades my property, he becomes an aggreffor, and puts himfelf into a ftate of war with me: I have a right to oppofe this invader; if I have not ftrength to repel him, I muft fubmit; but he acquires no right to my eftate which he has ufurped. Whenever I recover ftrength, I may renew my claim, and attempt to regain my poffeffion; if I am never ftrong enough, my fon, or his fon, may, when able, recover the natural right of his anceftor, which has been unjuftly taken from him.

I hope I fhall not be charged with infolence, in delivering the fentiments of an honeft mind with freedom: I am fpeaking of the *rights* of a people: *rights* imply *equality*, in the inftances to which they belong, and muft be treated without refpect to the dignity of the perfons concerned in them. If " the *Britifh* empire in *Europe* and in *America* is the fame " *power*;" if the " fubjects in both are the fame people, and " all equally participate in the adverfity and profperity of the " whole," what diftinctions can the difference of their fituations make, and why is this diftinction made between them? Why is the trade of the colonies more circumfcribed than the trade of *Britain*? And why are impofitions laid upon the one, which are not laid upon the other? If the parliament " have " a *right* to impofe taxes of *every kind* upon the colonies," they ought in juftice, as the fame people, to have the fame fources to raife them from: their commerce ought to be equally free with the commerce of *Britain*, otherwife it will be loading them with burthens, at the fame time that they are
deprived

deprived of ftrength to fuftain them; it will be forcing them to make bricks without ftraw. I acknowledge the parliament is the fovereign legiflative power of the *Britifh* nation, and that by a full exertion of their power, they can deprive the colonifts of the freedom, and other benefits of the *Britifh* conftitution, which have been fecured to them by our kings; they can abrogate all their civil rights and liberties; but by what *right* is it, that the parliament can exercife fuch a power over the colonifts, who have as natural a right to the liberties and privileges of *Englifhmen*, as if they were actually refident within the kingdom? The colonies are fubordinate to the authority of parliament; fubordinate I mean in degree, but not abfolutely fo: for if by a vote of the *Britifh* fenate, the colonifts were to be delivered up to the rule of a *French* or *Turkifh* tyranny, they may refufe obedience to fuch a vote, and may oppofe the execution of it by force. Great is the power of parliament, but, great as it is, it cannot, conftitutionally, deprive the people of their *natural* rights; nor, in virtue of the fame principle, can it deprive them of their *civil* rights, which are founded in compact, without their own confent. There is, I confefs, a confiderable difference between thefe two cafes, as to the right of refiftance: in the firft, if the colonifts fhould be difmembered from the nation, by act of parliament, and abandoned to another power, they have a natural right to defend their liberties by open force, and may lawfully refift; and, if they are able, repel the power to whofe authority they are abandoned. But in the other, if they are deprived of their civil rights, if great and manifeft oppreffions are impofed upon them by the ftate on which they are dependent, their remedy is to lay their complaints at the foot of the throne, and to fuffer patiently, rather than difturb the public peace, which nothing but a denial of juftice can excufe them in breaking. But if this juftice fhould be denied, if the moft humble and dutiful reprefentations fhould be rejected, nay, not even deigned to be received, what is to be done? To fuch a queftion, *Thucydides* would make the *Corinthians* reply, that if " a decent and " condefcending behaviour is fhown on the part of the colo- " nies it would be bafe in the mother-ftate to prefs too far " on fuch moderation:" And he would make the *Corcyreans* anfwer, that " every colony, whilft ufed in a proper man- " ner, ought to pay honour and regard to its mother ftate; " but, when treated with injury and violence, is become an " alien. They were not fent out to be the flaves, but to be " the equals of thofe that remain behind."

But,

But, according to your fcheme, the colonies are to be pro-hibited from uniting in a reprefentation of their general griev-ances to the common fovereign. This moment " the *Britifh* " empire in *Europe* and in *America* is the fame power ; its " fubjects in both are the fame people ; each is equally im-" portant to the other ; and mutual benefits, mutual necefii-" ties, cement their connection." The next moment " the " colonies are unconnected with each other, different in their " manners, oppofite in their principles, and clafh in their " interefts and in their views, from rivalry in trade, and the " jealoufy of neighbourhood. This happy divifion, which " was effected by accident, is to be continued throughout by " defign ; and all bond of union between them" is excluded from your vaft fyftem. *Divide et impera* is your maxim in colony adminiftration, left " an alliance fhould be formed " dangerous to the mother-country." Ungenerous infinua-tion ! deteftable thought ! abhorrent to every native of the colonies ! who, by an uniformity of conduct, have ever de-monftrated the deepeft loyalty to their king, as the father of his people, and an unfhaken attachment to the intereft of *Great-Britain.* But you muft entertain a moft defpicable opi-nion of the underftandings of the colonifts, to imagine, that they will allow divifions to be fomented between them about inconfiderable things, when the clofeft union becomes necef-fary to maintain, in a conftitutional way, their deareft inte-refts.

    Another writer *, fond of his new fyftem of placing *Great-Britain* as the center of attraction to the colonies, fays, that " they muft be guarded againft having or forming any prin-" ciple of coherence with each other, above that whereby " they cohere in the centre ; having no other principle of " intercommunication between each other, than that by " which they are in joint communication with *Great-Britain*, " as the common centre of all. At the fame time that they " are each, in their refpective parts and fubordinations, fo " framed, as to be acted by this firft mover, they fhould al-" ways remain incapable of any coherence, or of fo con-" fpiring amongft themfelves, as to create any other equal " force which might recoil back on this firft mover ; nor is " it more neceffary to preferve the feveral governments fub-" ordinate within their refpective orbs, than it is effential to " the prefervation of the empire to keep them difconnected " and independent of each other." But how is this " prin-" ciple of coherence," as this elegant writer calls it, between

---

   * *The Adminiftration of the Colonies by Governor Pownall.*

                the

the colonies, to be prevented ? The colonies upon the continent of *North-America*, lie united to each other in one tract
of country, and are equally concerned to maintain their common liberty.   If he will attend then to the laws of attraction
in natural as well as political philofophy, he will find, that
bodies in contact, and cemented by mutual interefts, cohere
more ftrongly than thofe which are at a diftance, and have no
common interefts to preferve.   But this natural law is to be
deftroyed ; and the colonies, whofe *real* interefts are the fame,
and therefore ought to be united in the clofeft communication, are to be disjoined, and all intercommunication between
them prevented.   But how is this fyftem of adminiftration to
be eftablifhed ? Is it to be done by a military force, quartered
upon private families ? Is it to be done by extending the jurifdiction of courts of admiralty, and thereby depriving the colonifts of legal trials in the courts of common law ? Or is it
to be done by harr. fling the colonifts, and giving overbearing
tax-gatherers an opportunity of ruining men, perhaps better
fubjects than themfelve°, by dragging them from one colony
to another, before prerogative judges, exercifing a defpotic
fway in inquifitorial courts? Oppreffion has produced very
great and unexpected events : the *Helvetick* confederacy, the
ftates of the *United Netherlands,* are inftances in the annals of
Europe, of the glorious actions a petty people, in comparifon,
can perform, when united in the caufe of liberty.   May the
colonies ever remain under a conftitutional fubordination to
Great-Britain ! It is their intereft to live under fuch a fubordination ; and it is their duty, by an exertion of all their
ftrength and abilities, when called upon by their common
fovereign, to advance the grandeur and the glory of the nation.   May the interefts of *Great-Britain* and her colonies be
ever united, fo as that whilft they are retained in a legal and
juft dependance, no unnatural or unlimited rule may be exercifed over them ; but that they may enjoy the freedom, and
other benefits of the *Britifh* conftitution, to the lateft page in
hiftory !

   I flatter myfelf, by what has been faid, your pofition of a *virtual* reprefentation is fufficiently refuted ; and that there is really
no fuch reprefentation known in the *Britifh* conftitution, and
confequently, that the colonies are not fubject to an *internal*
taxation by authority of parliament.

   I could extend this enquiry to a much greater length, by
examining into the policy of the late acts of parliament,
which impofe heavy and fevere taxes, duties, and prohibitions, upon the colonies : I could point out fome very difagreeable confequences, refpecting the trade and manufactures

of

of *Britain*, which muſt neceſſarily reſult from theſe acts; I could prove, that the revenues ariſing from the trade of the colonies, and the advantage of their exports to *Great-Britain*, in the balance of her trade with foreign nations, exceed infinitely all the expence ſhe has been at, all the expence ſhe can be at, in their protection; and perhaps I could ſhow, that the bounties given upon ſome articles exported from the colonies, were not intended, primarily, as inſtances of attention to their intereſt, but aroſe as well from the conſideration of the diſadvantageous dependance of *Great-Britain* upon other nations for the principal articles of her naval ſtores, as from her loſing trade for thoſe articles; I could demonſtrate, that theſe bounties are by no means adequate to her ſavings in ſuch foreign trade, if the articles upon which they are given, can be procured from the colonies, in quantities ſufficient to anſwer her conſumption; and that the exceſs of theſe ſavings is ſo much clear profit to the nation, upon the ſuppoſition that theſe bounties are drawn from it; but, as they will remain in it, and be laid out in its manufactures and exports, that the whole ſum which uſed to be paid to foreigners, for the purchaſe of theſe articles, will be ſaved to the nation. I ſay, I could extend my enquiry, by examining theſe ſeveral matters; but as the ſubject is delicate, and would carry me to a great length, I ſhall leave them to the reader's own reflection.

F I N I S

WILLIAMSBURG,
Printed by ALEXANDER PURDIE, and Co.
LONDON,
Re-printed for J. ALMON, oppoſite Burlington-Houſe, Piccadilly.
MDCCLXIX.

But, according to your fcheme, the colonies are to be pro-
hibited from uniting in a reprefentation of their general grievances to the common fovereign. This moment " the *Britiſh*
" empire in *Europe* and in *America* is the fame power; its
" fubjects in both are the fame people; each is equally im-
" portant to the other; and mutual benefits, mutual necefli-
" ties, cement their connection." The next moment " the
" colonies are unconnected with each other, different in their
" manners, oppofite in their principles, and clafh in their
" interefts and in their views, from rivalry in trade, and the
" jealoufy of neighbourhood. This happy divifion, which
" was effected by accident, is to be continued throughout by
" defign; and all bond of union between them" is excluded
from your vaft fyftem. *Divide et impera* is your maxim in
colony adminiftration, left " an alliance fhould be formed
" dangerous to the mother-country." Ungenerous infinua-
tion! deteftable thought! abhorrent to every native of the
colonies! who, by an uniformity of conduct, have ever de-
monftrated the deepeft loyalty to their king, as the father of
his people, and an unfhaken attachment to the intereft of
Great-Britain. But you muft entertain a moft defpicable opinion of the underftandings of the colonifts, to imagine, that
they will allow divifions to be fomented between them about
inconfiderable things, when the clofeft union becomes neceffary to maintain, in a conftitutional way, their deareft interefts.

Another writer *, fond of his new fyftem of placing *Great-*
Britain as the center of attraction to the colonies, fays, that
" they muft be guarded againft having or forming any prin-
" ciple of coherence with each other, above that whereby
" they cohere in the centre; having no other principle of
" intercommunication between each other, than that by
" which they are in joint communication with *Great-Britain*,
" as the common centre of all. At the fame time that they
" are each, in their refpective parts and fubordinations, fo
" framed, as to be acted by this firft mover, they fhould al-
" ways remain incapable of any coherence, or of fo con-
" fpiring amongft themfelves, as to create any other equal
" force which might recoil back on this firft mover; nor is
" it more neceffary to preferve the feveral governments fub-
" ordinate within their refpective orbs, than it is effential to
" the prefervation of the empire to keep them difconnected
" and independent of each other." But how is this " prin-
" ciple of coherence," as this elegant writer calls it, between

* *The Adminiftration of the Colonies by Governor Pownall.*

the

the colonies, to be prevented? The colonies upon the continent of *North-America*, lie united to each other in one tract of country, and are equally concerned to maintain their common liberty. If he will attend then to the laws of attraction in natural as well as political philosophy, he will find, that bodies in contact, and cemented by mutual interests, cohere more strongly than those which are at a distance, and have no common interests to preserve. But this natural law is to be destroyed; and the colonies, whose *real* interests are the same, and therefore ought to be united in the closest communication, are to be disjoined, and all intercommunication between them prevented. But how is this system of administration to be established? Is it to be done by a military force, quartered upon private families? Is it to be done by extending the jurisdiction of courts of admiralty, and thereby depriving the colonists of legal trials in the courts of common law? Or is it to be done by harrassing the colonists, and giving overbearing tax-gatherers an opportunity of ruining men, perhaps better subjects than themselves, by dragging them from one colony to another, before prerogative judges, exercising a despotic sway in inquisitorial courts? Oppression has produced very great and unexpected events: the *Helvetick* confederacy, the states of the *United Netherlands*, are instances in the annals of *Europe*, of the glorious actions a petty people, in comparison, can perform, when united in the cause of liberty. May the colonies ever remain under a constitutional subordination to *Great-Britain!* It is their interest to live under such a subordination; and it is their duty, by an exertion of all their strength and abilities, when called upon by their common sovereign, to advance the grandeur and the glory of the nation. May the interests of *Great-Britain* and her colonies be ever united, so as that whilst they are retained in a legal and just dependance, no unnatural or unlimited rule may be exercised over them; but that they may enjoy the freedom, and other benefits of the *British* constitution, to the latest page in history!

I flatter myself, by what has been said, your position of a *virtual* representation is sufficiently refuted; and that there is really no such representation known in the *British* constitution, and consequently, that the colonies are not subject to an *internal* taxation by authority of parliament.

I could extend this enquiry to a much greater length, by examining into the policy of the late acts of parliament, which impose heavy and severe taxes, duties, and prohibitions, upon the colonies: I could point out some very disagreeable consequences, respecting the trade and manufactures

of

of *Britain*, which muft neceffarily refult from thefe acts; I could prove, that the revenues arifing from the trade of the colonies, and the advantage of their exports to *Great-Britain*, in the balance of her trade with foreign nations, exceed infinitely all the expence fhe has been at, all the expence fhe can be at, in their protection; and perhaps I could fhow, that the bounties given upon fome articles exported from the colonies, were not intended, primarily, as inftances of attention to their intereft, but arofe as well from the confideration of the difadvantageous dependance of *Great-Britain* upon other nations for the principal articles of her naval ftores, as from her lofing trade for thofe articles; I could demonftrate, that thefe bounties are by no means adequate to her favings in fuch foreign trade, if the articles upon which they are given, can be procured from the colonies, in quantities fufficient to anfwer her confumption; and that the excefs of thefe favings is fo much clear profit to the nation, upon the fuppofition that thefe bounties are drawn from it; but, as they will remain in it, and be laid out in its manufactures and exports, that the whole fum which ufed to be paid to foreigners, for the purchafe of thefe articles, will be faved to the nation. I fay, I could extend my enquiry, by examining thefe feveral matters; but as the fubject is delicate, and would carry me to a great length, I fhall leave them to the reader's own reflection.

F I N I S

W I L L I A M S B U R G,
Printed by ALEXANDER PURDIE, and Co.
L O N D O N,
Re-printed for J. ALMON, oppofite Burlington-Houfe, Piccadilly.
MDCCLXIX.

THE INTEREST OF GREAT BRITAIN CONSIDERED

Benjamin Franklin, *The Interest of Great Britain Considered: with regard to her colonies and the acquisitions of Canada and Guadaloupe: To which are added, Observations Concerning the Increase of Mankind, the Peopling of Countries, &c.* (Boston, reprinted 1760), pp. 1–59.

This is Benjamin Franklin's most famous work on economics and population. Thomas Malthus cited the latter part of this essay, *Observations Concerning the Increase of Mankind*, in his *Essay on the Principle of Population* and some speculate that Adam Smith used Franklin's estimates of population and population growth in his chapter on the American colonies in *Wealth of Nations*.[1] The first part of this writing, *Interest of Great Britain Considered*, is devoted to convincing Great Britain to take Canada rather than Guadaloupe as a war settlement. Franklin's argument is based on the long-run importance of land and room for expansion in North America compared to an already developed sugar island that has no growth potential. Agriculture and population were the sources of wealth, Franklin argues, therefore Great Britain would benefit more from claiming Canada. Among other reasons, ousting the French from Canada would save on frontier defence.

The second part, *Observations Concerning the Increase of Mankind*, attempts to prove that the British trade restrictions on the colonies were detrimental to the British economy. Franklin deftly manipulates early classical and mercantile ideas – such as the labour theory of value and the determinants of wages – to show that the colonies did not drain off population from England (and thereby drive wages up) and that manufacturing in the colonies would not compete with British manufacturing. Franklin concludes that trade increases population, which was to the benefit of the British Empire. A variety of other issues are also addressed in this work. For example, Franklin argues against slavery, stating that slaves could never be used in manufacturing as it would be cheaper to hire labourers than to purchase and maintain slaves. Thus, in Franklin's view, England need not regard southern manufacturing as a threat.

---

[1] D. N. Logan, *Memoir of Dr. George Logan of Stenton*, ed. F. A. Logan (Philadelphia, Historical Society of Pennsylvania, 1899).

THE
INTEREST
OF
GREAT BRITAIN
CONSIDERED

With Regard to

Her COLONIES

AND THE ACQUISITIONS of

CANADA and GUADALOUPE.

To which are added,

ORSERVATIONS concerning the Increafe of Mankind, Peopling of Countries, &c.

☞ As the very ingenious, ufeful, and worthy Author of this Pamphlet [B——n F——n, LL. D.] is well-known and much efteemed by the principal Gentlemen in *England* and *America*; and feeing that his other Works have been received with univerfal Applaufe; the prefent Production needs no further Recommendation to a generous, a free, an intelligent and publick-fpirited People.

LONDON, *Printed.* MDCCLX.

BOSTON: *Reprinted, by* B. Mecom, *and Sold at the* New Printing-Office, *near the* Town-Houfe. 1760.

[Price ONE SHILLING.]

THE
INTEREST
OF
GREAT BRITAIN,
CONSIDERED

With Regard to Her COLONIES.

I Have perufed with no fmall pleafure the *Letter addreffed to Two Great Men*, and the *Remarks* on that letter. It is not merely from the beauty, the force and perfpicuity of expreffion, or the general elegance of manner confpicuous in both pamphlets, that my pleafure chiefly arifes; it is rather from this, that I have lived to fee fubjects of the greateft importance to this nation publickly difcuffed without party views, or party heat, with decency and politenefs, and with no other warmth than what a zeal for the honour and happinefs of our king and country may infpire;------and this by writers whofe underftanding (however they may differ from each other) appears not unequal to their candour and the uprightnefs of their intention.

But, as great abilities have not always the beft information, there are, I apprehend, in the *Remarks* fome opinions not well founded, and fome miftakes of fo important a nature, as to render a few obfervations on them neceffary for the better information of the publick.

The author of the *Letter*, who muft be every way beft able to fupport his own fentiments, will, I hope, excufe me, if I feem officioufly to interfere; when he confiders, that the fpirit of patriotifm, like

other

other qualities good and bad, is catching ; and that his long filence fince the *Remarks* appeared has made us defpair of feeing the fubject farther difcuffed by his mafterly hand. The ingenious and candid remarker, too, who muft have been mifled himfelf before he employed his fkill and addrefs to miflead others, will certainly, fince he declares he *aims at no feduction,*[*] be difpofed to excufe even the weakeft effort to prevent it.

And furely if the general opinions that poffefs the minds of the people may poffibly be of confequence in publick affairs, it muft be fit to fet thofe opinions right. If there is danger, as the remarker fuppofes, that " extravagant expectations" may embarrafs " a virtuous and able miniftry," and " render the negociation for peace a work of infinite difficulty ; " [†] there is no lefs danger that expectations too low, thro' want of proper information, may have a contrary effect, may make even a virtuous and able miniftry lefs anxious, and lefs attentive to the obtaining points, in which the honour and intereft of the nation are effentially concerned ; and the people lefs hearty in fupporting fuch a miniftry and its meafures.

The people of this nation are indeed refpectable, not for their numbers only, but for their underftanding and their publick fpirit : they manifeft the firft, by their univerfal approbation of the late prudent and vigorous meafures, and the confidence they fo juftly repofe in a wife and good prince, and an honeft and able adminiftration ; the latter they have demonftrated by the immenfe fupplies granted in parliament unanimoufly, and paid through the whole kingdom with chearfulnefs. And fince to this fpirit and thefe fupplies our " victories and fucceffes" [‡] have in great meafure
been

* Remarks, p. 6   † Remarks, p. 7.   ‡ Remarks, p. 7.

been owing, is it quite right, is it generous to fay, with the *remarker*, that the people " had no fhare in acquiring them ?" The mere mob he cannot mean, even where he fpeaks of the *madnefs of the people*; for the madnefs of the mob muft be too feeble and impotent, arm'd as the government of this country at prefent is, to " over-rule," * even in the flighteft inftances, the " virtue and moderation" of a firm and fteady miniftry.

While the war continues, its final event is quite uncertain. The Victorious of this year may be the Vanquifhed of the next. It may therefore be too early to fay, what advantages we ought abfolutely to infift on, and make the *fine quibus non* of a peace, If the neceffity of our affairs fhould oblige us to accept of terms lefs advantageous than our prefent fucceffes feem to promife us, an intelligent people, as ours is, muft fee that neceffity, and will ac- quiefce. But as a peace, when it is made, may be made haftily; and as the unhappy continuance of the war affords us time to confider, among feveral advantages gain'd or to be gain'd, which of them may be moft for our intereft to retain, if fome and not all may poffibly be retained ; I do not blame the public difquifition of thefe points, as premature or ufelefs. Light often arifes from a collifion of opinions, as fire from flint and fteel ; and if we can obtain the benefit of the *light*, without danger from the *heat* fometimes produc'd by controverfy, why fhould we difcourage it ?

Suppofing then, that heaven may ftill continue to blefs His Majefty's arms, and that the event of this juft war may put it in our power to retain fome of our conquefts at the making of a peace; let us confider whether we are to confine ourfelves to thofe poffeffions only that were " the *objects* for
which

* Remarks, p. 7.

which we began the war."* This the *remarker* feems to think right, when the queftion relates to ' *Canada*, properly fo called, it having never been ' mentioned as one of thofe objects in any of our ' memorials or declarations, or in any national or ' publick act whatfoever.' But the gentleman him-felf will probably agree, that if the ceffion of *Ca-nada* would be a real advantage to us, we may de-mand it under his fecond head, as an " *indemnifi-cation* for the charges incurred" in recovering our juft rights ; otherwife according to his own prin-ciples the demand of *Guadaloupe* can have no foun-dation.

That " our claims before the war were large " enough for poffeffion and for fecurity too,"† tho' it feems a clear point with the ingenious remarker, is, I own, not fo with me. I am rather of the con-trary opinion, and fhall prefently give my rea-fons. But firft let me obferve, that we did not make thofe claims becaufe they were large enough for fecurity, but becaufe we could rightfully claim no more. Advantages gained in the courfe of this war, may increafe the extent of our rights. Our claims before the war contain'd fome fecurity ; but that is no reafon why we fhould neglect acquiring more when the demand of more is become rea-fonable. It may be reafonable in the cafe of A-*merica* to afk for the fecurity recommended by the author of the letter, ‖ tho' it would be prepofterous to do it in many other cafes : his propos'd demand is founded on the little value of *Canada* to the *French* ; the right we have to afk, and the power we may have to infift on an indemnification for our expences ; the difficulty the *French* themfelves
will

---

* Remarks, p. 19. † Ibid. ‖ P. 30 of the *Letter*, and p. 21 of the *Remarks*.

will be under of reftraining their reftlefs fubjecls in *America* from encroaching on our limits and difturbing our trade ; and the difficulty on our parts of preventing encroachments that may poffibly exift many years without coming to our knowledge. But the remarker " does not fee why the " arguments employ'd concerning a fecurity for a " peaceable behaviour in *Canada*, would not be " equally cogent for calling for the fame fecurity " in *Europe*."* On a little farther reflection, he muft I think be fenfible, that the circumftances of the two cafes are widely different. Here we are feparated by the beft and cleareft of boundaries, the ocean, and we have people in or near every part of our territory. Any attempt to encroach upon us, by building a fort, even in the obfcureft corner of thefe iflands, muft therefore be known and prevented immediately. The aggreffors alfo muft be known, and the nation they belong to would be accountable for their aggreffion. In *America* it is quite otherwife. A vaft wildernefs thinly or fcarce at all peopled, conceals with eafe the march of troops and workmen. Important paffes may be feized within our limits and forts built in a month, at a fmall expence, that may coft us an age and a million to remove. Dear experience has taught us this. But what is ftill worfe, the wide extended forefts between our fettlements and theirs, are inhabited by barbarous tribes of favages that delight in war and take pride in murder, fubjecls properly neither of the *French* nor *Englifh*, but ftrongly attach'd to the former by the art and indefatigable induftry of priefts, fimiliarity of fuperftitions, and frequent family alliances. Thefe are eafily, and have been continually, inftigated to fall upon and maffacre our planters, even in times of full peace

between

* Remarks, p. 24.

between the two crowns, to the certain diminution of our people and the contraction of our settlements.* And tho' it is known they are supply'd by the *French* and carry their prisoners to them, we can by complaining obtain no redress, as the governors of *Canada* have a ready excuse, that the Indians are an independent people, over whom they have no power, and for whose actions they are there-

---

* A very intelligent writer of that country, Dr. *Clark*, in his *Observations on the late and present conduct of the French*, &c. printed at *Boston* 1755, says,

' The Indians in the *French* interest are, upon all proper op-
' portunities, instigated by their priests, who have generally the
' chief management of their publick councils, to acts of ho-
' stility against the *English*, even in time of profound peace be-
' tween the two crowns. Of this there are many undeniable
' instances. The war between the Indians and the colonies of
' the *Massachusets-Bay* and *New-Hampshire*, in 1723, by which
' those colonies suffered so much damage, was begun by the
' instigation of the *French* ; their supplies were from them, and
' there are now original letters of several Jesuits to be pro-
' duced, whereby it evidently appears, that they were continu-
' ally animating the Indians, when almost tired with the war,
' to a farther prosecution of it. The *French* not only excited
' the Indians, and supported them, but joined their own forces
' with them in all the late hostilities that have been committed
' within His Majesty's province of *Nova-Scotia*. And from an
' intercepted letter this year from the Jesuit at *Penobscot*, and
' from other information, it is certain that they have been using
' their utmost endeavours to excite the Indians to new acts of
' hostility, against His Majesty's colony of the *Massachusets-
' Bay*, and some have been committed.——The *French* not only
' excite the Indians to acts of hostility, but reward them for it,
' by buying the *English* prisoners of them ; for the ransom of
' each of which they afterwards demand of us the price that is
' usually given for a slave in these colonies. They do this un-
' der the specious pretence of rescuing the poor prisoners from
' the cruelties and barbarities of the savages ; but in reality to
' encourage them to continue their depredations, as they can
' by this means get more by hunting the *English* than by hunt-
' ing wild beasts ; and the *French* at the same time are thereby
' enabled to keep up a large body of Indians entirely at the ex-
' pence of the *English*."

therefore not accountable. Surely circumstances so widely different may reasonably authorise different demands of security in *America*, from such as are usual or necessary in *Europe*.

The *remarker*, however, thinks, that our real dependance for keeping " *France* or any other na-" tion true to her engagements, must not be in " demanding securities which no nation whilst *inde-*" *pendent* can give, but on our own strength and our " own viligance." * No nation that has carried on a war with disadvantage, and is unable to continue it, can be said, under such circumstances, to be *independent* ; and while either side thinks itself in a condition to demand an indemnification, there is no man in his senses, but will, *cæteris paribus*, prefer an indemnification that is a cheaper and more effectual security than any other he can think of. Nations in this situation demand and cede countries by almost every treaty of peace that is made. The *French* part of the island of St. *Cristopher's* was added to *Great Britain* in circumstances altogether similar to those in which a few months may probably place the country of *Canada*. Farther security has always been deemed a motive with a conqueror to be less moderate ; and even the vanquish'd insist upon security as a reason for demanding what they acknowledge they could not otherwise properly ask. The security of the frontier of *France* on the side of the *Netherlands*, was always considered, in the negotiation that began at *Getruydenburgh*, and ended with that war. For the same reason they demanded and had *Cape Breton*. But a war concluded to the advantage of *France* has always added something to the power, either of *France* or the house of *Bourbon*. Even that of 1733, which she commenced with declarations of

B

her

* Remarks, p. 25.

her having no ambitious views, and which finiſhed by a treaty at which the miniſters of *France* repeatedly declared that ſhe deſired nothing for herſelf, in effect gained for her *Lorrain*, an indemnification ten times the value of all her *North American* poſſeſſions.

In ſhort, ſecurity and quiet of princes and ſtates have ever been deemed ſufficient reaſons, when ſupported by power, for diſpoſing of rights ; and ſuch diſpoſition has never been looked on as want of moderation. It has always been the foundation of the moſt general treaties. The ſecurity of *Germany* was the argument for yielding conſiderable poſſeſſions there to the *Swedes :* and the ſecurity of *Europe* divided the *Spaniſh* monarchy, by the partition treaty, made between powers who had no *other* right to diſpoſe of any part of it. There can be no ceſſion that is not ſuppoſed at leaſt, to increaſe the power of the party to whom it is made. It is enough that he has a right to aſk it, and that he does it not merely to ſerve the purpoſes of a dangerous ambition. *Canada* in the hands of *Britain*, will endanger the kingdom of *France* as little as any other ceſſion ; and from its ſituation and circumſtances cannot be hurtful to any other ſtate. Rather, if peace be an advantage, this ceſſion may be ſuch to all *Europe.* The preſent war teaches us, that diſputes ariſing in *America*, may be an occaſion of embroiling nations who have no concerns there. If the *French* remain in *Canada* and *Louiſiana*, fix the boundaries as you will between us and them, we muſt border on each other for more than 1500 miles. The people that inhabit the frontiers, are generally the refuſe of both nations, often of the worſt morals and the leaſt diſcretion, remote from the eye, the prudence, and the reſtraint of government. Injuries are

are therefore frequently, in some part or other of so long a frontier, committed on both sides. Resentment provoked, the colonies first engaged, and then the mother countries. And two great nations can scarce be at war in *Europe*, but some other prince or state thinks it a convenient opportunity, to revive some ancient claim, seize some advantage, obtain some territory, or enlarge some power at the expence of a neighbour. The flames of war once kindled, often spread far and wide, and the mischief is infinite. Happy it prov'd to both nations, that the *Dutch* were prevailed on finally to cede the *New Netherlands* (now the province of *New York*) to us at the peace of 1674; a peace that has ever since continued between us, but must have been frequently disturbed, if they had retained the possession of that country, bordering several hundred miles on our colonies of *Pensylvania* westward, *Connecticut* and the *Massachusetts* eastward. Nor is it to be wondered at that people of different language, religion, and manners, should in those remote parts engage in frequent quarrels, when we find, that even the people of our own colonies have frequently been so exasperated against each other in their disputes about boundaries, as to proceed to open violence and bloodshed.

But the *remarker* thinks we shall be sufficiently secure in *America*, if we " raise *English* forts at ' such passes as may at once make us respectable to ' the *French* and to the *Indian* nations.' * The security desirable in *America*, may be considered as of three kinds; 1. A security of possession, that the *French* shall not drive us out of the country. 2. A security of our planters from the inroads of savages, and the murders committed by them. 3. A

* Remarks, p. 25.

3. A fecurity that the *Britiſh* nation fhall not be
oblig'd on every new war to repeat the immenſe
expence occaſion'd by this, to defend its poſſeſſions
in *America*.   Forts in the moſt important paſſes,
may, I acknowledge be of uſe to obtain the firſt
kind of fecurity : but as thoſe ſituations are far advanc'd beyond the inhabitants, the expence of
maintaining and ſupplying the garriſons, will be
very great, even in time of full peace, and immenſe
on every interruption of it ; as it is eaſy for ſkulk-
ing parties of the enemy in ſuch long roads thro' the
woods, to intercept and cut off our convoys, unleſs guarded continually by great bodies of men.
The ſecond kind of fecurity, will not be obtained by ſuch forts, unleſs they are connected by a
wall like that of *China*, from one end of our ſettlements to the other.   If the *Indians* when at war,
march'd like the *Europeans*, with great armies,
heavy cannon, baggage, and carriages, the paſſes
thro' which alone ſuch armies could penetrate our
country, or receive their ſupplies, being ſecur'd, all
might be ſufficiently ſecure ; but the caſe is widely
different.   They go to war, as they call it, in
ſmall parties, from fifty men down to five.   Their
hunting life has made them acquainted with the
whole country, and ſcarce any part of it is impracticable to ſuch a party.   They can travel thro'
the woods even by night, and know how to conceal their tracks.   They paſs eaſily between your
forts undiſcover'd ; and privately approach the
ſettlements of your frontier inhabitants.   They
need no convoys of proviſions to follow them ; for
whether they are ſhifting from place to place in
the woods, or lying in wait for an opportunity to
ſtrike a blow, every thicket and every ſtream furniſhes ſo ſmall a number with ſufficient ſubſiſtence.
When they have ſurpriz'd ſeparately, and murder'd
and

and fcalp'd a dozen families, they are gone with inconceivable expedition thro' unknown ways, and 'tis very rare that purfuers have any chance of coming up with them.＊ In fhort, long experience has taught our planters, that they cannot rely upon forts as a fecurity againft *Indians:* The inhabitants of *Hackney* might as well rely upon the tower of *London*

to

* ＊ ' Although the *Indians* live fcattered, as a hunter's life requires, they may be collected together from almoft any diftance, as they can find their fubfiftence from their gun in their travelling. But let the number of the *Indians* be what it will, they are not formidable merely on account of their numbers; there are many other circumftances that give them a great advantage over the *Englifh*. The *Englifh* inhabitants, though numerous, are extended over a large tract of land, 500 leagues in length on the fea-fhore; and altho' fome of their trading towns are thick fettled, their fettlements in the country towns muft be at a diftance from each other: befides, that in a new country, where lands are cheap, people are fond of acquiring large tracts to themfelves; and therefore in the out fettlements, they muft be more remote: and as the people that move out are generally poor, they fit down, either where they can eafieft procure land, or fooneft raife a fubfiftence. Add to this, that the *Englifh* have fixed fettled habitations, the eafieft and fhorteft paffages to which the *Indians*, by conftantly hunting in the woods, are perfectly well acquainted with; whereas the *Englifh* know little or nothing of the *Indian* country, nor of the paffages thro' the woods that lead to it. The *Indian* way of making war is by fudden attacks upon expofed places; and as foon as they have done mifchief, they retire, and either go home by the fame or fome different rout, as they think fafeft; or go to fome other place at a diftance, to renew their ftroke. If a fufficient party fhould happily be ready to purfue them, it is a great chance, whether in a country, confifting of woods and fwamps, which the *Englifh* are not acquainted with, the enemy do not lie in ambufh for them in fome convenient place, and from thence deftroy them. If this fhould not be the cafe, but the *Englifh* fhould purfue them, as foon as they have gained the rivers, by means of their canoes, to the ufe of which they are brought up from their infancy, they prefently get out of their reach: further, if a body of men were

' to

to fecure them againft highwaymen and houfebreak-
ers. As to the third kind of fecurity, that we fhall
not in a few years, have all we have now done
to do over again in *America* ; and be oblig'd to
employ the fame number of troops, and fhips, at
the fame immenfe expence to defend our poffeffions there, while we are in proportion weaken'd
here :

' to march into their country, to the places where they are
' fettled, they can, upon the leaft notice, without great dif-
' advantage, quit their prefent habitations, and betake them-
' felves to new ones.'   *Clark's Obfervations p.* 13.

' It has been already remarked, that the tribes of the *In-*
' *dians* living upon the lakes and rivers that run upon the back
' of the *Englifh* fettlements in *North-America*, are very numerous,
' and can furnifh a great number of fighting men, all per-
' fectly well acquainted with the ufe of arms as foon as capable
' of carrying them, as they get the whole of their fubfiftence
' from hunting; and that this army, large as it may be, can be
' maintained by the French without any expence. From their
' numbers, their fituation, and the rivers that run into the
' *Englifh* fettlements, it is eafy to conceive that they can at any
' time make an attack upon, and conftantly annoy as many of
' the expofed *Englifh* fettlements as they pleafe, and thofe at
' any diftance from each other. The effects of fuch incurfions
' have been too feverely felt by many of the *Britifh* colonies,
' not to be very well known. The entire breaking up places
' that had been for a confiderable time fettled at a great ex-
' pence, both of labour and money; burning the houfes, de-
' ftroying the ftock, killing and making prifoners great num-
' bers of the inhabitants, with all the cruel ufage they meet
' with in their captivity, is only a part of the fcene. All other
' places that are expofed are kept in continual terror; the
' lands lie wafte and uncultivated from the danger that attends
' thofe that fhall prefume to work upon them : befides the
' immenfe charge the governments muft be at in a very inef-
' fectual manner to defend their extended frontiers; and all
' this from the influence the *French* have had over, but com-
' paratively, a few of the *Indians*. To the fame or greater
' evils ftill will every one of the colonies be expofed, when-
' ever the fame influence fhall be extended to the whole body
' of them.'   *Ibid. p.* 20.

here : such forts I think cannot prevent this. During a peace, it is not to be doubted the *French*, who are adroit at fortifying, will likewise erect forts in the most advantageous places of the country we leave them, which will make it more difficult than ever to be reduc'd in case of another war. We know by the experience of this war, how extremely difficult it is to march an army thro' the *American* woods, with its necessary cannon and stores, sufficient to reduce a very slight fort. The accounts at the treasury will tell you what amazing sums we have necessarily spent in the expeditions against two very trifling forts, *Duquesne* and *Crown Point*. While the *French* retain their influence over the *Indians*, they can easily keep our long extended frontier in continual alarm, by a very few of those people ; and with a small number of regulars and militia, in such a country, we find they can keep an army of ours in full employ for several years. We therefore shall not need to be told by our colonies, that if we leave *Canada*, however circumscrib'd, to the *French*, " *we have done* " *nothing* ; * we shall soon be made sensible our-selves of this truth, and to our cost.

I would not be understood to deny that even if we subdue and retain *Canada*, some few forts may be of use to secure the goods of the traders, and protect the commerce, in case of any sudden mis-understanding with any tribe of *Indians* : but these forts will be best under the care of the colonies in-terested in the *Indian* trade, and garrison'd by their provincial forces, and at their own expence. Their own interest will then induce the *American* govern-ments to take care of such forts in proportion to their importance ; and see that the officers keep their corps full, and mind their duty. But any

troops

* Remarks, p. 26.

troops of ours plac'd there and accountable here, would, in such remote and obscure places and at so great a distance from the eye and inspection of superiors, soon become of little consequence, even tho' the *French* were left in possession of *Canada*. If the four independent companies maintained by the Crown in *New York* more than forty years, at a great expence, consisted, for most part of the time, of faggots chiefly ; if their officers en-joy'd their places as *fine cures*, and were only, as a writer * of that country stiles them, a kind of *military monks* ; if this was the state of troops posted in a populous country, where the imposition could not be so well conceal'd ; what may we expect will be the case of those that shall be posted two, three or four hundred miles from the inhabitants, in such obscure and remote places as *Crown Point, Oswego, Duquesne,* or *Niagara ?* they would scarce be even faggots ; they would dwindle to meer names upon paper, and appear no where but upon the muster rolls.

Now all the kinds of security we have mention'd are obtain'd by subduing and retaining *Canada*. Our present possessions in *America*, are secur'd ; our planters will no longer be massacred by the *Indians*, who depending absolutely on us for what are now become the necessaries of life to them, guns, powder, hatchets, knives, and cloathing ; and having no other *Europeans* near, that can ei-ther supply them, or instigate them against us ; there is no doubt of their being always dispos'd, if we treat them with common justice, to live in perpetual peace with us. And with regard to *France,* she cannot in case of another war, put us to the immense expence of defending that long extended frontier ; we shall then, as it were, have

our

* Douglass.

our backs againft a wall in *America*, the fea-coaft will be eafily protected by our fuperior naval power; and here " our own watchfulnefs and our own ftrength" will be properly, and cannot but be fuccefsfully employed.   In this fituation the force now employ'd in that part of the world, may be fpar'd for any other fervice here or elfewhere; fo that both the offenfive and defenfive ftrength of the *Britifh* empire on the whole will be greatly increafed.

But to leave the *French* in poffeffion of *Canada* when it is in our power to remove them, and depend, as the remarker propofes, on our own " *ftrength and watchfulnefs* " * to prevent the mifchiefs that may attend it, feems neither fafe nor prudent.   Happy as we now are, under the beft of kings, and in the profpect of a fucceffion promifing every felicity a nation was ever blefs'd with : happy too in the wifdom and vigour of every part of the adminiftration, particularly that part whofe peculiar province is the *Britifh* plantations, a province every true *Englifhman* fees with pleafure under the principal direction of a nobleman, as much diftinguifh'd by his great capacity, as by his unwearied and difinterefted application to this important department ; we cannot, we ought not to promife ourfelves the uninterrupted continuance of thofe bleffings.   The fafety of a confiderable part of the ftate, and the intereft of the whole are not to be trufted to the wifdom and vigor of future adminiftrations, when a fecurity is to be had more effectual, more conftant, and much lefs expenfive.   They who can be moved by the apprehenfion of dangers fo remote as that of the future independence of our colonies (a point I fhall hereafter confider) feem fcarcely confiftent

C   with

* P. 25.

with themſelves when they ſuppoſe we may rely on the wiſdom and vigour of an adminiſtration for their ſafety.

I ſhould indeed think it leſs material whether *Canada* were ceded to us or not, if I had in view only the *ſecurity of poſſeſſion* in our colonies. I entirely agree with the Remarker, that we are in *North America* " a far greater continental as well " as naval power ; " and that only cowardice or ignorance can ſubject our colonies there to a *French* conqueſt. But for the ſame reaſon I diſagree with him widely upon another point. I do not think that our " blood and treaſure has been expended," as he intimates, " *in the cauſe of the colonies*," and that we " are making conqueſts *for them :* "* yet I believe this is too common an error. I do not ſay they are altogether unconcerned in the event. The inhabitants of them are, in common with the other ſubjects of *Great Britain*, anxious for the glory of her crown, the extent of her power and commerce, the welfare and future repoſe of the whole *Britiſh* people. They could not therefore but take a large ſhare in the affronts offered to *Britain*, and have been animated with a truely *Britiſh ſpirit* to exert themſelves beyond their ſtrength, and againſt their evident intereſt. Yet ſo unfortunate have they been, that their virtue has made againſt them ; for upon no better foundation than this, have they been ſuppoſed the authors of a war carried on *for their advantage only.* It is a great miſtake to imagine that the *American* country in queſtion between *Great Britain* and *France*, is claimed as the property of any individuals or publick body in *America*, or that the poſſeſſion of it by *Great-Britain*, is likely, in any lucrative view, to redound at all to the advantage of any perſon there.

On

* Remarks, p. 26.

On the other hand, the bulk of the inhabitants of *North America* are land-owners, whose lands are inferior in value to those of *Britain*, only by the want of an equal number of people. It is true the accession of the large territory claimed before the war began, especially if that be secured by the possession of *Canada*, will tend to the increase of the *British* subjects, faster than if they had been confin'd within the mountains : yet the increase within the mountains only, would evidently make the comparative population equal to that of *Great Britain*, much sooner than it can be expected when our people are spread over a country six times as large. I think this is the only point of light in which this question is to be viewed, and is the only one in which any of the colonies are concerned. No colony, no possessor of lands in any colony, therefore wishes for conquests, or can be benefited by them, otherwise than as they may be a means of securing peace on their borders. No considerable advantage has resulted to the colonies by the conquests of this war, or can result from confirming them by the peace, but what they must enjoy in common with the rest of the *British* people; with this evident drawback from their share of these advantages, that they will necessarily lessen, or at least prevent the increase of the value of what makes the principal part of their private property. A people spread thro' the whole tract of country on this side the *Mississipi*, and secured by *Canada* in our hands, would probably for some centuries find employment in agriculture, and thereby free us at home effectually from our fears of *American* manufactures. Unprejudic'd men well know that all the penal and prohibitory laws that ever were thought on, will not be sufficient to prevent manufactures in a country whose inhabitants

furpass

surpass the number that can subsist by the husbandry of it. That this will be the case in *America* soon, if our people remain confined within the mountains, and almost as soon should it be unsafe for them to live beyond, tho' the country be ceded to us, no man acquainted with political and commercial history can doubt. Manufactures are founded in poverty. It is the multitude of poor without land in a country, and who must work for others at low wages or starve, that enables undertakers to carry on a manufacture, and afford it cheap enough to prevent the importation of the same kind from abroad, and to bear the expence of its own exportation. But no man who can have a piece of land of his own, sufficient by his labour to subsist his family in plenty, is poor enough to be a manufacturer, and work for a master. Hence while there is land enough in *America* for our people, there can never be manufactures to any amount or value. It is a striking observation of a very *able pen*, that the natural livelihood of the thin inhabitants of a forest country, is hunting; that of a greater number, pasturage; that of a middling population, agriculture; and that of the greatest, manufactures; which last must subsist the bulk of the people in a full country, or they must be subsisted by charity, or perish. The extended population, therefore, that is most advantageous to *Great Britain*, will be best effected, because only effectually secur'd by our possession of *Canada*. So far as the being of our present colonies in *North America* is concerned, I think indeed with the re-marker, that the *French* there are not " *an enemy* " *to be aprehended*," * but the expression is too vague to be applicable to the present, or indeed to any other case. *Algiers, Tunis,* and *Tripoli,* un-

* Remarks, p. 27.

equal

equal as they are to this nation in power and numbers of people, are enemies to be ſtill apprehended; and the *Highlanders* of *Scotland* have been ſo for many ages by the greateſt princes of *Scotland* and *Britain*. The wild *Iriſh* were able to give a great deal of diſturbance even to Queen *Elizabeth*, and coſt her more blood and treaſure than her war with *Spain*. *Canada* in the hands of *France* has always ſtinted the growth of our colonies: In the courſe of this war, and indeed before it, has diſturb'd and vex'd even the beſt and ſtrongeſt of them, has found means to murder thouſands of their people, and unſettle a great part of their country. Much more able will it be to ſtarve the growth of an infant ſettlement. *Canada* has alſo found means to make this nation ſpend two or three millions a year in *America*; and a people, how ſmall ſoever, that in their preſent ſituation, can do this as often as we have a war with them, is methinks, " *an ene-* " *my to be apprehended*."

Our *North American* colonies are to be conſidered as the frontier of the *Britiſh* empire on that ſide. The frontier of any dominion being attack'd, it becomes not merely " *the cauſe*" of the people immediately affected, (the inhabitants of that frontier) but properly " *the cauſe*" of the whole body. Where the frontier people owe and pay obedience, there they have a right to look for protection. No political propoſition is better eſtabliſhed than this. It is therefore invidious to repreſent the " blood and treaſure" ſpent in this war, as ſpent in " the " cauſe of the colonies" only, and that they are " abſurd and ungrateful" if they think we have done nothing unleſs we " make conqueſts for " them," and reduce *Canada* to gratify their " vain ambition," &c. It will not be a conqueſt for them, nor gratify any vain ambition of theirs.

It

It will be a conqueſt for the whole, and all our people will, in the increaſe of trade and the eaſe of taxes, find the advantage of it. Should we be obliged at any time to make a war for the protection of our commerce, and to ſecure the exportation of our manufactures, would it be fair to repreſent ſuch a war merely as blood and treaſure ſpent in the cauſe of the weavers of *Yorkſhire*, *Norwich*, or the *Weſt*, the cutlers of *Sheffield*, or the button-makers of *Birmingham?* I hope it will appear before I end theſe ſheets, that if ever there was a *national war*, this is truly ſuch a one : a war in which the intereſt of the *whole* nation is directly and fundamentally concerned.

Thoſe who would be thought deeply ſkilled in human nature, affect to diſcover ſelf-intereſted views every where at the bottom of the faireſt, the moſt generous conduct. Suſpicions and charges of this kind, meet with ready reception and belief in the minds even of the multitude; and therefore leſs acuteneſs and addreſs than the *remarker* is poſ-ſeſſed of, would be ſufficient to perſuade the nation generally, that all the zeal and ſpirit manifeſted and exerted by the colonies in this war, was only in " their own cauſe" to " make conqueſts for " themſelves," to engage us to make more for them, to gratify their own " vain ambition." But ſhould they now humbly addreſs the mother country in the terms and the ſentiments of the *remarker*, return her their grateful acknowledgments for the blood and treaſure ſhe had ſpent in " *their* " *cauſe*," confeſs that enough had been done " *for them*;" allow that " *Engliſh* forts raiſed in " proper paſſes, will, with the wiſdom and vigour " of her adminiſtration" be a ſufficient future protection; expreſs their deſires that their people may be confined within the mountains, left if they are
ſuffered

suffered to spread and extend themselves in the fertile and pleasant country on the other side, they should " *increase infinitely from all causes,*" " live " wholly on their own labour" and become independent; beg therefore that the *French* may be suffered to remain in possession of *Canada*, as their neighbourhood may be useful to prevent our increase; and the removing them may " in its conse- " quences be even dangerous *. " I say, should such an address from the colonies make its appearance here, though, according to the *remarker*, it would be a most just and reasonable one; would it not, might it not with more justice be answered; We understand you, gentlemen, perfectly well : you have only your own interest in view : you want to have the people confined within your present limits, that in a few years the lands you are possessed of may increase tenfold in value ! you want to reduce the price of labour by increasing numbers on the same territory, that you may be able to set up manufactures and vie with your mother country ! you would have your people kept in a body, that you may be more able to dispute the commands of the crown, and obtain an independency. You would have the *French* left in *Canada*, to exercise your military virtue, and make you a warlike people, that you may have more confidence to embark in schemes of disobedience, and greater ability to support them ! You have tasted too, the sweets of TWO OR THREE MILLIONS *Sterling per annum* spent among you by our fleets and forces, and you are unwilling to be without a pretence for kindling up another war, and thereby occasion a repetition of the same delightful doses ! But, gentlemen, allow us to understand

our

* Remarks, p. 50, 51.

our intereſt a little likewiſe: we ſhall remove the *French* from *Canada* that you may live in peace, and we be no more drained by your quarrels. You ſhall have land enough to cultivate, that you may have neither neceſſity nor inclination to go into manufactures, and we will manufacture for you, and govern you.

A reader of the remarks may be apt to ſay ; if this writer would have us reſtore *Canada* on principles of moderation, how can we conſiſtent with thoſe principles, retain *Guadaloupe*, which he repreſents of ſo much greater value ! I will endeavour to explain this, becauſe by doing it I ſhall have an opportunity of ſhowing the truth and good ſenſe of the anſwer to the intereſted application I have juſt ſuppoſed. The author then is only *apparently* and not *really* inconſiſtent with himſelf. If we can obtain the credit of moderation by reſtoring *Canada*, it is well : but we ſhould, however, reſtore it at all events ; becauſe it would not only be of no uſe to us, but " the poſſeſſion of it (in his opinion) " may in its conſequence be dangerous*." as how ? Why, plainly, (at length it comes out) if the *French* are not left there to check the growth of our colonies, " they will extend themſelves almoſt without " bounds into the inland parts, and increaſe in- " finitely from all cauſes ;---becoming a numerous, " hardy, *independent* people, poſſeſſed of a ſtrong " country, communicating little or not at all with " *England*, living wholly on their own labour, and " in proceſs of time knowing little and enquiring " little about the mother country." In ſhort, according to this writer, our preſent colonies are large enough and numerous enough, and the *French* ought to be left in *North America* to prevent their increaſe, leſt they become not only *uſeleſs* but *dangerous* to *Britain*. ᴦ

* Remarks, p. 50, 51.

I agree with the gentleman, that with *Canada* in our possession, our people in *America* will increase amazingly. I know that their common rate of increase, where they are not molested by the enemy, is doubling their numbers every twenty-five years by natural generation only, exclusive of the accession of foreigners.* I think this increase continuing, would probably in a century more, make the number of *British* subjects on that side the water more numerous than they now are on this ; but I am far from entertaining, on that account, any fears of their becoming either *useless* or *dangerous* to us ; and I look on those fears to be merely imaginary and without any probable foundation. The *remarker* is reserv'd in giving his reasons, as in his opinion this " is not a fit subject for discussion." I shall give mine, because I conceive it a subject necessary to be discussed ; and the rather, as those fears, how groundless and chimerical soever, may, by possessing the multitude, possibly induce the ablest ministry to conform to them against their own judgment, and thereby prevent the assuring to the *British* name and nation, a stability and permanency that no man acquainted with history durst have hoped for, till

our

---

* The reason of this greater increase in *America* than in *Europe*, is, that in old settled countries, all trades, farms, offices, and employments are full, and many people refrain marrying till they see an opening, in which they can settle themselves, with a reasonable prospect of maintaining a family : but *in America*, it being easy to obtain land which with moderate labour will afford subsistence and something to spare, people marry more readily and earlier in life, whence arises a numerous offspring and the swift population of those countries. 'Tis a common error that we cannot fill our provinces or increase the number of them, without draining this nation of its people. The increment alone of our present colonies is sufficient for both those purposes.

our *American* poffeffions opened the pleafing profpect.

The remarker thinks that our people in *America*, " finding no check from *Canada*, would ex-
" tend themfelves almoft without bounds into the
" inland parts, and increafe infinitely from all
" caufes." The very reafon he affigns for their fo
extending, and which is indeed the true one, their
being " invited to it by the pleafantnefs, fertility
" and plenty of the country," may fatisfy us, that
this extenfion will continue to proceed as long as
there remains any pleafant fertile country within
their reach. And if we even fuppofe them confin'd by the waters of the *Miffiffipi* weftward,
and by thofe of *St. Laurence* and the lakes to the
northward, yet ftill we fhall leave them room e-
nough to increafe, even in the *fparfe* manner of
fettling now practis'd there, till they amount to
perhaps a hundred millions of fouls. This muft
take fome centuries to fulfil, and in the mean time,
this nation muft neceffarily fupply them with the
manufactures they confume, becaufe the new fettlers
will be employed in agriculture, and the new fettlements will fo continually draw off the fpare hands
from the old, that our prefent colonies will not,
during the period we have mention'd, find themfelves in a condition to manufacture even for their
own inhabitants, to any confiderable degree, much
lefs for thofe who are fettling behind them. Thus
our *trade* muft, till that country becomes as fully
peopled as *England*, that is, for centuries to come,
be continually increafing, and with it our naval
power ; becaufe the ocean is between us and them,
and our fhips and feamen muft increafe as that
trade increafes.

The human body and the political differ in
this, that the firft is limited by nature to a certain
ftature,

ftature, which, when attain'd, it cannot, ordinarily, exceed ; the other by better government and more prudent police, as well as by change of manners and other circumftances, often takes frefh ftarts of growth, after being long at a ftand ; and may add tenfold to the dimenfions it had for ages been confined to. The mother being of full ftature, is in a few years equalled by a growing daughter : but in the cafe of a mother country and her colonies, it is quite different. The growth of the children tends to encreafe the growth of the mother, and fo the difference and fuperiority is longer preferv'd.

Were the inhabitants of this ifland limited to their prefent number by any thing in nature, or by unchangeable circumftances, the equality of population between the two countries might indeed fooner come to pafs : but fure experience in thofe parts of the ifland where manufactures have been introduced, teaches us, that people increafe and multiply in proportion as the means and facility of gaining a livelihood increafe ; and that this ifland, if they could be employed, is capable of supporting ten times its prefent number of people. In proportion, therefore, as the demand increafes for the manufactures of *Britain*, by the increafe of people in her colonies, the numbers of her people at home will increafe, and with them the ftrength as well as the wealth of the nation. For fatisfaction in this point let the reader compare in his mind the number and force of our prefent fleets, with our fleet in queen *Elizabeth*'s time * before we had colonies. Let him compare the ancient with the prefent ftate of our towns and ports on our weftern coaft, *Manchefter, Liverpool, Kendal, Lancafter, Glafgow*, and the countries round them, that trade with and manufacture for our colonies,

not

---

* *Viz.* Forty fail, none of more than 40 guns.

not to mention *Leeds*, *Halifax*, *Sheffield* and *Birmingham*, and consider what a difference there is in the numbers of people, buildings, rents, and the value of land and of the produce of land, even if he goes back no farther than is within man's memory. Let him compare those countries with others on this same island, where manufactures have not yet extended themselves, observe the present difference, and reflect how much greater our strength may be, if numbers give strength, when our manufacturers shall occupy every part of the island where they can possibly be subsisted.

But, say the objectors, " there is a certain distance from the sea, in *America*, beyond which the expence of carriage will put a stop to the sale and consumption of your manufactures ; and this, with the difficulty of making returns for them, will oblige the inhabitants to manufacture for themselves ; of course, if you suffer your people to extend their settlements beyond that distance, your people become useless to you : " and this distance is limited by some to 200 miles, by others to the *Apalackian* mountains. Not to insist on a very plain truth, that no part of a dominion, from whence a government may on occasion draw supplies and aids both of men of money, tho' at too great a distance to be supply'd with manufactures from some other part, is therefore to be deem'd useless to the whole ; I shall endeavour to show that these imaginary limits of utility, even in point of commerce, are much too narrow.

The inland parts of the continent of *Europe* are much farther from the sea than the limits of settlement proposed for *America*. *Germany* is full of tradesmen and artificers of all kinds, and the governments there, are not all of them always favourable to the commerce of *Britain*,, yet it is a
well-

well-known fact, that our manufactures find their
way even into the heart of *Germany*. Afk the great
manufacturers and merchants of the *Leeds*, *Sheffield*,
Birmingham, *Manchester* and *Norwich* goods, and they
will tell you that fome of them fend their riders
frequently through *France* or *Spain* and *Italy*, up to
Vienna, and back through the middle and northern
parts of *Germany*, to fhow famples of their wares
and collect orders, which they receive by almoft
every mail, to a vaft amount. Whatever charges
arife on the carriage of goods, are added to the
value, and all paid by the confumer. If thefe nations over whom we have no government, over
whofe confumption we can have no influence, but
what arifes from the cheapnefs and goodnefs of our
wares; whofe trade, manufactures, or commercial
connections are not fubject to the controul of our
laws, as thofe of our colonies certainly are in fome
degree: I fay, if thefe nations purchafe and confume fuch quantities of our goods, notwithftanding the remotenefs of their fituation from the fea;
how much lefs likely is it that the fettlers in *America*, who muft for ages be employed in agriculture chiefly, fhould make cheaper for themfelves
the goods our manufacturers at prefent fupply
them with; even if we fuppofe the carriage five, fix,
or feven hundred miles from the fea as difficult and
expenfive as the like diftance into *Germany* :
whereas in the latter, the natural diftances are frequently doubled by political obftructions, I mean
the intermix'd territories and clafhing interefts of
princes. But when we confider that the inland parts
of *America* are penetrated by great navigable rivers;
that there are a number of great lakes, communicating with each other, with thofe rivers and with
the fea, very fmall portages here and there ex-
cepted;

cepted ; * that the fea coafts (if one may be allow'd the expreffion) of thofe lakes only, amount
at leaft to 2700 miles, exclufive of the rivers run-
ing into them ; many of which are navigable to a
great extent for boats and canoes, thro' vaft tracts
of country ; how little likely is it that the expence
on the carriage of our goods into thofe countries,
fhould prevent the ufe of them.   If the poor *Indians* in thofe remote parts are now able to pay for
the linnen, woolen and iron wares they are at prefent furnifh'd with by the *French* and *Englifh* traders, tho' *Indians* have nothing but what they get
by hunting, and the goods are loaded with all the
impofitions fraud and knavery can contrive to in-
hance their value ; will not induftrious *Englifh*
farmers, hereafter fettled in thofe countries, be
much better able to pay for what fhall be brought
them in the way of fair commerce?

If it is afked, what can fuch farmers raife,
wherewith to pay for the manufactures they may
want from us ? I anfwer, that the inland parts of
America in queftion are well known to be fitted for
the production of hemp, flax, potafh, and above
all, filk ; the fouthern parts may produce olive-
oil, raifins, currans, indigo, and cochineal.   Not
to mention horfes and black cattle, which may eafily be driven to the maritime markets, and at
the

---

* From *New York* into lake *Ontario*, the land carriage
of the feveral portages altogether, amounts to but about 27
miles.   From lake *Ontario* into lake *Erie*, the land carriage at
Niagara is but about 12 miles.   All the lakes above *Niagara*
communicate by navigable ftraits, fo that no land carriage is
neceffary, to go out of one into another. From *Prefqu'ifle* on lake
Erie, there are but 15 miles land-carriage, and that a good wag-
gon road, to *Reef River* a branch of the *Obio*, which brings you
into a navigation of many thoufand miles inland, if you take
together the *Obio*, the *Miffiffipi*, and all the great rivers and
branches that run into them.

the fame time affift in conveying other commodities. That the commodities firft mention'd,
may eafily by water or land carriage be brought to
the fea ports from interior *America*, will not feem
incredible, when we reflect, that hemp' formerly
came from the *Ukraine* and moft fouthern parts of
Ruffia to *Wologda*, and down the *Dwina* to *Archangel*, and thence by a perilous navigation round
the *North Cape* to *England* and other parts of *Europe*. It now comes from the fame country up the
Dnieper and down the *Duna* with much land carriage. Great part of the *Ruffia* iron, no high-
priced commodity, is brought 3000 miles by land
and water from the heart of *Siberia*. Furs, [the
produce too of *America*] are brought to *Amfterdam*
from all parts of *Siberia*, even the moft remote,
Kamfchatfka. The fame country furnifhes me with
another inftance of extended inland commerce. It
is found worth while to keep up a mercantile communication between *Peking* in *China*, and *Peterfburgh*. And none of thefe inftances of inland commerce exceed thofe of the courfes by which, at
feveral periods, the whole trade of the *Eaft* was
carried on. Before the profperity of the *Mama-
luke* dominion in *Egypt* fixed the ftaple for the
riches of the *Eaft* at *Cairo* and *Alexandria*, whither they were brought from the *Red Sea*, great
part of thofe commodities were carried to the cities
of *Cafhgar* and *Balk*. This gave birth to thofe
towns, that ftill fubfift upon the remains of their
ancient opulence, amidft a people and country equally wild. From thence thofe goods were carried down
the *Amû*, the ancient *Oxus*, to the *Cafpian* fea, and
up the *Wolga* to *Aftrachan*, from whence they were
carried over to, and down the *Don* to the mouth
of that river, and thence again the *Venetians* directly, and the *Genoefe* and *Venetians* indirectly by way
of

of *Kaffa* and *Trebifonde*, difpers'd them thro' the
Mediterranean and fome other parts of *Europe*.
Another part of thofe goods was carried over-land
from the *Wolga* to the rivers *Duna* and *Neva*; from
both they were carried to the city of *Wifluy* in the
Baltick, fo eminent for its fea-laws; and from the
city of *Ladoga* on the *Neva*, we are told they were
even carried by the *Dwina* to *Archangel*, and from
thence round the *North Cope*.

If iron and hemp will bear the charge of carriage
from this inland country, other metals will as well
as iron; and certainly filk, fince 3d. *per lb.* is not
above 1 *per cent.* on the value, and amounts to
L. 28 *per* ton.

If the growths of a country find their way out
of it, the manufactures of the countries where they
go, will infallibly find their way into it.   They who
underftand the œconomy and principles of manufactures, know, that it is impoffible to eftablifh
them in places not populous; and even in thofe
that are populous, hardly poffible to eftablifh them
to the prejudice of the places already in poffeffion of them.   Several attempts have been made in
France and *Spain*, countenanced by the Government,
to draw from us and eftablifh in thofe countries, our
hard-ware and woolen manufactures, but without
fuccefs.   The reafons are various.   A manufacture
is part of a great fyftem of commerce, which takes
in conveniences of various kinds, methods of providing materials of all forts, machines for expedit-
ing and facilitating labour, all the channels of correfpondence for vending the wares, the credit and
confidence neceffary to found and fupport this
correfpondence, the mutual aid of different artizans, and a thoufand other particulars, which time
and long experience have gradually eftablifhed.   A
part of fuch a fyftem cannot fupport itfelf without
the whole, and before the whole can be obtained
the

the part perishes. Manufactures where they are in perfection, are carried on by a multiplicity of hands, each of which is expert only in his own part, no one of them a master of the whole; and if by any means spirited away to a foreign country, he is lost without his fellows. Then it is a matter of the extremest difficulty to persuade a complete set of workmen, skilled in all parts of a manufactory, to leave their country together and settle in a foreign land. Some of the idle and drunken may be enticed away, but these only disappoint their employers, and serve to discourage the undertaking. If by royal munificence, and an expence that the profits of the trade alone would not bear, a complete set of good and skilful hands are collected and carried over, they find so much of the system imperfect, so many things wanting to carry on the trade to advantage, so many difficulties to overcome, and the knot of hands so easily broken, by death, dissatisfaction and desertion, that they and their employers are discouraged together, and the project vanishes into smoke. Hence it happens, that established manufactures are hardly ever lost, but by foreign conquest, or by some eminent interior fault in manners or government; a bad police oppressing and discouraging the workmen, or religious persecutions driving the sober and industrious out of the country. There is in short, scarce a single instance in history of the contrary, where manufactures have once taken firm root. They sometimes start up in a new place, but are generally supported like exotic plants at more expence than they are worth for any thing but curiosity, until these new seats become the refuge of the manufacturers driven from the old ones. The conquest of *Conflantinople* and final reduction of the *Greek* empire, dispersed many curious manufacturers.

rers into different parts of *Chriſtendom*. The former conqueſts of its provinces had before done the
ſame. The loſs of liberty in *Verona, Milan, Florence,
Piſa, Piſtoia,* and other great cities of *Italy*, drove
the manufacturers of woolen cloth into *Spain* and
Flanders. The latter firſt loſt their trade and manufacturers to *Antwerp* and the cities of *Brabant,*
from whence by perſecution for religion they were
ſent into *Holland* and *England.* The civil wars
during the minority of *Charles* the firſt of *Spain,*
which ended in the loſs of the liberty of their great
towns, ended too in the loſs of the manufactures of
Toledo, Segovia, Salamanca, Medina del Campo, &c.
The revocation of the edict of *Nantes*, communicated, to all the Proteſtant parts of *Europe*, the
paper, ſilk, and other valuable manufactures of
France, almoſt peculiar at that time to that country,
and till then in vain attempted elſewhere.

To be convinced that it is not ſoil and climate,
or even freedom from taxes, that determines the
reſidence of manufacturers, we need only turn our
eyes on *Holland*, where a multitude of manufactures are ſtill carried on (perhaps more than on the
ſame extent of territory any where in *Europe*) and
ſold on terms upon which they cannot be had in any
other part of the world. And this too is true
of thoſe growths, which by their nature and the
labour required to raiſe them, come the neareſt to
manufactures.

As to the common-place objection to the *North
American* ſettlements, that they are in the ſame
climate and their produce the ſame as that of *England* ; in the firſt place it is not true ; it is particularly not ſo of the countries now likely to be added to
our ſettlements ; and of our preſent colonies, the
products, lumber, tobacco, rice, and indigo, great
articles of commerce, do not interfere with the products

ducts of *England*: in the next place, a man muſt know very little of the trade of the world, who does not know, that the greater part of it is carried on between countries whoſe climate differs very little. Even the trade between the different parts of theſe *Britiſh* iſlands, is greatly ſuperior to that between *England* and all the *Weſt-India* iſlands put together.

If I have been ſucceſsful in proving that a conſiderable commerce may and will ſubſiſt between us and our future moſt inland ſettlements in *North America*, notwithſtanding their diſtance, I have more than half proved no other inconveniency will ariſe from their diſtance. Many men in ſuch a country, muſt " *know*," muſt " *think*" and muſt " *care*" about the country they chiefly trade with. The juridical and other connections of government are yet a faſter hold than even commercial ties, and ſpread directly and indirectly far and wide. Buſineſs to be ſolicited and cauſes depending, create a great intercourſe even where private property is not divided into different countries, yet this diviſion will always ſubſiſt where different countries are ruled by the ſame government. Where a man has landed property both in the mother country and a province, he will almoſt always live in the mother country: this, though there were no trade, is ſingly a ſufficient gain. It is ſaid, that *Ireland* pays near a million *Sterling* annually to its abſentees in *England*: The ballance of trade from *Spain* or even *Portugal* is ſcarcely equal to this.

Let it not be ſaid we have no abſentees from *North America*. There are many to the writer's knowledge; and if there are at preſent but few of them that diſtinguiſh themſelves here by great expence, it is owing to the mediocrity of fortune among the inhabitants of the *Northern colonies*; and a more equal divifion of landed property, than in the *Weft-India* iflands, fo that there are as yet but few large eftates. But if thofe who have fuch eftates, refide upon and take care of them themfelves, are they worfe fubjects than they would be if they lived idly in *England?* Great merit is affumed for the gentlemen of the *Weft-Indies* * , on the fcore of their refiding and fpending their money in *England*. I would not depreciate that merit ; it is confiderable, for they might, if they pleafed fpend their money in *France:* but the difference between their fpending it *here* and *at home* is not fo great. What do they fpend it in when they are here, but the produce and manufactures of this country ; and would they not do the fame if they were at home? Is it of any great importance to the *Englifh* farmer, whether the *Weft-India* gentleman comes to *London* and eats his beef, pork, and tongues, frefh, or has them brought to him in the *Weft-Indies* falted ; whether he eats his *Englifh* cheefe and butter or drinks his *Englifh* ale at *London* or in *Barbadoes?* Is the clothier's, or the mercer's, or the cutler's, or the toy-man's profit lefs, for their goods being worn and confumed by the fame perfons refiding on the other fide of the ocean? Would not the profits of the merchant and mariner be rather greater, and fome addition made to our navigation, fhips and feamen? If the *North American* gentleman ftays in his own country, and lives there in that degree of luxury and expence with regard to the ufe of *Britifh* manufactures, that his fortune entitles him to ; may not his example (from the imitation of fuperiors fo natural to mankind) fpread the ufe of thofe manufactures among hundreds of families around him, and occafion

Remarks p. 47, 48 &c.

occasion a much greater demand for them, than it would do if he should remove and live in *London?*

However this may be, if in our views of immediate advantage, it seems preferable that the gentlemen of large fortunes in *North America* should reside much in *England*, 'tis what may surely be expected as fast as such fortunes are acquired there. Their having "colleges of their own for "the education of their youth," will not prevent it: A little knowledge and learning acquired, increases the appetite for more, and will make the conversation of the learned on this side the water more strongly desired. *Ireland* has its university likewise; yet this does not prevent the immense pecuniary benefit we receive from that kingdom. And there will always be in the conveniencies of life, the politeness, the pleasures, the magnificence of the reigning country, many other attractions besides' those of learning, to draw men of substance there, where they can, apparently at least, have the best bargain of happiness for their money.

Our trade to the *West-India* islands is undoubtedly a valuable one: but whatever is the amount of it, it has long been at a stand. Limited as our sugar planters are by the scantiness of territory, they cannot increase much beyond their present number; and this is an evil, as I shall show hereafter, that will be little helped by our keeping *Guadaloupe*. The trade to our *Northern Colonies*, is not only greater, but yearly increasing with the increase of people: and even in a greater proportion, as the people increase in wealth and the ability of spending as well as in numbers. I have already said, that our people in the *Northern Colonies* double in about 25 years, exclusive of the accession of strangers. That I speak within bounds, I appeal to the
                                                    authentic

authentic accounts frequently required by the board of trade, and tranfmitted to that board by the refpective governors; of which accounts I fhall felect one as a fample, being that from the colony of *Rhode-Ifland* *; a colony that of all the others receives the leaft addition from ftrangers. For the increafe of our trade to thofe colonies, I refer to the accounts frequently laid before Parliament, by the officers of the cuftoms, and to the cuftom-houfe books: from which I have alfo felected one account, that of the trade from *England* (exclufive of *Scotland*) to *Penfilvania* †; a colony moft remarkable

---

* *Copy of the Report of Governor Hopkins to the Board of Trade, on the Numbers of People in Rhode-Ifland.*

In obedience to your lordfhip's commands, I have caufed the within account to be taken by officers under oath. By it there appears to be in this colony at this time 35,939 white perfons, and 4697 blacks, chiefly negroes.

In the year 1730, by order of the then lords commiffioners of trade and plantations, an account was taken of the number of people in this colony, and then there appeared to be 15,302 white perfons, and 2633 blacks.

Again in the year 1748, by like order, an account was taken of the nmber of people in this colony, by which it appears there were at that time 29,755 white perfons, and 4373 blacks.

STEPHEN HOPKINS.

Colony of Rhode-Ifland,
Dec. 24. 1755.

† *An Account of the Value of the Exports from England to Penfylvania, in one Year, taken at different Periods, viz.*

In	1723	they amounted only to	*L.* 15,992 : 19 : 4
	1730	they were	48,592 : 7 : 5
	1737		56,690 : 6 : 7
	1742		75,295 : 3 : 4
	1747		82,404 : 17 : 7
	1752		201,666 : 19 : 11
	1757		268,426 : 6 : 6

N. B. The account for 1758 and 1759 are not yet compleated; but thofe acquainted with the *North American*
trade,

markable for the plain frugal **manner of living of** its inhabitants, and the moſt ſuſpected of carrying on manufactures on account of the number of *Ger-man* artizans, who are known to have tranſplanted themſelves into that country, though even theſe, in truth, when they come there, generally apply themſelves to agriculture as the ſureſt ſupport and moſt advantageous employment. By this account it appears, that the exports to that province have in 28 years, increaſed nearly in the proportion of 17 to 1 ; whereas the people themſelves, who by other authentic accounts appear to double their numbers (the ſtrangers who ſettle there included) in about 16 years, cannot in the 28 years have in-creaſed in a greater proportion than as 4 to 1 : the additional demand then, and conſumption of goods from *England*, of 13 parts in 17 more than the additional number would require, muſt be owing to this, that the people having by their in-duſtry mended their circumſtances, are enabled to indulge themſelves in finer cloaths, better furni-ture, and a more general uſe of all our manufac-tures than heretofore. In fact, the occaſion for *Engliſh* goods in *North America*, and the inclination . to have and uſe them, is, and muſt be for ages to come, much greater than the ability of the people to pay for them ; they muſt therefore, as they now do, deny themſelves many things they would other-wiſe chuſe to have, or increaſe their induſtry to obtain them ; and thus, if they ſhould at any time manufacture ſome coarſe article, which on account of

trade, know, that the increaſe in thoſe two years, has been in a ſtill greater proportion ; the laſt year being ſuppoſed to exceed any former year by a third ; and this owing to the increaſed ability of the people to ſpend, from the greater quantities of money circulating among them by the war.

of its bulk or some other circumstance, cannot so
well be brought to them from *Britain*, it only
enables them the better to pay for finer goods
that otherwise they could not indulge themselves
in : so that the exports thither are not diminished
by such manufacture but rather increased. The
single article of manufacture in these colonies mentioned by the *remarker*, is *hats* made in *New England*. It is true there have been ever since the
first settlement of that country, a few hatters
there, drawn thither probably at first by the
facility of getting beaver, while the woods
were but little clear'd, and there was plenty of
those animals. The case is greatly altered now.
The beaver skins are not now to be had in
New England, but from very remote places, and
at great prices. The trade is accordingly declining there, so that, far from being able to make
hats in any quantity for exportation, they cannot
supply their home demand; and it is well known
that some thousand dozens are sent thither yearly
from *London*, and sold there cheaper than the inhabitants can make them of equal goodness. In
fact, the colonies are so little suited for establishing
of manufactures, that they are continually losing
the few branches they accidentally gain. The
working brasiers, cutlers, and pewterers, as well
as hatters, who have happened to go over from
time to time and settle in the colonies, gradually
drop the working part of their business, and import their respective goods from *England*, whence
they can have them cheaper and better than they
can make them. They continue their shops indeed, in the same way of dealing, but become *sel-
lers* of brasiery, cutlery, pewter, hats, &c. brought
from *England*, instead of being *makers* of those
goods.

Thus

Thus much as to the apprehenfion of our colonies becoming *ufelefs* to us. I fhall next confider the other fuppofition, that their growth may render them *dangerous*. Of this I own, I have not the leaft conception, when I confider that we have already fourteen feparate governments on the maritime coaft of the continent, and if we extend our fettlements fhall probably have as many more behind them on the inland fide. Thofe we now have, are not only under different governors, but have different forms of government, different laws, different interefts, and fome of them different religious perfuafions and different manners. Their jealoufy of each other is fo great that however necoffary an union of the colonies has long been, for their common defence and fecurity againft their enemies, and how fenfible foever each colony has been of that neceffity, yet they have never been able to effect fuch an union among themfelves, nor even to agree in requefting the mother country to eftablifh it for them. Nothing but the immediate command of the crown has been able to produce even the imperfect union but lately feen there, of the forces of fome colonies. If they could not agree to unite for their defence againft the *French* and *Indians,* who were perpetually haraffing their fettlements, burning their villages, and murdering their people; can it reafonably be fuppofed there is any danger of their uniting againft their own nation, which protects and encourages them, with which they have fo many connections and ties of blood, intereft and affection, and which 'tis well known they all love much more than they love one another? In fhort, there are fo many caufes that muft operate to prevent it, that I will venture to fay, an union amongft them for fuch a purpofe is not merely improbable, it is impoffible; and if the union of
the

the whole is impoffible, the attempt of a part muft be madnefs: as thofe colonies that did not join the rebellion, would join the mother country in fuppreffing it.

When I fay fuch an union is impoffible, I mean without the moft grievous tyranny and oppreffion. People who have property in a country which they may lofe, and privileges which they may endanger; are generally difpos'd to be quiet; and even to bear much, rather than hazard all. While the government is mild and juft, while important civil and religious rights are fecure, fuch fubjects will be dutiful and obedient. The waves do not rife, but when the winds blow. What fuch an adminiftration as the Duke of *Alva's* in the *Netherlands*, might produce, I know not; but this I think I have a right to deem impoffible. And yet there were two very manifeft differences between that cafe, and ours, and both are in our favour. The firft, that *Spain* had already united the feventeen provinces under one vifible government, tho' the ftates continued independent: The fecond, that the inhabitants of thofe provinces were of a nation, not only different from, but utterly unlike the *Spaniards*. Had the *Netherlands* been peopled from *Spain*, the worft of oppreffion had probably not provoked them to wifh a feparation of government. It might and probably would have ruined the country, but would never have produced an independent fovereignty. In fact, neither the very worft of governments, the worft of politicks in the laft century, nor the total abolition of their remaining liberty, in the provinces of *Spain* itfelf, in the prefent, have produced any independency that could be fupported. The fame may be obferved of *France*. And let it not be faid that the neighbourhood of thefe to the feat of government has

prevented

prevented a feparation. While our ftrength at fea continues, the banks of the *Obio* (in point of eafy and expeditious conveyance of troops) are nearer to *London*, than the remote parts of *France* and *Spain* to their refpective capitals ; and much nearer than *Connaught* and *Ulfter* were in the days of Queen *Elizabeth*. No body foretels the diffolution of the *Ruffian* monarchy from its extent, yet I will venture to fay, the eaftern parts of it are already much more inacceffiable from *Peterfburgh*, than the country on the *Miffiffipi* is from *London* ; I mean more men, in lefs time, might be conveyed the latter than the former diftance. The rivers *Oby*, *Jenefea* and *Lena*, do not facilitate the communication half fo well by their courfe, nor are they half fo practicable as the *American* rivers. To this I fhall only add the obfervation of *Macbiavel*, in his *Prince*, that a government feldom long preferves its dominion over thofe who are foreigners to it ; who on the other hand fall with great eafe, and continue infeparably annex'd to the government of their own nation, which he proves by the fate of the *Englifh conquefts* in *France*.

Yet with all thefe difadvantages, fo difficult is it to overturn an eftablifhed government, that it was not without the affiftance of *France* and *England*, that the *United Provinces* fupported themfelves : which teaches us, that if the vifionary danger of independence in our colonies is to be feared, nothing is more likely to render it fubftantial than the neighbourhood of foreigners at enmity with the fovereign government, capable of giving either aid or an afylum, as the event fhall require. Yet againft even thefe difadvantages, did *Spain* preferve almoft ten provinces, merely through their want of union, which indeed could never have taken place among the others, but for caufes, fome
of

of which are in our cafe impoffible, and others it is impious to fuppofe poffible.

The *Romans* well underftood that policy which teaches the fecurity arifing to the chief government from feparate ftates among the governed, when they reftored the liberties of the ftates of *Greece*, (oppreffed but united under *Macedon*) by an edict that every ftate fhould live under its own laws.* They did not even name a governor. *Independence of each other, and feparate interefts*, tho' among a people united by common manners, language, and I may fay religion, inferior neither in wifdom, bravery, nor their love of liberty to the *Romans* themfelves, was all the fecurity the fovereigns wifhed for their fovereignty. It is true, they did not call themfelves fovereigns ; they fet no value on the title ; they were contented with poffeffing the thing ; and poffefs it they did, even without a ftanding army. What can be a ftronger proof of the fecurity of their poffeffion ? And yet by a policy fimilar to this throughout, was the *Roman* world fubdued and held : a world compos'd of above an hundred languages and fets of manners different from thofe of their mafters.† Yet this dominion was unfhakeable, till the lofs of liberty and corruption of manners overturned it.   But

---

* *Omnes Græcorum civitates, quæ in Europa, quæque in Afia effent, libertatem ac fuas leges haberent, &c.*   Liv. lib. 33. c. 30.

† When the *Romans* had fubdu'd *Macedon* and *Illyricum*, they were both form'd into republicks by a decree of the fenate, and *Macedon* was thought fafe from the danger of a revolution, by being divided, into a divifion common among the *Romans*, as we learn from the tetrarchs in fcripture. *Omnium primum liberos effe placebat Macedonas atque Illyrios ; ut omnibus gentibus apareret, arma populi Romani non liberis fervitutem, fed contra fervientibus libertatem afferre. Ut et in libertate gentes quæ effent, tutam eam fibi perpetuamque fub tutela populi Romani effe : & quæ fub regibus viverent, & in prefens tempus mitiores eos juftiorefque refpectu populi Romani habere fe ; & fi quando bellum*

But what is the prudent policy inculcated by the *remarker*, to obtain this end, security of dominion over our colonies: It is, to leave the *French* in *Canada*, to " *check*" their growth, for otherwise our people may " increase infinitely from all " causes." * We have already seen in what manner the *French* and their *Indians check the growth* of our colonies. 'Tis a modest word this, *check*, for massacring men, women and children. The writer would, if he could, hide from himself as well as from the public, the horror arising from such a proposal, by couching it in general terms : 'tis no wonder he thought it a " subject not fit for dif- " cussion" in his letter, tho' he recommends it as " a point that should be the constant object of the " minister's attention !"------But if *Canada* is restored on this principle, will not *Britain* be guilty of all the blood to be shed, all the murders to be committed in order to check this dreaded growth of our own people ? Will not this be telling the *French* in plain terms, that the horrid barbarities they perpetrate with their *Indians* on our colonists, are agreeable to us ; and that they need not apprehend the resentment of a government with whose views they so happily concur ? Will not the colonies view it in this light ? Will they have reason to consider themselves any longer as subjects and children, when they find their cruel enemies halloo'd upon them by the country from whence they sprung, the government that owes them protection

lum cum populo Romano regibus fuisset sui?, exisum ejus victoriam Romanis, sibi libertatem allaturum crederent.——In quatuor regiones describi Macedoniam, ut suum quæque concilium haberet, placuit : & dimidium tributi quàm quod regibus ferre soliti erant, populo Romano pendere. Similia his & in Illyricum mandata.

Liv. lib. 45. c. 18.

* Remarks, p. 50, 51.

tection as it requires their obedience? Is not this the moſt likely means of driving them into the arms of the *French*, who can invite them by an offer of that ſecurity their own government chuſes not to afford them? I would not be thought to inſinuate that the *remarker* wants humanity. I know how little many good-natured perſons are affected by the diſtreſſes of people at a diſtance and whom they do not know. There are even thoſe, who, being preſent, can ſympathize ſincerely with the grief of a lady on the ſudden death of her favourite bird, and yet can read of the ſinking of a city in *Syria* with very little concern. If it be, after all, thought neceſſary to *check* the growth of our colonies, give me leave to propoſe a method leſs cruel. It is a method of which we have an example in ſcripture. The murder of huſbands, of wives, of brothers, ſiſters and children, whoſe pleaſing ſociety has been for ſome time enjoyed, affects deeply the reſpective ſurviving relations : but grief for the death of a child juſt born is ſhort and eaſily ſupported. The method I mean is that which was dictated by the *Egyptian* policy, when the " infinite increaſe" of the *children of Iſrael* was apprehended as dangerous to the ſtate.* Let an act of parliament, then be made, enjoining the colony midwives to ſtifle in the birth every third or fourth child. By this means you may keep the colonies to their preſent ſize. And if they were under the hard alternative of ſubmitting to one or the other of theſe ſchemes

for

---

* And *Pharoah* ſaid unto his people, behold the people of the children of *Iſrael* are more and mightier than we ; come on, let us deal *wiſely* with them ; *leſt they multiply* and it come to paſs that when there falleth out any war, they join alſo unto our enemies and fight againſt us, and ſo get them up out of the land. ——And the king ſpake to the *Hebrew* midwives, &c.

Exodus, Chap. 1.

for *checking* their growth, I dare anfwer for them, they would prefer the latter.

But all this debate about the propriety or impropriety of keeping or reftoring *Canada*, is poffibly too early. We have taken the capital indeed, but the country is yet far from being in our poffeffion ; and perhaps never will be : for if our M- ----rs are perfuaded by fuch counfellors as the *remarker*, that the *French* there are " not the worft of neighbours," and that if we had conquered *Canada*, we ought for our own fakes to reftore it, as a *check* to the growth of our colonies, I am then afraid we fhall never take it. For there are many ways of avoiding the completion of the conqueft, that will be lefs exceptionable and lefs odious than the giving it up.

The objection I have often heard, that if we had *Canada*, we could not people it without draining *Britain* of its inhabitants, is founded on ignorance of the nature of population in new countries. When we firft began to colonize in *America*, it was neceffary to fend people, and to fend feed-corn ; but it is not now neceffary that we fhould furnifh, for a new colony, either one or the other. The annual increment alone of our prefent colonies, without diminifhing their numbers, or requiring a man from hence, is fufficient in ten years to fill *Canada* with double the number of *Englifh* that it now has of *French* inhabitants.* Thofe who are proteftants among the *French*, will probably chufe to remain under the *Englifh* government ; many will chufe to remove, if they can be allowed to fell their lands, improvements and effects : the reft in that thinfettled

---

* In fact, there has not gone from *Britain* to our colonies thefe 20 years paft, to fettle there, fo many as 10 families a year ; the new fettlers are either the offspring of the old, or emigrants from *Germany* or the north of *Ireland*.

fettled country, will in lefs than half a century, from the crouds of *Englifh* fettling round and among them, be blended and incorporated with our people both in language and manners.

In *Guadaloupe* the cafe is fomewhat different; and though I am far from thinking * we have fugar-land enough †, I cannot think *Guadaloupe* is fo defirable an increafe of it, as other objects the enemy would probably be infinitely more ready to part with. A country *fully inhabited* by any nation is no proper poffeffion for another of different language, manners and religion. It is hardly ever tenable at lefs expence than it is worth,—But the ifle of *Cayenne*, and its appendix *Equinoctial-France*, would indeed be an acquifition every way fuitable to our fituation and defires. This would hold all that migrate from *Barbadoes*, the *Leeward Iflands*, or *Jamaica*. It would certainly recal into an *Englifh* government (in which there would be room for millions) all who have before fettled or purchafed in *Martineco*, *Guadaloupe*, *Santa-Cruz* or *St. John's*; except fuch as know not the value of an *Englifh* government, and fuch I am fure are not worth recalling.

But fhould we keep *Guadaloupe*, we are told it would enable us to export £. 300,000 in fugars. Admit it to be true, though perhaps the amazing increafe of *Englifh* confumption might ftop moft of it here, to whofe profit is this to redound? to

the

* Remark, p. 30, 34.

† It is often faid we have plenty of fugar-land ftill unemployed in *Jamaica*: but thofe who are all well acquainted with that ifland, know, that the remaining vacant land in it is generally fituated among mountains, rocks and gullies, that make carriage impracticable, fo that no profitable ufe can be made of it unlefs the price of fugars fhould fo greatly increafe as to enable the planter to make very expenfive roads, by blowing up rocks, erecting bridges, &c. every 2 or 300 yards.

the profit of the *French* inhabitants of the iſland : except a ſmall part that ſhould fall to the ſhare of the *Engliſh* purchaſers, but whoſe whole purchaſe-money muſt firſt be added to the wealth and circulation of *France.*

I grant, however, much of this £. 300,000 would be expended in *Britiſh* manufactures. Perhaps, too, a few of the land-owners of *Guadaloupe* might dwell and ſpend their fortunes in *Britain,* (though probably much fewer than of the inhabitants of *North America*). I admit the advantage ariſing to us from theſe circumſtances, (as far as they go) in the caſe of *Guadaloupe,* as well as in that of our other *Weſt India* ſettlements Yet even this conſumption is little better than that of an allied nation would be, who ſhould take our manufactures and ſupply us with ſugar, and put us to no expence in defending the place of growth.

But though our own colonies expend among us almoſt the whole produce of our ſugar, * can we or ought we to promiſe ourſelves this will be the caſe of *Guadaloupe.* One 100,000 £. will ſupply them with *Britiſh* manufactures ; and ſuppoſing we can effectually prevent the introduction of thoſe of *France,* (which is morally impoſſible in a country uſed to them) the other 200,000 will ſtill be ſpent in *France,* in the education of their children and ſupport of themſelves ; or elſe be laid up there, where they will always think their home to be.

Beſides this conſumption of *Britiſh* manufactures, much is ſaid of the benefit we ſhall have from the ſituation of *Guadaloupe,* and we are told of a trade to the *Caraccas* and *Spaniſh Main.* In what reſpect *Guadaloupe* is better ſituated for this trade than *Jamaica,* or even any of our other iſlands, I am at a loſs to gueſs. I believe it to be

not

* Remarks, p. 47.

not so well situated for that of the windward coast, as *Tobago* and *St. Lucia*, which in this as well as other respects, would be more valuable possessions, and which, I doubt not, the peace will secure to us. Nor is it nearly so well situated for that of the rest of the *Spanish Main* as *Jamaica*. As to the greater safety of our trade by the possession of *Guadaloupe*, experience has convinced us that in reducing a single island, or even more, we stop the privateering business but little. Privateers still subsist in equal if not greater numbers, and carry the vessels into *Martinico* which before it was more convenient to carry into *Guadaloupe*. Had we all the *Caribbees*, it is true, they would in those parts be without shelter. Yet upon the whole I suppose it to be a doubtful point and well worth consideration, whether our obtaining possession of all the *Caribbees*, would be more than a temporary benefit, as it would necessarily soon fill the *French* part of *Hispaniola* with *French* inhabitants, and thereby render it five times more valuable in time of peace, and little less than impregnable in time of war; and would probably end in a few years in the uniting the whole of that great and fertile island under a *French* government. It is agreed on all hands, that our conquest of *St. Christopher's*, and driving the *French* from thence, first furnish'd *Hispaniola* with skilful and substantial planters, and was consequently the first occasion of its present opulence. On the other hand, I will hazard an opinion, that valuable as the *French* possessions in the *West Indies* are, and undeniable the advantages they derive from them, there is somewhat to be weighed in the opposite scale. They cannot at present make war with *England*, without exposing those advantages while divided among the numerous islands they now have, much more than they would, were they possessed

feffed of *St. Domingo* only ; their own fhare of which would, if well cultivated, grow more fugar, than is now grown in all their *Weft India* iflands.

I have before faid I do not deny the utility of the conqueft, or even of our future poffeffion of *Guadaloupe*, if not bought to dear. The trade of the *Weft Indies* is one of our moft valuable trades. Our poffeffions there deferve our greateft care and attention. So do thofe of *North America*. I fhall not enter into the invidious tafk of comparing their due eftimation. It would be a very long and a very difagreeable one, to run thro' every thing material on this head. It is enough to our prefent point, if I have fhown, that the value of *North America* is capable of an immenfe increafe, by an acquifition and meafures, that muft neceffarily have an effect the direct contrary of what we have been induftrioufly taught to fear ; and that *Guadaloupe* is, in point of advantage, but a very fmall addition to our *Weft India* poffeffions, rendered many ways lefs valuable to us than it is to the *French*, who will probably fet more value upon it than upon a country that is much more valuable to us than to them.

There is a great deal more to be faid on all the parts of thefe fubjects ; but as it would carry me into a detail that I fear would tire the patience of my readers, and which I am not without apprehenfions I have done already, I fhall referve what remains till I dare venture again on the indulgence of the publick.

IN Confirmation of the Writer's Opinion concerning *Population, Manufactures, &c.* he has thought it not amifs to add an Extract from a Piece written fome years fince in *America*, where the Facts muft be well known, on which the Reafonings are founded.   It is intitled

OBSERVATIONS concerning the Increafe of Mankind, Peopling of Countries, *&c.*   Written in *Penfylvania*, 1751.

1. TABLES of the proportion of marriages to births, of deaths to births, of marriages to the numbers of inhabitants, *&c.* formed on obfervations made upon the bills of mortality, chriftenings, *&c.* of populous cities, will not fuit countries; nor will tables formed on obfervations made on full fettled old countries, as *Europe*, fuit new countries, as *America*.

2. For people increafe in proportion to the number of marriages, and that is greater in proportion to the eafe and convenience of fupporting a family.   When families can be eafily fupported, more perfons marry, and earlier in life.

3. In cities, where all trades, occupations and offices are full, many delay marrying, till they can fee how to bear the charges of a family; which charges are greater in cities, as luxury is more common; many live fingle during life, and continue fervants to families, journeymen to trades, *&c.* hence cities do not by natural generation fupply themfelves with inhabitants; the deaths are more than the births.

4. In countries full fettled, the cafe muft be nearly the fame; all lands being occupied and improved to the heighth; thofe who cannot get land, muft labour for others that have it; when labourers are plenty, their wages will be low; by low wages a family is fupported with difficulty; this difficulty deters many from marriage, who therefore long continue fervants and fingle.— Only as the cities take fupplies of people from the country, and thereby make a little more room in the country, marriage is a little more encouraged there, and the births exceed the deaths.

5. Great part of *Europe* is full fettled with hufbandmen, manufacturers, *&c.* and therefore cannot now much increafe in people: *America* is chiefly occupied by *Indians*, who fubfift moftly by hunting.———But as the hunter, of all men, requires the greateft quantity of land from whence to draw his fubfiftence, (the hufbandmen fubfifting on much lefs, the Gardener on ftill lefs,

lefs, and the manufacturer requiring leaft of all) the *Europeans* found *America* as fully fettled as it well could be by hunters; yet thefe having large tracts, were eafily prevailed on to part with portions of territory to the new comers, who did not much interfere with the natives in hunting, and furnifhed them with many things they wanted.

6. Land being thus plenty in *America*, and fo cheap as that a labouring man, that underftands hufbandry, can in a fhort time fave money enough to purchafe a piece of new land fufficient for a plantation, whereon he may fubfift a family; fuch are not afraid to marry; for if they even look far enough forward to confider how their children when grown up are to be provided for, they fee that more land is to be had at rates euually eafy, all cirmcumftances confidered.

7. Hence marriages in *America* are more general, and more generally early, than in *Europe*. And if it is reckoned there, that there is but one marriage *per annum* among 100 perfons, perhaps we may here reckon two; and if in *Europe* they have but four births to a marriage (many of their marriages being late) we may here reckon eight; of which if one half grow up, and our marriages are made, reckoning one with another, at twenty years of age, our people muft at leaft be doubled every twenty years.

8. But notwithftanding this increafe, fo vaft is the territory of *North America*, that it will require many ages to fettle it fully; and till it is fully fettled, labour will never be cheap here, where no man continues long a labourer for others, but gets a plantation of his own; no man continues long a journeyman to a trade, but goes among thofe new fettlers, and fets up for himfelf, *&c.* Hence labour is no cheaper now, in *Penfilvania*, than it was thirty years ago, tho' fo many thoufand labouring people have been imported from *Germany* and *Ireland*.

9. The danger therefore of thefe colonies interfering with their mother country in trades that depend on labour, manufactures, *&c.* is too remote to require the attention of *Great Britain*.

10. But in proportion to the increafe of the colonies, a vaft demand is growing for *Britifh* manufactures; a glorious market wholly in the power of *Britain*, in which foreigners cannot interfere, which will increafe in a fhort time even beyond her power of fupplying, tho' her whole trade fhould be to her colonies. * *
* * * * * * *

12. 'Tis an ill-grounded opinion that by the labour of flaves, *America* may poffibly vie in cheapnefs of manufactures with *Britain*. The labour of flaves can never be fo cheap here as the labour of working men is in *Britain*. Any one may compute it. Intereft of money is in the colonies from 6 to 10 *per Cent.* Slaves one with another coft 30 *l.* Sterling *per* head.

Reckon

Reckon then the intereſt of the firſt purchaſe of a ſlave, the inſurance or riſque on his life, his cloathing and diet, expences in his ſickneſs and loſs of time, loſs by his neglect of buſineſs (neglect is natural to the man who is not to be benefited by his own care or diligence) expence of a driver to keep him at work, and his pilfering from time to time, almoſt every ſlave being from the nature of ſlavery a thief, and compare the whole amount with the wages of a manufacturer of iron or wool in *England*, you will ſee that labour is much cheaper there than it ever can be by negroes here.   Why then will *Americans* purchaſe ſlaves ? Becauſe ſlaves may be kept as long as a man pleaſes, or has occaſion for their labour; while hired men are continually leaving their maſter (often in the midſt of his buſineſs) and ſetting up for themſelves. § 8.

13. As the increaſe of people depends on the encouragement of marriages, the following things muſt diminiſh a nation, *viz.* 1. The being conquered ; for the conquerors will engroſs as many offices, and exact as much tribute or profit on the labour of the conquered, as will maintain them in their new eſtabliſhment ; and this diminiſhing the ſubſiſtence of the natives, diſcourages their marriages, and ſo gradually diminiſhes them, while the foreigners increaſe.   2. Loſs of territory.   Thus the *Britons* being driven into *Wales*, and crouded together in a barren country inſufficient to ſupport ſuch great numbers, diminiſhed till the people bore a proportion to the produce, while the *Saxons* increaſed on their abandoned lands, till the iſland became full of *Engliſh*.   And were the *Engliſh* now driven into *Wales* by ſome foreign nation, there would in a few years be no more *Engliſhmen* in *Britain*, than there are now people in *Wales*.   3. Loſs of trade.   Manufactures exported, draw ſubſiſtence from foreign countries for numbers ; who are thereby enabled to marry and raiſe families.   If the nation be deprived of any branch of trade, and no new employment is found for the people occupy'd in that branch, it will ſoon be deprived of ſo many people.   4. Loſs of food.   Suppoſe a nation has a fiſhery, which not only employs great numbers, but makes the food and ſubſiſtence of the people cheaper : if another nation becomes maſter of the ſeas, and prevents the fiſhery, the people will diminiſh in proportion as the loſs of employ, and dearneſs of proviſion makes it more difficult to ſubſiſt a family.   5. Bad government and inſecure property.   People not only leave ſuch a country, and ſettling abroad incorporate with other nations, loſe their native language, and become foreigners ; but the induſtry of thoſe that remain being diſcouraged, the quantity of ſubſiſtence in the country is leſſened, and the ſupport of a family becomes more difficult.   So heavy taxes tend to diminiſh a people.   6. The introduction of ſlaves.   The negroes brought into the *Engliſh* ſugar iſlands,
have

have greatly diminished the whites there; the poor are by this means deprived of employment, while a few families acquire vast estates, which they spend on foreign luxuries, and educating their children in the habit of those luxuries; the same income is needed for the support of one, that might have maintained one hundred. The whites, who have slaves, not labouring, are enfeebled, and therefore not so generally prolific; the slaves being worked too hard, and ill fed, their constitutions are broken, and the deaths among them are more than their births; so that a continual supply is needed from *Africa.* The northern colonies having few slaves, encrease in whites. Slaves also pejorate the families that use them; the white children become proud, disgusted with labour, and being educated in idleness, are rendered unfit to get a living by industry.

14. Hence the prince that acquires new territory, if he finds it vacant, or removes the natives to give his own people room; the legislator that makes effectual laws for promoting of trade, increasing employment, improving land by more or better tillage, providing more food by fisheries, securing property, &c. and the man that invents new trades, arts or manufactures, or new improvements in husbandry, may be properly called *Fathers of their Nation*, as they are the cause of the generation of multitudes, by the encouragement they afford to marriage.

15. As to privileges granted to the married, (such as the *jus trium liberorum* among the *Romans*) they may hasten the filling of a country that has been thinned by war or pestilence, or that has otherwise vacant territory, but cannot increase a people beyond the means provided for their subsistence.

16. Foreign luxuries and needless manufactures imported and used in a nation, do, by the same reasoning, increase the people of the nation that furnishes them, and diminish the people of the nation that uses them.——Laws therefore that prevent such importations, and on the contrary promote the exportation of manufactures to be consumed in foreign countries, may be called (with respect to the people that make them) *generative laws*, as by increasing subsistence they encourage marriage. Such laws likewise strengthen a country doubly, by increasing its own people and diminishing its neighbours.

17. Some *European* nations prudently refuse to consume the manufactures of *East-India*:—They should likewise forbid them to their colonies; for the gain to the merchant is not to be compared with the loss by this means of people to the nation.

18. Home luxury in the great increases the nation's manufacturers employed by it, who are many, and only tends to diminish the families that indulge in it, who are few. The greater the common fashionable expence of any rank of people, the more cautious they are of marriage. Therefore luxury should never be suffered to become common. 19.

19. The great increase of offspring in particular families, is not always owing to greater fecundity of nature, but sometimes to examples of industry in the heads, and industrious education; by which the children are enabled to provide better for themselves, and their marrying early is encouraged from the prospect of good subsistence.

20. If there be a sect therefore, in our nation, that regard frugality and industry as religious duties, and educate their children therein, more than others commonly do; such sect must consequently increase more by natural generation, than any other sect in *Britain.*——

21. The importation of foreigners into a country that has as many inhabitants as the present employments and provisions for subsistence will bear, will be in the end no increase of people, unless the new comers have more industry and frugality than the natives, and then they will provide more subsistence and increase in the country; but they will gradually eat the natives out.——Nor is it necessary to bring in foreigners to fill up any occasional vacancy in a country; for such vacancy (if the laws are good, § 14, 16) will soon be filled by natural generation. Who can now find the vacancy made in *Sweden*, *France*, or other warlike nations, by the plague of heroism 40 years ago; in *France*, by the expulsion of protestants; in *England*, by the settlement of her colonies; or in *Guinea*, by 100 years exportation of slaves that has blackened half *America* ?——The thinness of the inhabitants in *Spain*, is owing to national pride and idleness, and other causes, rather than to the expulsion of the *Moors*, or to the making of new settlements.

22. There is in short no bound to the prolific nature of plants or animals, but what is made by their crowding and interfering with each other's means of subsistence. Was the face of the earth vacant of other plants, it might be gradually sowed and overspread with one kind only; as for instance, with Fennel; and were it empty of other inhabitants, it might in a few ages be replenished from one nation only as for instance with *Englishmen*. Thus there are supposed to be now upwards of one Million *English* souls in *North America*, (tho' 'tis thought scarce 80,000 have been brought over sea) and yet perhaps there is not one the fewer in *Britain*, but rather many more, on account of the employment the colonies afford to manufacturers at home. This million doubling, suppose but once in 25 years, will in another century be more than the people of *England*, and the greatest number of *Englishmen* will be on this side the water.

What an accession of power to the *British* empire by sea as well as land! What increase of trade and navigation! What numbers of ships and seamen! We have been here but little more than 100 years, and yet the force of our privateers in the late war, united, was greater, both in men and guns, than that of the whole *British* navy in queen *Elizabeth's* time. ———— How important an affair then to *Britain*, is the present treaty † for settling the bounds between her colonies and the *French*, and how careful should she be to secure room enough, since on the room depends so much the Increase of her people?

23. In fine, a nation well regulated is like a polypus; ‡ take away a limb, its place is soon supply'd; cut it in two, and each deficient part shall speedily grow out of the part remaining. Thus if you have room and subsistence enough, as you may by dividing, make ten polypuses out of one, you may of one make ten nations, equally populous and powerful; or rather increase a nation tenfold in numbers and strength. * * * * * * * * *

† 1751.   ‡ *A water-insect, well-known to naturalists.*

SINCE the foregoing fheets were printed off, the writer has obtained accounts of the Exports to *North America*, and the *Weft India Iflands*, by which it appears, that there has been fome increafe of trade to thofe *Iflands* as well as to *North America*, though in a much lefs degree. The following extract from thefe accounts will fhow the reader at one view the amount of the exports to each, in two different terms of five years; the terms taken at ten years diftance from each other, to fhow the increafe, *viz.*

Firft Term, from 1744 to 1748, inclufive.

Northern Colonies.	Weft India Iflands.
1744—£.640,114 12 4	£.796,112 17 9
1745——534,316 2 5	——503,669 19 9
1746——754,945 4 3	——472,994 19 7
1747——726,648 5 5	——856,463 18 6
1748——830,243 16 9	——734,095 15 3

Total, £. 3,486,268   1   2   Tot. £. 3,363,337 10 10
Difference,   122,930 10   4

£.3,486,268   1   2

Second Term, from 1754 to 1758, inclufive.

Northern Colonies.	Weft India Iflands.
1754——1,246,615 1 11	——685,675 3 0
1755——1,177,848 6 10	——694,667 13 3
1756——1,428,720 18 10	——733,453 16 3
1757——1,727,924 2 10	——776,488 0 6
1758——1,832,948 13 10	——877,571 19 11

Total, £.7,414,57   4   3   Tot. £.3,767,841 12 11
Difference 3,646,215 11   4

£.7,414,057   4   3

Ia

In the firſt term, total for *Weſt India Iſlands*, 3,363,337 10 10
In the ſecond Term, *ditto*, - - - - 3,767,841 12 11

Increaſe only £.0,404,504 2 1

In the firſt Term, total for *Northern Colonies*, 3,486,268 1 2
In the ſecond Term, *ditto*, - - - - 7,414,057 4 3

Increaſe, £.3,927,789 3 1

By theſe accounts it appears, that the Exports to the *Weſt India Iſlands* and to the *Northern Colonies* were in the firſt term nearly equal; the difference being only 122,936*l*. 10*s*. 4*d*. and in the ſecond term, the exports to thoſe iſlands had only increaſed 404,504*l*. 2*s*. 1*d*.--------Whereas the increaſe to the *Northern Colonies* is 3,927,789*l*. 3*s*. 1*d*. almoſt FOUR MILLIONS.

Some part of this increaſed demand for *Engliſh* goods, may be aſcribed to the armies and fleets we have had both in *North America*, and the *Weſt Indies*; not ſo much for what is conſumed by the ſoldiery; their cloathing, ſtores, ammunition, &c. ſent from hence on account of the government, being (as is ſuppoſed) not included in theſe accounts of merchandize exported; but, as the war has occaſioned a great plenty of money in *America*, many of the inhabitants have increaſed their expence.

Theſe accounts do not include any exports from *Scotland* to *America*, which are doubtleſs proportionably conſiderable; nor the exports from *Ireland*.

THE END.

THE CAUSES OF THE PRESENT DISTRACTIONS IN AMERICA EXPLAINED

Benjamin Franklin, *The Causes of the Present Distractions in America Explained: in Two Letters to a Merchant in London* (New York, 1774), pp. 1–16.

From the first publication of *Observations Concerning the Increase of Mankind* in 1760 to the publication of this piece in 1774, Franklin's views on the relationship between the colonies and Great Britain underwent some dramatic changes. By 1774, Franklin increasingly supported the movement for independence, realising that the colonists would never receive fair representation in Parliament. Further, Franklin recognised that the colonists would never succumb to the increasing restrictive trade and tax regulations. *The Causes of the Present Distractions in America Explained* was written as two anonymous letters, addressed to a 'merchant in London'. While some have attributed this writing to Sir Francis Bernard, it is more generally believed that Franklin is the author. These letters spell out the colonial grievances in a manner that attracts the attention of London merchants – who relied on the American trade for their livelihood – in an attempt to win support for American demands for freer trade in England.

THE
CAUSES
OF THE
PRESENT DISTRACTIONS
IN
AMERICA
EXPLAINED:
IN
TWO LETTERS
TO A
MERCHANT
IN LONDON.

By F—— B——

Printed in the Year 1774.

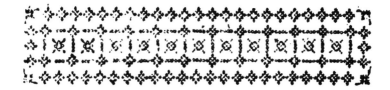

The Caufes of the prefent Dif-tractions explained, in two Letters to a Merchant in London.

LETTER I.

S I R,

AS the caufe of the prefent ill-humour in America, and of the Refolutions taken there to purchafe lefs of our manufactures, does not feem to be generally underftood, it may afford fome fatisfaction to you, if I give them the following fhort hiftorical ftate of facts.

From the time that the Colonies were firft confidered as capable of granting aids to the Crown, down to the end of the laft war; it is faid that the conftant mode of obtaining thofe aids was by requifition made from the Crown through its Governors to the feveral Affemblies,

in

in circular letters from the Secretary of State in his Majefty's name, fetting forth the occafion, requiring them to take the matter into confideration, and expreffing a reliance on their prudence, duty and affection to his Majefty's government, that they would grant fuch fums, or raife fuch numbers of men, as were fuitable to their refpective circumftances.

The colonies being accuftomed to this method, have from time to time granted money to the Crown, or raifed troops for its fervice, in proportion to their abilities, and, during all the laft war, beyond their abilities, fo that confiderable fums were returned them yearly by Parliament, as exceeding their proportion.

Had this happy method been continued (a method which left the King's fubjects in thofe remote countries the pleafure of fhewing their zeal and loyalty, and of imagining that they recommended themfelves to their Sovereign by the liberality of their voluntary grants) there is no doubt but all the money that could reafonably be expected to be raifed from them, in any manner, might have been obtained from them, without the leaft heart-burning, offence, or breach of the harmony of affections and interefts that fo long fubfifted between the two countries.

It

It has been thought wisdom in a government, exercising sovereignty over different kinds of people, to have some regard to prevailing and established opinions among the people to be governed, wherever such opinions might in their effects promote or obstruct public measures.—If they tend to obstruct public service, they are to be changed before we act against them, and they can only be changed by reason and persuasion.—But if public service can be carried on without thwarting those opinions, if they can be on the contrary made subservient to it, they are not unnecessarily to be thwarted, how absurd soever such popular opinions may be in their natures.

This had been the wisdom of our government, with respect to raising money in the colonies. It was well known that the colonists universally were of opinion, that no money could be levied from English subjects, but by their own consent, given by themselves or their chosen representatives. That therefore, whatever money was to be raised from the people in the colonies, must first be granted by their assemblies, as the money raised in Britain is first to be granted by the House of Commons. That this right of granting their own money was essential to English liberty; and that if any man, or body of men, in which they had no representative of their choosing, could

could tax them at pleafure, they could not be faid to have any property, any thing they could call their own.   But as thefe opinions did not hinder their granting money voluntarily and amply, whenever the Crown, by its fervants, came into their affemblies (as it does into its Parliaments of Britain and Ireland) and demanded aids, therefore that method was chofen, rather than the baneful one of arbitrary taxes.

I do not undertake here to fupport thofe opinions; they have been refuted by a late act of Parliament, declaring its own power; which very Parliament, however, fhewed wifely fo much tender regard to thofe inveterate prejudices, as to repeal a tax that had odioufly militated againft them.—And thefe prejudices are ftill fo fixed and rooted in the Americans, that it is fuppofed not a fingle man among them has been convinced of his error by that act of parliament.

The Minifter, therefore, who firft projected to lay afide the accuftomed method of requifition, and to raife money en America by ftamps, feems not to have acted wifely in deviating from that method (which the colonifts looked upon as conftitutional) and thwarting unneceffarily, the general fixed prejudices of fo great a number of the King's fubjects.   It was not,

not, however, for want of knowledge that what he was about to do would give them great offence; he appears to have been very sensible of this, and apprehensive that it might occasion some disorders, to prevent or suppress which he projected another bill, that was brought in the same session with the stamp act, whereby it was to be made lawful for military officers in the colonies to quarter their soldiers in private houses. This seemed intended to awe the people into a compliance with the other act. Great opposition, however, being raised here against the bill, by the agents from the colonies, and the merchants trading thither, the colonists declaring that, under such a power in the army, no one could look on his house as his own, or think he had a home, when soldiers might be thrust into it, and mixed with his family, at the pleasure of an officer, that part of the bill was dropt; but there still remained a clause, when it passed into a law, to oblige the several assemblies to provide quarters for the soldiers, furnishing them with fire, beds, candles, small beer or rum, and sundry other articles, at the expence of the several provinces.—And this act continued in force when the stamp-act was repealed, though, if obligatory on the assemblies, it equally militated against the American principle abovementioned, that money is not to be raised on English subjects without their consent.

The

The colonies neverthelefs, being put into high good humour by the repeal of the ftamp-act, chofe to avoid a frefh difpute upon the other, it being temporary, and foon to expire, never (as they hoped) to revive again; and in the mean time they, by various ways, provided for the quartering of the troops, either by acts of their own affemblies, without taking notice of the acts of Parliament, or by fome variety or fmall diminution (as of falt and vinegar) in the fupplies required by the Act, that what they did might appear a voluntary act of their own, and not done in obedience to an act of parliament, which they thought contrary to right, and therefore void in itfelf.

It might have been well if the matter had thus paffed without notice; but an officious Governor having written home an angry and aggravating letter upon this conduct in the affembly of his province, the outed projector of the ftamp-act, and his adherents, then in the oppofition, raifed fuch a clamour againft America, as in rebellion, &c. and againft thofe who had been for the repeal of the ftamp-act, as having thereby been encouragers of this fuppofed rebellion, that it was thought neceffary to enforce the quartering act by another act of Parliament, taking away from the province of New-York, which had been moft explicit in its refufal, all the powers of legiflation, till it

fhould

fhould have complied with that act : The news of which greatly alarmed the people every where in America, as the language of fuch an act feemed to be Obey implicitly laws made by the Parliament of Great Britain, to force money from you without your confent, or you fhall enjoy no rights or privileges at all.

At the fame time the late Chancellor of the Exchequer, defirous of ingratiating himfelf with the oppofition, or driven to it by their clamours, projected the levying more money from America, by new duties on various articles of our own manufacture, as glafs, paper, painters colours, &c. appointing a new board of cuftoms, and fending over a fet of commiffioners (with large falaries) to be eftablifhed at Bofton, who were to have the care of collecting thefe duties ; and which were, by the act, exprefsly mentioned to be intended for the payment of the falaries of Governors, Judges, and other officers of the Crown in America, it being a pretty general opinion here, that thofe officers ought not to depend on the people there for any part of their fupport.

It is not my intention to combat this opinion ; but perhaps it may be fome fatisfaction to you to know what ideas the Americans have on the fubject. They fay then, as to Governors, that they are not like Princes whofe
posterity

posterity have an inheritance in the government of a nation, and therefore an interest in
its prosperity ;, they are generally strangers to
the provinces they are sent to govern ; have
no estate, natural connection, or relation there,
to give them an affection for the country ; that
they come only to make money as fast as they
can, are frequently men of vicious characters
and broken fortunes, sent merely to get them
off the hands of a minister somewhere out of
the way ; as that they intend staying in the
country no longer than their government continues, and purpose to leave no family behind
them, they are apt to be regardless of the good
will of the people, and care not what is said
or thought of them after they are gone. Their
situation gives them many opportunities of being vexatious, and they are often so, notwithstanding their dependance on the assemblies
for all that part of their support that does not
arise from fees established by law, but would
probably be much more so if they were to be
fully supported by money drawn from the
people, without the consent or good will of
the people, which is the professed design of
this act. That if by means of the enforced
duties, government is to be supported in America, without the intervention of the assemblies, their assemblies will soon be looked upon
as useless, and a Governor will not call them,
as having nothing to hope from their meeting,

and

and perhaps fomething to fear from their en-
quiries into, and remonftrances againft his mal-
adminiftration; that thus the people will be
deprived of their moft effential rights; that its
being, as at prefent, a Governor's intereft to
cultivate the good will, by promoting the
welfare of the people he governs, can be attended with no prejudice to the Mother-Country, fince all the laws he may be prevailed to
give his affent to, are fubject to a revifion here,
and if reported againft by the Board of Trade,
as hurtful to the intereft of this country, may,
and are immediately repealed by the Crown;
nor dare he pafs any law contrary to his inftructions, as he holds his office during the
pleafure of the Crown, and his Securities are
liable for the penalties of their bonds, if he
contravenes thofe inftructions.

This is what they fay as to Governors.

As to Judges, they alledge, that being appointed from hence by the Crown, and holding their commiffions, not during good behaviour, as in Britain, but during pleafure, all
the weight of intereft would be thrown into
one of the fcales (which ought to be held
even) if the falaries are alfo to be paid out of
duties forced from the people without their
confent, and independent of their Affemblies
approbation or difapprobation of the Judges
behaviour;

behaviour; that where the Crown will grant commiffions to able and honeft Judges during good behaviour, the Affemblies will fettle permanent and ample falaries on them during their commiffions; but at prefent they have no other means of getting rid of an ignorant, unjuft Judge (and fome of fcandalous characters have, they fay, been fent them) but by ftarving him out.

I do not fuppofe thefe reafonings of the Americans will have much weight in them. I do not produce them with an expectation of convincing you. I relate them merely in purfuance of the tafk I have impofed on myfelf, to be an impartial Hiftorian of American facts and opinions.

L E T T E R   II.

THE Colonifts being greatly alarmed, as I obferved in my laft, by news of the act for abolifhing the legiflature of New-York, and the impofition of thefe new duties, profeffedly for fuch difagreeable, and to them appearing dangerous purpofes; accompanied by a new fet of Revenue officers, with large appointments, which gave ftrong fufpicion

that

that more bufinefs of the fame kind was foon
to be provided for them, that they might earn
thofe falaries, began ferioufly to confider their
fituation, and to revolve afrefh in their minds,
grievances, which from t eir refpect and love
for this country, they had long borne, and
feemed almoft willing to forget. They re-
flected how lightly the interefts of all America had been efteemed here, when the
intereft of a few inhabitants of Great-Britain
happened to have the fmalleft competition with
it. That thus the whole American people
were forbidden the advantage of a direct importation of wine, oil, and fruit from Portugal,
but muft take them loaded with all the expences of a voyage of one thoufand leagues
round about, being to be landed firft in England, to be re-fhipped for America: expences
amounting, in war-time, at leaft to thirty per
cent. more than otherwife they would have
been charged with, and all this, merely that
a few Portugal merchants in London might
gain a commiffion on thofe goods paffing
through their hands.—Portugal Merchants,
by the bye, who complain loudly of the fmal-
eft hardfhips laid on their trade by foreigners,
and yet even the laft year, could oppofe with
all their influence the giving eafe to their fellow-fubjects under fo heavy an oppreffion—
That on a frivolous complaint of a few Virginia Merchants, nine colonies were reftrained
from

from making paper-money, though become absolutely neceſſary for their internal commerce, from the conſtant remittance of their gold and ſilver to Britain.—But not only the intereſt of a particular body of merchants, the intereſt of any ſmall body of Britiſh tradeſmen or artificers, has been found, they ſay, to outweigh that of all the King's ſubjects in the colonies.

There cannot be a ſtronger natural right than that of a man's making the beſt profit he can of the natural produce of his lands, provided he does not thereby injure the State in general. Iron is to be found every where in America, and beaver furs are the natural produce of that country. Hats and nails, and ſteel, are wanted there as well as here. It is no importance to the common welfare of the Empire, whether a ſubject gets his living by making hats on this or that ſide of the water; yet the hatters of England have prevailed! ſo far as to obtain an act in their own favour, reſtraining that manufacture in America, in order to oblige the Americans to ſend their beaver to England, to be manufactured, and purchaſe back the hats loaded with the charges of a double tranſportation. In the ſame manner have a few Nail-makers, and ſtill a ſmaller number of Steel-makers (perhaps there are not half a dozen of theſe in England) prevailed

totally

totally to forbid, by an act of Parliament, the erecting of flitting-mills, and steel-furnaces in America, that the Americans may be obliged to take nails for their buildings, and steel for their tools from these artificers under the same disadvantages. Added to these, the Americans remembered the act authorizing the most cruel insult that perhaps was ever offered by one people to another, that of emptying our gaols into their settlements (Scotland too, has within these few years, obtained the privilege it had not before, of sending its rogues and villains to the plantations) an insult aggravated by that barbarous, ill-placed sarcasm in a report of the Board of Trade, when one of the provinces complained of the act. " It " is necessary that it should be continued for " the better peopling of your Majesty's colo- " nies." I say, reflecting on those things, the Americans said to one another (their news papers are full of discourses) these people are not content with making a monopoly of us, forbidding us to trade with any other country of Europe, and compelling us to buy every thing of them, though in many articles we could furnish ourselves 10, 20, and even 50 per cent. cheaper elsewhere ; but now they have as good as declared they have a right to tax us, *ad libitum*, internally and externally ; and that our constitution and liberties shall all be taken away if we do not submit to that claim. They

are

are not content with the high prices at which they sell us their goods, but have now begun to enhance those prices by new duties; and by the expensive apparatus of a new set of officers, they appear to intend an augmentation and multiplication of those burthens that shall still be more grievous to us. Our people have been foolishly fond of their superfluous modes and manufactures, to their impoverishing our country, carrying off all our cash, and loading us with debt; they will not suffer us to restrain the luxury of our inhabitants as they do that of their own, by laws; they can make laws to discourage or pr hibit the importation of French superfluities; but though those of England are as ruinous to us as the French ones are to them; if we make a law of that kind, they immediately repeal it. Thus they get all our money from us by trade, and every profit we can any where make by our fishery, our produce, and our commerce, centers finally with them! But this does not satisfy. It is time then to take care of ourselves, by the best means in our power. Let us unite in solemn resolutions and engagements with and to each other, that we will give these new officers as little trouble as possible by not consuming the British manufactures, on which they are to levy the duties. Let us agree to consume no more of their expensive gew-gaws; let us live frugally; and let us industriously

manu-

manufacture what we can for ourfelves; thus we fhall be able honourably to difcharge the debts we already owe them, and after that, we may be able to keep fome money in our country, not only for the ufes of our internal commerce, but for the fervice of our gracious Sovereign, whenever he fhall have occafion for it, and think proper to require it of us in the old conftitutional manner. For notwithftanding the reproaches thrown out againft us in the public papers and pamphlets; notwithftanding we have been reviled in their Senate as rebels and traitors, we are truly a loyal people. Scotland has had its rebellions, and England its plots, againft the prefent royal family; but America is untainted with thofe crimes; there is in it fcarce a man, there is not a fingle native of our country who is not firmly attached to his King by principle and by affection. But a new kind of loyalty feems to be required of us, a loyalty to Parliament; a loyalty that is to extend, it feems, to a furrender of all our properties, whenever a Houfe of Commons, in which there is not a fingle member of our choofing, fhall think fit to grant them away without our confent, and to a patient fuffering the lofs of our privileges as Englifhmen, if we cannot fubmit to make fuch furrender. We were feparated too far from Britain by the ocean, but we were united ftrongly to it by refpect and love, fo that we could at any time

freely

freely have fpent our lives and little fortunes in its caufe; but this unhappy new fyftem of politics tends to diffolve thofe bands of union, and to fever us forever. Woe to the man that firft adopted it! Both countries will long have caufe to execrate his memory.

Thefe are the wild ravings of the at prefent half diftracted Americans. To be fure no reafonable man in England can approve of fuch fentiments, and, as I faid before, I do not pretend to fupport or juftify them; but I fincerely wifh, for the fake of the manufactures and commerce of Great-Britain, and for the fake of the ftrength a firm union with our growing colonies would give us, that thofe people had never been thus needlefsly driven out of their fenfes.

F. B.

F I N I S.

REFLECTIONS ON THE PRINCIPLE OF TRADE IN GENERAL

[Benjamin Franklin or George Whatley], *Reflections on the Principle of Trade in General. Freedom and Protection, its best Support: Industry, the only Means to render Manufactures cheap: Of Coins; and the Scarcity of Silver Coin: Of Exchange: Bountys considered: That on Corn discussed* (London, 1769), pp. 1–58.

The authorship of this piece is generally assigned to either George Whatley (d. 1791) or Benjamin Franklin (1706–90), with the consensus being that both contributed to the piece in some way. Unfortunately, very little biographical information survives on Whatley.

In *Principle of Trade*, various issues of commerce, bounties, money supply and British commercial restrictions on colonial trade are addressed. However, the main theme of this tract, for which it is most famous, was the defence of free trade using both Physiocratic and Mercantilist arguments. The argument is that all British trade restrictions on the American colonies should be abolished since free trade has never shown evidence of destroying a nation, no matter how disadvantageous it may appear to be. Here, free trade is supported to an extreme degree, arguing that nations at war should not limit their trade, as trade is advantageous to both. The enemy could obtain the same supplies elsewhere, therefore why should the nation not supply them for profit?

This piece was certainly of some influence, as it was cited in J.-B. Say's *Treatise on Political Economy*[1] . Further, Jacob Viner identifys the authors of this piece as being of the very few who were true free traders before Adam Smith.[2]

---

[1] J.-B. Say, *A Treatise on Political Economy: or, The Production, Distribution and Consumption of Wealth* (Philadelphia: Claxton, Remsen & Haffelfinger, 1880).

[2] Jacob Viner, 'English Theories of Foreign Trade Before Adam Smith', *Journal of Political Economy*, 38 (1930) pp. 404–57; see p. 433.

REFLECTIONS

ON THE

PRINCIPLE

OF

TRADE

IN GENERAL.

FREEDOM and PROTECTION, its beſt
Support : INDUSTRY, the only Means
to render Manufactures cheap : Of
COINS ; and the Scarcity of SILVER
COIN : Of EXCHANGE : BOUNTYS
conſidered : That on CORN diſcuſſed.

BY

A WELL-WISHER

TO HIS

KING and COUNTRY.

*Commerce is generally underſtood to be
the Baſis, on which the Power of this
Country hath been raiſed; and on which
it muſt, ever, ſtand.*

*Tous les Sujets doivent leurs Soins, et leurs
Lumieres, à l'Etat.*

LONDON

Printed, and Sold by all BOOKSELLERS.

MDCCLXIX.

THE
CONTENTS,

REFLECTIONS

ON

TRADE in GENERAL.

1. *TRADE*, or *Commerce*, is the *Intercourse*, as well between Nation and Nation, as between one Man and another.

2. The *Spring*, or *Movement* of such *Intercourse*, is,

and

and ever muſt be, *Gain:* which Word carries with it, *whatſo-ever may be thought, or under-ſtood to be, of Uſe, or Delight ; whether real or ideal.*

3. *Gain* being the *Principle* of *Action,* inaſmuch as neither the Public, or the Individual, purpoſedly, and intentionally, would purſue any *unprofitable Intercourſe,* the whole *Myſtery* of *Trade* muſt conſiſt *in proſe-cuting Methods, whereby Gain,* or *Advantage, may be ob-tained.*

4. *Freedom* and *Protection,* are moſt indiſputable *Principles* whereon the *Succeſs* of *Trade* muſt

muſt depend; as clearly as an open good Road tends towards a ſafe and ſpeedy Intercourſe: nor has it a greater Enemy than Conſtraint.

5. *Governments* which have adopted thoſe *plain Simple Principles* have been greatly benefited.

6. Were Princes, in general, to aboliſh all Sorts of prohibitory Laws, *Trade, in general,* would flouriſh moſt in thoſe Countries, where *the happy Situation; the mildneſs of the Climate; the Activity and Induſtry of the Inhabitants; would furniſh Means for a ſpeedy and an uſeful In-*

ter-

tercourſe, reciprocally to ſupply any real, or ideal Want.

7. We are no more to expect this, than that the whole World ſhould be governed by the ſame Laws. In our Opinion, however, *no Laws that the Art of Man can deviſe, will, or can, hinder, or entirely ſtop the Current of, a gainful Trade*; any more than the ſevereſt Laws, could prevent the ſatisfying of Hunger, when any Chance, or Opportunity, offered to gratify it.

8. Neverthelefs, as far as it is poſſible, according to the different Modes, and Conſtitutions

tions of each State, *Freedom and Protection, should be ever had in View, by its respective Government.*

9. For whatever Law is enacted; *abridging a Freedom, or Liberty, which the true Interest of the State demands; or does not grant Protection, where it may be wanted, must clearly be detrimental.*

10. Though we are well aware, that in many Cases, *Individuals* may endeavour at an *Intercourse or Trade*, whereby the Public, *in one particular Point*, may seem *detrimented;* yet if it be out of *the Power of the*

the State to hinder it, without breaking in upon *the Freedom of Trade*; the Dutchman, who when Antwerp was befieged, furnifhed Arms, Ammunition, and Provifion to the Spaniards, and glory'd in it, though a chief Magiftrate of Amfter-dam, was not fo very wrong in his Principles, in general, as at firft Sight might appear: for this Dutchman ran the Rifk of lofeing his Ammuni-tion, &c. which, if taken, were indeed his Lofs; but a Gain to the Captors his Countrymen; and if fold, and delivered to the Enemy, were a Profit to him, and in confequence to

the

the State of which he was a Member.

This Man, to evince how much he held Freedom in Trade to be effential, ufed a very ftrong Figure; when glorying in, and owning his having furnifhed the Enemy of the State with Ammunition, &c. he added; that he wou'd, to profecute his Trade, fail thro' Hell, at the Rifk of fingeing his Sails.

11. We have, as *a firft Principle*, laid down what we apprehend every one who thinks or confiders of it, muſt do; *that Gain, or the Hopes of Gain,*

Gain, are the *Mover* of all *Intercourse or Trade.* Herein, as above hinted, muſt be comprehended, *all Matters of Uſe, in the firſt Inſtance;* and then, *Matters of Ambition; Delight; Opinion;* in one Word, *Luxury.*

12. Now of *real Uſe,* to us Mortals, there can only be, what ſerves for *Meat,* for *Drink,* and for *Clotheing.* The ſeveral Contingencies relative to theſe, every ones Mind can ſuggeſt: to enumerate them would, almoſt, be endleſs.

13. In a Country where Corn, Fruits, and Cattle, can
be

be raifed, and bred ; the inhabitants muſt be wanting in *Induſtry*, to cultivate the Lands,
or they cannot, in the common
courſe of things, want help
from their Neighbours, *forSuſ-
tenance*.

The fame of *Drink* ; if for
it they will content themfelves, with the *Beverage*
made of their own Corn, and
Fruits.

And fo of *Clotheing* ; if they
can be fatisfy'd to be clad, with
the *Manufactures* made from
the Produce of their own
Country.

14. The

14. The *real Want* of àll thefe *Neceſſaries*, muſt, and ever will be, an Incentive to *Labor*; either by every Individual himſelf, in the Community; or by thoſe, to whom an *Equivalent* is given, for their *Labor*.

15. When *Ambition*; *Delight*; *Opinion*; otherwiſe *Luxury*, come to be conſidered, the Field is extreamly enlarged; and it will require a copious Deliberation, and Aſcertainment.

16. For we preſume, this ſame *Luxury*, may be carry'd to ſuch a *Heighth*, *as to be*

thought

thought, *by some*, to be prejudicial to the State ; tho' we,
in *a general Sense*, cannot well
apprehend it can : inafmuch,
as what we call *Riches*, *must*
be the Cause of Luxury, *taken*
in all its Branches.

17. Now *Riches*, as we conceive them, confift, *in what-*
ever, either a State, or an Indi-
vidual, have, more, than is ne-
ceffary to procure the above Ef-
fentials, of only real use ; Meat,
and *Drink*, and *Cloths.*

This *more* or *abundance*,
from whatfoever Cause it may
proceed, after the bartering
for, and procuring thofe Effen-
tials.

tials, wou'd, *absolutely, and to all Intents, be useless, and of no manner of Avail,* were it not, that *Delight,* and *Opinion,* came in Aid, to cause what we will call *an ideal Want:* which *Want,* our Paffions put into our Make by the Almighty Hand that formed us, cause us to be almoft as folicitous to provide for, and, to fupply, as if fuch *Wants* were real.

18. We therefore muft repeat that from Motives to acquire what may be thought of *real* or *ideal Ufe,* fpring the *Intercourfe or Trade between Nations,* as well as between *Individuals:* and it feems to be

felf-

felf-evident that the *Produce* of the *Land*, and of *Induſtry* in *general*, muſt fupply all our Wants; and confequently our *Trade*.

19. Now, tho' it is hardly to be expected, as above hinted, that *Princes* ſhould allow of a *General Free Trade* or *Inter-courſe*; yet it does not fol-low that *fundamental Maxims* ſhould not be attended to in governing of an *induſtrious People*. Some, as Principles, we beg Leave to hint.

20. Land, to bring forth its Increaſe, muſt be cultivated by Man and Beaſt. It is therefore the

the *Duty* and *Interest* of the
State to rear both; and in
their respective Classes to nou-
rish and cherish them.

21. *Industry* in all Shapes
should be encouraged and protected. *Indolence* by every pos-
fible Method rooted out.

22. Whatever can *contri-*
bute towards procuring from
the Land, and by Industry, a
Produce wherewith other Nations may be supply'd, ought
highly to be encouraged.

23. *Materials* wanting in a
Country to *employ* its inhabitants, ought by all means to
be

be procured. Gold and Silver, thofe Tokens of Riches (ufed as fuch, and otherwife of little Ufe) are not near fo eftimable. The bartering of them for fuch Materials is manifeftly advantageous.

24. Thefe, as we apprehend, are uncontrovertible Principles, on which a wife Government will found its Refolutions.

25. That the Ufe of the Produce of other Countries for *ideal Wants* ought to be difcouraged; particularly when the Produce of the Land, or of Induftry, are not given in Ex-

Exchange for them, has been ſtrongly urged by many. On the grand Principle of Freedom in Trade, we can't well admit it: for it is plain the Luxurious will uſe, and the Trader, to proſecute his Gain, will procure ſuch foreign Produce: nor do prohibitory Laws or heavy Duties hinder. Nevertheleſs, to allow for a Moment the Doctrine, we will remark, that only the eſtabliſh-ing it as a Mode or Faſhion amongſt the Opulent and Great, can poſſibly effectuate a Diſuſe or Diſcouragement.

We here think it neceſſary to obſerve, and to point out as

erro-

erroneous, though often ſtre-
nuouſly inſiſted on, that the
Cheapneſs of Proviſions muſt
render Manufactures cheap ;
and that Plenty of Money con-
duces to the Benefit of Trade.
We ſhall endeavour to prove
that Induſtry alone does both.

26. The all-wiſe Creator
of all things allows there
ſhould be Rich and Poor a-
mongſt Mankind ; and that
they ſhould be actuated by
real or *ideal* Wants : ſo that it
is next to impoſſible for the
Rich to be without Deſires,
or Wiſhes for greater Acquiſitions ; or the Poor, to be,
without being neceſſitated to
                    acquire

acquire what muft fupply his real Wants. If the Rich curtail his Defires, or Wifhes, his Riches ferve, in Proportion to his not ufing them, no more than Ore in an unworked Mine. If the Poor by *one* Day's Labor can fupply his real Want for *two* Days, and fits idle the Half of his Time, he becomes, in fuch idle Time, as a Monk or a Cripple to the Community. If a Thirft for Acquifition move the Rich, he induftrioufly employs all his Riches. If the Scarcity of Provifions compel the Poor to work his whole Time, he affuredly, by his Induftry, muft make more Manufactures than

only

only working Half of it.
Hence we conclude, that it is
Gain is the firſt Mover; and
Induſtry, and the Deſire of
ſupplying our Wants, the intermediate Movers of all Intercourſe or Trade. We however muſt obſerve, that Government truly wiſe ſhould
always, as far as the general
Good allows, be as ſollicitous
to procure Plenty of Proviſion,
whereby both Man and Beaſt,
may be kept in good Health
and Strength, as to encourage
Induſtry.

27. As to Plenty of Money
being a Benefit to Trade and
Manufactures, we apprehend,
every

every one converfant therein, muft know that the Coin, by which we generally underftand Money, of every refpective State, is, by no means the Mover of the Intercourfe or Tradings of the World in general. Gold and Silver in Bullion, or in an uncoined Mafs, are rather more fo; being in point of Value a Merchandize lefs liable to Variation than any other. It is true that Coin may be liable, in the Fluctuation of Trade, to be made a Merchandize of; but as by conftant Ufe, they become lighter than their original Weight, they thereby are lefs fit for Merchandize. We therefore may

advance

advance that Coins, in general, can no otherwife be ufeful than as a common-agreed-on-underftood Meafure between Man and Man, as ferving to barter againft, or exchange for, all Kinds of Commodities. It is evident they cannot be rank'd amongft thofe Things we have laid down above, as the ones of *only real ufe*. Let us therefore call them Counters: and to fimplify the Matter ftill more, fuppofe every Manufacturer to have of thefe Counters whatever Sum poffible, will it follow, that any Sort of Manufacture fhall be induftrioufly attended to, or more Work done than when no more Counters

Counters than juſt enough to barter for the real Wants of Meat, and Drink and Cloths, can be procured by Labor? Surely no.   It muſt be Induſtry, or the Deſire of ſupplying our Wants, as above hinted, that ſets Trade a going, and that only can procure Plenty of Manufactures.

28. It is, neverthelefs, the Duty of Government to ſtamp Coins or Counters of different Sorts and Denominations, ſo that *Time, of all Things the moſt precious,* be not waſted in ſettling the reſpective Exchangings amongſt Mankind. Neverthelefs the Plenty or Scarcity

city of them cannot entirely
depend on any Government;
but on the general Circulation
and Fluctuation of Trade:
which may make them a Merchandize, without the leaft
Detriment; as it muft, on all
Hands, be allowed, that the
precious Metals of Gold and
Silver, of which they principally are compofed, are no o-
ther than Merchandize acquired from Countries where there
are Mines, by thofe Countries
which have none, in Exchange
for the Produce of their Land,
or of their Manufactures :

29. That the Welfare of any
State depends, on its keeping
all

all its Gold, and Silver, either in Bullion, or in Coin; muſt be founded on a very narrow Principle indeed. All Republicks, we know of, wiſely think otherwiſe. Spain, the grand Source of Silver, has, of late Years, very juſtly, allow'd the free Exportation of it, paying a Duty, as in Great Britain, Lead, and Tin do : nor prior to this Permiſſion cou'd their Penal Laws, in Spain, hinder its being exported : for it was a Commodity that Kingdom, neceſſarily, muſt give, as an E-quivalent, for what was furniſhed to them by other Countries.

30. We

29. We muſt beg leave here, to obſerve, that in Great Britain, the Silver Coin bearing a Diſproportion to Gold more than in neighbouring States, of about *Five* in the Hundred, muſt, by that Diſproportion, become Merchandize, as well for abroad, as for the Manufactures wherein Silver is employ'd at home; more than if it remained in the Maſs uncoined. This might be remedy'd without injuring the Public, or touching the preſent Standard; only by enacting that *Sixty-five* Shillings ſhould be cut out of One Pound Weight of Standard Silver, inſtead of *Sixty-two*, which

which are the Number now
ordained by Law. We muſt
however remark, neverthelefs;
that whenever, by any extraordinary Demand for Silver, a
Pound Weight, bought even
for *Sixty-five* Shillings, can be
fent abroad to Advantage; or
melted down for Manufac-
tures; no prohibitory Laws
will hinder its Exportation, or
melting, and ſtill becoming a
Merchandize.

30. Coiners for Gain, tho' at
the Riſk of the Gallows,
have ſhewn, what in a lefs Degree ought to be done, by
circulating their Shillings,
whereby they profit from *Ten*

to

to *Fourteen* in the Hundred,
and upwards; as out of a
Pound of Standard Silver they
cut *Sixty-eight* or *Seventy-one*
Shillings. That these light
Shillings or Counters are useful, tho' the Public be so
greatly imposed on, is evident.
It must be presumed, that every Thing is put in Practice by
Government to detect and stop
this manifest Roguery. If so,
can it on the one Hand be supposed the public Purse should
bear the Burden of this Fraud?
yet, on the other, having no
Supply of legal Shillings or
Counters, the Utility of the
illegal ones forces them, as it
were, on the Public. The
Power

Power of the Legiſlature to correct the erroneous Proportion of *Five* in the Hundred, as above-mentioned, is indubitable ; but whether every private Perſon poſſeſs'd of theſe Counters, or the public Purſe, ſhould a Recoinage of Silver be ordained, be obliged to bear the Loſs, ſeems a Difficulty ; as it may be alledged, that every private Perſon has it in his Power, to accept, or refuſe any Coin, under the Weight, as by Law enacted, for each Denomination. If the former, he does it in his own Wrong ; and muſt take the Conſequences.   The Individual, on the other Hand, has

to

to alledge, the almoft-total-Want of lawful Counters; together with the Impoffibility, or Neglect, of hindering thofe of an inferior Weight from being fuffer'd to be current. Our Idea is; that as the Ufe of Coin is for public Utility, they are of public Concern in all Shapes. What feems felf-evident to us, is; that after a certain Period, even thofe Coins that have been iffued from the Mint, under the Sanction of Law; and are by time worn yea even filed, or fweated; fhould be called in at their nominal Values, and recoined at the Charge of the Public. We are well aware what a

Lati-

Latitude fuch a Refolution might give, to the Coiners of Shillings; the Filers; and the Sweaters of Gold; but by taking proper Meafures before-hand, this Evil might, we think, in a great Degree be prevented.

31. In the Beginning of his prefent Majefty's Reign, Quarter Guineas were wifely ordered to be coined; whereby the Want of Silver Coin was in fome Degree fupply'd: which wou'd ftill be more fo, were Thirds and Two-Thirds of Guineas to be coined. We cannot conceive why this be not done; except that thefe

Deno-

Denominations are not fpeci-
fy'd in his Majefty's Indenture
with the Mafter of the Mint ;
which in our humble Opinion
ought to be rectify'd.

32. We think it not improper
here to add that it matters not,
whether *Silver*, or *Gold*, be
called the *Standard Money;*
but it feems *moft rational* that
the moft fcarce precious Metal
fhou'd be the Unit or Standard.

That as to Copper, it is as fit
for Money, or a Counter, as
Gold or *Silver*; provided it be
coined of a proper Weight, and
Finenefs : and juft fo much
will

will be ufeful as will ferve to make up *fmall Parts* in *Exchange*, between Man, and Man, and no more.

As to Paper circulating as Money, it is *highly profitable*, as its quick paffing from one to another is *a Gain* of *Time* and we may add an Affiftant towards an Augmentation of People : inafmuch as thofe, who wou'd be employ'd in telling and weighing, may be ufed for other Purpofes. The Iffuers or Coiners of Paper, are underftood to have an Equivalent to anfwer what it is iffued for, or valued at; nor more can

any

any Metal or Coin do, than find its Value.

33. As some Principles relative to Exchange, according to our Notion, have been confusedly handled; and not only so but some have been advanc'd that tend to mislead; we shall here briefly lay down, what, according to our Opinion, are self-evident Principles.

34. Exchange, by Bills, between one Country or City and another, we conceive to be this. One Person wants to get a Sum from any Country or City; consequently has

his

his Bill or Draft to fell : another wants to fend a Sum thither; and therefore agrees to buy fuch Bill, or Draft. He has it at an agreed-for Price, the Courfe of the Exchange. It is with this Price for Bills, as with Merchandize; when there's a Scarcity, Dearnefs follows; when Plenty, a Cheapnefs.

35. We judge it needlefs, to enter into the feveral Courfes, and Denominations of Exchanges, which Cuftom hath eftablifhed : they are taught at School. But we think we muft offer a few Words to deftroy an Error that

that has misled some, and con-
fused others: which is, that
by Authority, a certain Par,
or fix'd Price of Exchange,
should be settled, between
each respective Country:
thereby rendering the Currency of Exchange, as fixed,
as the Standard of Coin.

36. We have above hinted,
that Plenty, and Scarcity,
must govern the Course of
Exchange. Which Principle,
duly considered, wou'd suffise
on the Subject; but we will
add, that no human Foresight,
can absolutely judge of, the
almost numberless Fluctuations in Trade; which vary,
                        some

sometimes directly, sometimes indirectly, between Countrys: consequently no State, or Potentate, can, by Authority, any more pretend to settle the Currency of the Prices of the several Sorts of Merchandize, sent to, and from, their respective Dominions, than they can, a Par of Exchange.   In Point of Merchandize indeed, when there is a Monopoly: and that Monopoly, possest of one particular Commodity, an Exception must be allowed; but that holds not at all for Trade in general; for which we cannot too often repeat, that *Freedom and Protection*

are

*are essentially its greatest En-
couragement.*

37. Another specious Doc-
trine, much labored by Theo-
rists, in Consequence of that
relating to the Par, is, that the
Exchange between any particular Country, being above,
or below, Par, always shews
whether their reciprocal
Trade be advantageous or
disadvantageous. It is, and
must be, allowed, that in
Trade, nothing is given without adequate Returns, or Com-
pensations; but these are so
various, and so fluctuating,
between Countrys, as often
indirectly, as directly, that
there

there is no Poſſibility of fixing a Point from whence to
argue; ſo that ſhou'd there
happen a Variation of *Two* or
Three, or more, in the Hundred, at any certain Period,
in the Exchange, above or
below what is called the Par,
or Equality, of the Money of
one Country, to that of another; influenced by the Fluctuations, and Circulations in
Trade; it does not follow,
that a Trade is advantageous,
or diſadvantageous, excepting
momentarily, if one may ſo
ſay; which can be of no Conſequence to the Public, in general; as, from advantageous,
it may become diſadvantageous,

ours, and vice verfa ; and confequently, the deducing of
Reafons, from what *in its Nature* muft be fluctuating, can
only help to embarrafs, if not,
miflead.

38. To return to Trade in
general. Our Principles, we
apprehend, may hold good for
all Nations. It lays with their
Legiflations always to have an
Eye towards them. We will
not difcufs every particular
Point : nor is it to our Purpofe to examine the pretended
Principles of Utility, whereon
Monopolies are generally eftablifhed. That the Wifdom
of Government fhou'd weigh
and

and nicely confider any propofed Regulation, on thofe
Principles, we humbly judge
to be felf-evident; whereby
may be feen, whether it coin-
cides with the General Good.
Solomon advifeth *not to coun-*
fel with a Merchant for Gain.
This, we prefume, relates to
the Merchants own particular
Profit; which, we repeat,
muft ever be the Spring of his
Actions: Government ought,
notwithftanding, to endeavour
to procure particular Informa-
tions from every one; not only
from thofe actually employed,
or thofe who have been concerned, in particular Branches
of Trade; but even from Perfons,

fons, who may have confidered of it, theoretically, and fpeculatively.

39. Tho' we wave a Difcuffion on particular Branches of Trade, as the Field is too large for what we ever purpofed entering into; and that particular Laws, and Regulations, may require Variation, as the different Intercourfes, and even Interefts of States, by manifold Fluctuations, may alter; yet, as what relates to Bountys or Premiums, which the Legiflature of Great Britain has thought fit to grant, hath been, by fome, deemed, if not ill-judged, unneceffary; we

we hope our Time not ill-
beſtowed, to conſider of the
Fitneſs, and Rectitude of the
Principle, on which, we ap-
prehend, theſe Bountys, or
Premiums, have been granted.

40. It muſt, we think, on
all Hands be allowed, that the
Principle whereon they are
founded muſt be *an Encouragement, tending to a general
Benefit*, tho' granted, on Commoditys ; Manufactures ; or
Fiſherys ; carry'd on in particular Places, and Countrys,
*judg'd to require Aid from the
public Purſe for farther Improvement.*

Of

Of the Bountys, fome hav-
ing had the propofed Effect,
are difcontinued : others are
continued, for the very Reafon they were firft given.

In our Opinion, no doubt
can arife, as to the Utility of
thefe Grants from the Public Purfe, to Individuals ; in -
afmuch as their Incentive is
Gain : (our grand Principle of
Action) for as every Individual,
makes a Part of the Whole
Public, if we may be allowed
the Expreffion, confequently,
whatever benefits the Individual, muft benefit the Public :
hereby the Wifdom of the
Legiflature is moft evident,

nor

nor fhou'd it in any wife be arraigned, though ill Succefs attended any particular Commodity ; Manufacture ; or Fifhery.

We are well aware that it is not impoffible for Gain, the purpofe of Bounty may have been perverted ; but it lays with the Legiflature to enact Laws fo as to prevent fuch Iniquity : which no ways, however, invalidates the Firft Principle for allowing a Bounty.

41. So much we apprehend may ferve in regard to every Article whereon a Bounty or Premium has been granted;

except

except Wheat, and other Grain, which we fhall confider, and enlarge on, as being of a complicate Nature ; and in regard to which, Mankind have, at particular Times, been divided, in Opinion.

42. It feems to us that this Bounty on Grain, was intended, *not only to Encourage the Cultivating of Land for the raifing of it, in Abundance, in this Kingdom, for the Ufe of its Inhabitants ; but alfo to furnifh our Neighbours, whenever the kind Hand of Providence fhould be pleafed to grant a Superfluity.*

43. It

43. It never can be presumed, that the Encouragement, by the Bounty, insures to the Community an uninterrupted constant Plenty: Yet, when the Grower of Grain knows, he may, by such Bounty, have a Chance of a foreign Market for any Excess he may have, more than the usual Home Consumption, he, the more willingly, labors; and improves his Land; upon the Presumption of having a Vent of his Superfluity, by a Demand in foreign Countrys; so that he will not, probably, be distressed by Abundance: which, strange as it may seem to some, might be the Case by

his

his Want of Sale; and his great Charges of gathering in his Crop.

44. As there are no public Granarys in this Kingdom; the Legiſlature cou'd deviſe no better Means, than to fix *ſtated Prices* under which, the Bounty, or Encouragement from the Public Purſe, ſhould be allowed.   Whenever the current Prices exceeded thoſe ſtipulated; then ſuch Bounty ceaſes.

45. Few conſider, or are affected, but by the preſent. They ſee Grain, by reaſon of ſcanty Crops, dear; therefore

all

all the Doors for Gain, to the Cultivator of it, muſt always be kept ſhut. The common Out-cry is that *the exporting our Wheat, furniſhes Bread to our Neighbours, cheaper than it can be afforded to our Poor at home; which affects our Manufactures as they can thereby work cheaper.* To this laſt Alegation we muſt refer to what we have ſaid, Sec. 26; though the former, that Wheat is, by the Bounty, aforded to our Neighbours cheaper than to us, at home; muſt, in general, be without Foundation: for the ſeveral Items of Charge, atending the Exportation of Grain; ſuch as Carriage; Factorage;

torage; Commiſſion; Porter-
age; &c.   The Freight paid
to *our own Shipping*, to which
alone, the Bounty is reſtrained;
muſt, when duly conſidered,
very ſufficiently counterbalance the Bounty; ſo that,
more than what is given out
of the public Purſe, is put into
the Pockets of Individuals, for
the Carriage, &c. as above:
therefore, we think, we may
advance, that in general, Grain
exported, comes dearer to the
Foreigner, than to the Con-
ſumer, in Great Britain,

46. Nothing can be more
evident, we apprehend, than
that the Superfluity of our
Grain

Grain being exported, is, *a clear Profit to the Kingdom*; as much as any other Produce of our Labor, in Manufactures; in Tin; or any Commoditys, whatsoever.

47. It behoves us, however, indubitably, to have an Eye towards having a Suficiency of Grain for Food in this Country, as we have laid down Sec. 26; and our Opinion is, that were the Legislature to enact, that the Justices of the Peace, at the Christmas Quarter Session, shou'd have Power to summons all Growers of Grain, or Dealers therein, and upon Oath to examine them

as

as to the Quantity, then remaining. Returns to be made to the Lords of His Majefty's Treafury, to be laid before Parliament. The Legiflature wou'd, upon fuch Returns, be able to judge, whether it wou'd be neceffary to enable His Majefty, with the Advice of his Council, to put a Stop to any farther Exportation at fuch Times, as might be thought proper.

48. Or, whether the Legiflature, upon duly weighing every Thing in the feveral Lights their Wifdom wou'd fuggeft to them, fhou'd not re-

peal

peal the Act, alowing the prefent Bounty on the feveral
Sorts of Grain at the now
fixed Prices, and reduce thefe
Prices as follow :

On Wheat from Forty-
eight to Thirty-fix or Thirty-
two Shillings.

On Barley from Twenty-
four to Eighteen or Sixteen a
Quarter; and fo in Proportion
for other Grain. In fhort, diminifh the prefent ftandard
Prices, under which the Bounty is granted, one Quarter, or
one Third.

49. In

49. In our humble Opinion, this laſt Method wou'd be by much the moſt ſimple, and eligible; as conſiſtent with our Grand Principle of *Freedom in Trade,* which wou'd be cramp'd, if dependent on annual, parliamentary, deliberation.

50. The Advocates for not lowering the preſent ſtipulated Prices that command the Bountys from the public Purſe, may aledge; that our Anceſtors deemed them neceſfary, on the Principle for granting any Bounty at all, which we have above hinted,

Sec.

Sec. 42. We controvert not the Wisdom of the Principle, for granting a Bounty: for it must have been, and ever will be, an Encouragement to Cultivation; and consequently, it wou'd be highly improper, wholly, to discontinue it; nevertheless if it have answered one great End proposed, which was Cultivation, and Improvement; and that it is uncontrovertable, the Cultivator has, by the Improvements made by the Encouragement of the Bounty, a living Profit at the reduced Prices of Thirty-two, or Thirty-six Shillings; Sixteen or Eighteen, &c. as above-

above-faid, which, peradventure, when our Anceftors enacted the Law for granting the Bounty, they underftood the Cultivators cou'd not have: It feems clear, that there ought to be the propofed Change, and Reduction of the Bounty Prices as above-faid.

51. The French, intent on Trade, have, a few Years fince, rectify'd a very grofs Miftake they labored under, in Regard to their Commerce in Grain. One County or Province in France fhou'd abound, and the neighbouring one,

one, tho' starving, almost, shou'd not be permitted to get Grain from the plentiful Province, without particular Licence from Court, which cost no small Trouble and Expence. In Sea Port Towns, Wheat shou'd be imported; and soon after, without Leave of the Magistrates, the Owner shou'd only have Liberty to export one Quarter, or one Third, of it. They are now wiser; and thro' all the Kingdom the Corn Trade is quite free: and what is more, all Sorts of Grain may be exported (upon French bottoms *only*, for their Encouragement,

copying

copying we prefume our Law)
whenever the Market Prices
for three following Days fhall
not exceed about *Forty-five*
Shillings Sterling a Quarter
for Wheat: Our Reafon for
mentioning this, is only to
fhew, that other Nations are
changing their deftructive
Meafures; and that it be-
hoves us to be careful that
we mind our effential Intereft
in all Shapes.

We fhall here end thefe
Reflections, with our moft
ardent Wifhes for the Profperity of our Country; and
our Hopes, that the Doctrine
we

we have ſo often urged *of all possible Protection and Free-dom in Trade,* may, for the public Weal, *be ever the grand Point in View, and the Foun-dation of all the Reſolutions of the Legiſlature.*

F I N I S.

OBSERVATIONS ON SEVERAL ACTS OF PARLIAMENT

Association of the Merchants of Boston, *Observations on Several Acts of Parliament, Passed in the 4th, 6th and 7th Years of his present Majesty's Reign: and also, on the Conduct of the Officers of the Customs, since Those Acts were passed, and the Board of Commissioners appointed to Reside in America*, (Boston, 1769), pp. 1–24

In *Observations on Several Acts of Parliament*, the economic dangers of the strengthened Navigation Acts are spelled out by a group of Boston merchants. They argue that if the colonies suffer great economic hardship through their decreasing trade, particularly with Spain and Portugal, the losses would also be felt in Great Britain owing to the decreased colonial consumption of English-manufactured products. Although the colonial requests for a reduction in the duty on sugar products and for the repeal of the Stamp Act were heeded, the British Parliament replaced the current taxes with new duties under the Townshend Acts, and expanded the lower duty on sugar to include imports from the British sugar islands. It was becoming increasingly apparent that the British mercantilist policy was not designed to be beneficial for the American colonists. In *Observations*, the merchants argue that their small profit margins would be eliminated altogether by the increase in duties and taxes, which would lead to Boston's financial ruin.

OBSERVATIONS

ON

Several Acts of Parliament,

PASSED

In the 4th, 6th and 7th Years of his present Majesty's Reign:

AND ALSO,

ON

The Conduct of the Officers of the Customs,

SINCE

Those Acts were paffed,

AND

The Board of Commiffioners appointed

TO

Refide in AMERICA.

Publifhed by the Merchants of BOSTON.

Printed by EDES & GILL,

M,DCC,LXIX.

OBSERVATIONS

On feveral Acts of Parliament, &c.

THE representative body of this people having very fully and repeatedly remonftrated againft thefe acts as unconftitutional and as infringing the rights and privileges of the fubject, it is unneceffary to add any thing upon that head ; but we fhall confine our Remarks to fuch parts of thefe acts as affect the trading intereft.

By thefe acts certain rates and duties are impofed on molaffes, fugars, wine, tea, glafs, paper and many other articles, commonly imported into the Britifh colonies in America, and feveral leading articles which procured remittances to Great-Britain are now either brought into the clafs of enumerated articles, or fubjected to the duty, rifque and ex-pence of being landed in Great-Britain; which em-barrafsments on the trade of the colonies muft greatly

greatly diminifh if not wholly deftroy feveral branches of it, and fo far leffen the demand for Britifh manufactures great quantities of which are annually imported into this province, (more than the amount of our exports to Gfeat-Britain) for the payment of which we depend not only upon what is produced among ourfelves, but alfo upon what is caught out of the fea, or is obtained by a circuity of commerce abroad. To collect this revenue, the government is at a very great expence, equal at leaft (and including the charge of men of war and cutters to guard the coaft, vaftly fuperior) to all the revenue that could be collected, had our trade been as extenfive as it was before thofe Acts were made, which is not the cafe now, and never will be, while they remain in force.

One principal branch of the trade of this province is the fifhery, carried on to the banks, in which there are upwards of three hundred veffels employ'd, befides a great number of boats in the bay, and about ninety fail in the mackrel fifhery, the amount the fifh thefe veffels cure, with the pickled fifh and liver oil is upwards of *one hundred and fixty thoufand pounds* fterling per annum, about two fiths of the bank fifh turns out merchantable, and is fent to Spain, Portugal and Italy, and the nett Proceeds remitted to Great-Britain ; the other three fifths being unfit for any market in Europe, is fent with the pickled fifh and mackrel to the iflands in the Weft-Indies : And as the Englifh iflands do not confume more than is made

made by the boats in the bay, being about one fifth and one fourth of the mackrel and pickled fish, the remaining two fifths made by the bankers, together with three quarters of the mackrel and pickled fish is carried to the French and other foreign islands, in return for which we receive molasses, and some ordinary sugars. —This valuable branch of our trade the fishery, almost, if not wholly depends on our trade to the foreign islands in the West-Indies—As we cannot cure fish for the European markets seperate from the other sort sent there, and as we have no other market for what is made by the bankers, it will be lost if not sent to the foreign islands, and this loss must intirely destroy the whole bank fishery.

Another considerable branch of the trade of this province is lumber of all kinds, also provisions, horses and many other articles suitable for the West-India markets, in which trade there are upwards of an hundred & eighty vessels annually employed, most of which make two voyages in a year; these vessels call first at the English islands, and when they are supplied, the remainder is carried to the foreign islands—A quantity of oak timber, staves, and other lumber is sent to Ireland, some to Madera and the Western Islands, to purchase wines, and some few cargoes are sent to Spain, Portugal and England, but none to any foreign port to the northward of Cape Finister—The first cost of these cargoes of lumber being very small, the whole profits are not more than a bare freight for the vessels, but this

freight

freight is a great encouragement to ship-building, which is another very confiderable branch of trade in this province, wherein there have been upwards of three hundred fail built in a year, before the late embarrafsments were laid on the trade, fince which this number has been reduced at leaft two thirds, and the tradefmen formerly employ'd in this branch of bufinefs are now obliged to procure a livelihood in fome manufacture, or ftarve—Some of thefe fhips went direct to Europe with fifh, oil, pot and pearl afh, naval ftores and lumber, but the greateft part went to the Weft-Indies with lumber, fifh and other articles of our produce, the proceeds of which, with the freights from thence to England, together with the veffels, were remitted to Great Britain, to pay for the goods we received from thence—and by having timber plenty and building fo many veffels, we became carriers for other parts of America; befides the trade to the Weft-Indies many of our fhips formerly went to Virginia, North and South-Carolina, where they carried large quantities of rum to purchafe rice, tobacco and naval ftores, and took in freight for Great-Britain, where the proceeds of the whole, (and indeed of all our trade) centers.

Another confiderable branch of our trade is that carried on to Africa, where we fend large quantities of New-England rum, not only for our own trade, but to fupply the traders in fhips from Great-Britain, with whom we exchange this commodity for other European articles brought out by them fuitable for that trade, by means of which they are enabled to
carry

carry on their trade to greater advantage than they would otherwise do without this neceſſary article— And as the ſlaves purchaſed there, are chiefly ſold in the Weſt-Indies for bills on London, the proceeds of this trade conſequently are remitted to Great-Britain.

All theſe ſeveral branches of trade are greatly obſtructed by the duties impoſed, and the reſtrictions to which they are ſubjected by the aforementioned acts.—The duty on molaſſes, tho' reduced to one penny per gallon, which at firſt ſight may appear but ſmall, yet as it is one tenth part of the value (when brought to market) is really large, and will be a diſcouragement to a trade which has inſinuated itſelf into, and is a great ſpring to every branch of buſineſs among us. ——The fiſhery, the lumber trade and ſhip-building are greatly promoted by the importation of molaſſes, and diſtilling it into rum, and the trade to Africa wholly depends on this article ; ſo that any act which hath a tendency to obſtruct the importation of molaſſes, muſt be prejudicial to Great-Britain.—The former acts impoſing duties on molaſſes, were intended only as a regulation of trade, and to encourage our own iſlands ; and the duty was only on foreign molaſſes : But by theſe acts, it is impoſed on all molaſſes, and expreſly for the purpoſe of raiſing a revenue.

The duty of five ſhillings per hundred on brown, and twenty-two ſhillings on white ſugars, is a great burden on our trade to the foreign iſlands ; if we confine

confine ourselves to molasses, a sufficient return'd cargo cannot always be obtain'd ; and the aforesaid duties upon sugars are so heavy as to render the import of them so unprofitable, that we cannot pursue a trade by which we disposed of the superfluous produce of our country.

By these acts we are restrained from exporting sugars to a foreign market, without first landing them in Great-Britain, or obtaining a licence from thence to carry them direct to a foreign market.—If we go first to Great Britain and land them there, it will prove so expensive by the delay and charges of unloading & reshipping, & also of a double freight and insurance, that the trade cannot be carried on to any advantage, especially in a time of war.—If we carry these sugars direct to a foreign market by licence from Great-Britain, the difficulties and embarrassments are still greater, as the vessel in which any sugars are to be shipt, must first go to Great-Britain, and the master enter into bonds there, before a licence can be procured, during which the sugars are to remain in the King's stores here, and after they are delivered in a foreign port, the vessel must return to Great Britain to cancel the bonds, before she can proceed on any other voyage—tho' the liberty granted to carry these sugars directly to foreign ports by licence, might be intended as an encouragement to the trade, the regulations and restrictions are such as will effectually defeat this very design ; whereas if we were allowed to export these sugars (after being stored here under the care of custom-house officers) to foreign markets

in

in our own veffels, free of duty, it would encourage the bringing them here, and in time might become a very confiderable branch of trade ; and in particular would enable us to employ our fifh-fhips to better advantage, as they carry no fifh between decks, and confequently might be partly laden with fugars. But under the prefent regulations, none will ever be bro't here in order to be exported to a foreign market in Europe, either in our own veffels or any other.

Here it may be proper to obferve, that fhould we be allowed the free importation of foreign fugars even for our own confumption, the trade of G. Britain would not be injured, but greatly benefitted ; for in this cafe, more of the fugars made in the Englifh iflands might be carried to Great-Britain, and what they did not confume, would be exported from thence to foreign markets, which would employ a greater number of fhips, and thereby increafe the commerce of Great-Britain, without leffoning that of the Colonies—and all the fugars we procured from the French iflands, and carried to foreign markets in Europe, muft neceffarily leffen their navigation, and increafe that of Great-Britain.

Formerly we made confiderable remittances to Great-Britain with fugars the produce of the Englifh iflands, which we received in return for our own produce fold there : But by the Act of the 6th of his prefent Majefty, we find fuch a diftinction made in favor of our fellow fubjects in the iflands, that while they may import Britifh plantation fugars into Great Britain

Britain *as fuch*, that which is imported from North-America muft be deemed *French*, by which means we are cut off from an article of export which hath been heretofore confiderable, and might be fo ftill, were it not for this regulation.

Logwood and mohogany have been by a circuity of trade the means of large remittances to Great-Britain—thefe we have obtained by fmall cargoes of provifions produced among ourfelves, together with fome Britifh manufactures, by which many of our veffels have been employ'd ; but now by being obliged to carry them firft to England, fuch heavy expences will be incurred by reafon of their bulk, and the fmallnefs of their value, as muft put an end to this branch of bufinefs, and confequently the trade muft fall into the hands of foreigners.

The reafons given for thefe regulations as mention'd in the act of the 6th of George the Third, were " the more effectually to prevent enumerated " goods being privately carried from the Britifh co-" lonies into foreign parts of Europe in veffels that " clear'd out with non-enumerated goods ; and alfo " to prevent the clandeftine importation of foreign " European goods into faid Britifh colonies." Upon the firft of thefe reafons we would obferve, that the great care and vigilance of the cuftom-houfe officers here might anfwer the purpofe, and effectually prevent any fuch enumerated goods from being exported to foreign parts—With refpect to the fecond, it is difficult to conceive how the obliging a veffel to
                                                            ftop

ftop at England upon an outward-bound voyage, can have any influence in preventing the importation of illicit Goods upon her return, efpecially when fufficient care was before taken to prevent fuch illicit importation, by obliging all veffels that have any foreign goods on board to ftop at Great-Britain on their return.

Another great embarrafsment to the trade of the colonies, is the multiplicity of bonds required by the aforefaid acts of his prefent Majefty, in addition to the bond for enumerated goods, required by an act made in the 12th year of the reign of Charles the fecond, the condition of which bond is, that fuch enumerated goods fhall be landed either in G. Britain or fome part of his Majefty's dominions ; and by an act of the 4th of George the 3d, Coffee, Piemento, Cocoa, Hides, Skins, Pot and Pearl Afh, and feveral other articles are added to the lift of enumerated goods—befides which, no mafter of a veffel is allowed to take in any non-enumerated goods without firft giving another bond with one furety ; the condition of which is, that none of faid non-enumerated goods fhall be landed in any port of Europe to the northward of Cape-Finiftere, except in Great-Britain ; by which we are excluded from carrying even non-enumerated goods to Ireland, without firft calling at fome port in G. Britain. If any iron, or lumber are laden on board any veffel, the mafter muft give a third bond, on the fame condition as that required for non-enumerated goods ; and in cafe any rum is laden on board, a fourth
bond

bond is required, the condition of which i·, that such rum shall not be landed in the Isle of Man.

These bonds the officers of the customs in this port require for all vessels loading any of these articles, not only for such as are going to Europe, the West-Indies, and other colonies on the continent, but even for coasters going from one town to another in the same province, and sometimes for vessels under twenty tons going to another town within the district of the same custom-house where the bonds are given ; so that no lumber can be brought from the place of its growth in the eastern parts of this province, to this or any other market for exportation, until such bond is given, though no custom-house officer reside within 40 or 50 and sometimes 100 miles of the place where the coaster takes in his lumber : This is a very great embarrassment to the trade of this province, in which there are a great number of vessels employ'd in the coasting business, and upwards of one thousand sail are annually enter'd and cleared at the several offices : This restriction appears the more unaccountable, as it is not known that one single vessel ever carried a cargo of lumber to any foreign port to the northward of Cape-Finistere ; had such a trade formerly been carried on, the coasting vessels are not capable of prosecuting such a voyage, and the charge of these bonds and certificates to cancel them, amount annually to a very large sum.——Besides these several bonds, every master of a vessel, even a coaster, is obliged to take out a sufferance and cocket for every article laden

laden on board ; and in cafe he takes in any goods for which bond is required, he muft have a certificate from the collector of his having given bond for thofe articles ; and in cafe he neglects taking fuch certificate, not only the goods for which bonds are required, but even the veffel and the reft of the cargo are forfeited ; this has been feverely felt by fome traders here, who have loft both veffel and cargo to a very confiderable value, only for want of fuch certificate, tho' the cocket for thofe goods mentioned that bonds were taken, but the certificate was either miflaid or never delivered by the Collector.——The fureties in thefe bonds are likewife greatly expofed, fhould the mafter neglect to fend a certificate of the landing the goods for which he has given bonds, or fhould the collector refufe or difapprove of the certificate he may fend, as being improper, (tho' there fhould be no reafon to fufpect the goods were carried to any port they were excluded from,)the fureties may be profecuted in the court of admiralty, and obliged to pay confiderable cofts at leaft, if not the whole penalty, as has heretofore been experienced in that court, and is fuch an infupportable burden on trade, as will prevent many from engaging in it.

Before a cocket can be taken out for any goods, and fome even of Britifh manufacture, oath muft be made when, by whom, and in what veffel the article intended to be exported, was imported, this in many cafes is impoffible, and will prevent fome towns from being fupply'd with fuch goods as they want,

and

and induce others to set up manufactures of their own, and thereby lessen the consumption of British manufactures in the colonies, which must be severely felt by the manufacturers in Great-Britain.

Another great discouragement to the trade of America is the unlimited power given to officers of the customs—The act passed in the 4th year of George the 3d ordains, That in case any information shall be commenced and brought to tryal in America, on account of the seizure of any ship or goods as forfeited, wherein a verdict shall be given for the claimer, the defendant if the judge certifies that there was a probable cause of seizure, shall not be intitled to any costs of suit whatsoever—and further in case an action shall be brought against any officer for seizing any ship or goods, where no information shall be commenced, or brought to tryal to condemn the same, and a verdict shall be given against the defendant, the plaintiff, besides his ship or goods so seized, or the value thereof, shall not be entitled to above two pence damages, nor to any cost of suit. But if the plaintiff shall be non-suited or discontinue his action, or if judgment shall be given upon any verdict or demurrer against the plaintiff, the defendant shall recover triple costs. By these clauses in this act, and the power and extention of the courts of *vice-admiralty*, the whole trade of America lies at the mercy of the officers of the customs and judge of said court, the former being impower'd to seize the ships or goods of the American merchants at their pleasure;

and

and tho' they never profecute the fame, or act ever fo arbitrarily or unjuftly, the merchant has no remedy, the officer not being fubject to any damage, or even to coft of fuit, while the diftreffed claimant, tho' ever fo much injured, if he fhou'd be nonfuited or difcontinue his action, muft pay triple cofts. And as the Governor, as well as the officers of the cuftoms and judge of the admiralty, are interefted in thofe feizures, it is natural to conclude they will always encourage and promote the fame ; and many inftances may be produced, where both veffel and goods have been condemned as forfeited, only for a fmall miftake or neglect of the mafter, and the induftrious trader thereby ruined, which feverities are not exercifed towards our fellow fubjects in Great-Britain.

Since the appointment of a board of commiffioners to refide in America, the reftrictions and embarrafsments on the trade have been greatly increafed by the attendance and delay in entering and clearing of veffels at the collector's office, where fome mafters have been obliged to wait two or three days before they could obtain an entry or permit to unload ; the many oaths and certificates required before any veffel can be cleared out have occafion'd the fame delay to our outward-bound veffels.

Another difficulty attending the entry of veffels, particularly from the Weft-Indies, is the mafter's being required to make an exact report of their cargoes on their firft arrival (even at any out-ports they

they may put into by contrary winds) and denying them liberty to make a post entry.——In Great-Britain the masters are allow'd to make reports from day to day as they find any goods omitted, but this *justice* is denied the Americans, and the board of commissioners have publickly advertiz'd that no allowance for the future shall be made for mistakes or omissions in the first report, even for adventures belonging to the seamen; this is an hardship, or rather a cruelty, as the seamen frequently get aboard more than the masters are acquainted with, and as the masters purchase their molasses on shore in teirces and shift it into other casks of their own when bro't on board the vessel, and are often filling up those casks, its sometimes difficult for them exactly to ascertain the number and contents of the casks they have filled——The fees taken at the collector's office, particularly for coasters, and obliging them to enter and clear in the same manner as vessels bound on foreign voyages, and to give bonds for every trifling article they carry for private families, even for a few pounds of tea or sugar, or a few gallons of rum or molasses purchased of retailers, for which they must produce certificates on oath in what vessel these trifles were imported, and by whom the duties were paid, which is often impossible, are such embarrassments on this branch of business, as if continued, it must intirely destroy it.——Formerly the coasters were not required to take cockets for every trifling article, and the fees both entering and clearing was only *one shilling* sterling, whereas the expence now is from *ten shillings* to
sixteen

fifteen shillings, which is more ready money than they sometimes receive for their whole freight ; and as they frequently take in only a few articles, the charge of clearing those articles at the custom-house is more than the freight.————The appointment of an almost incredible number of inferior officers, as tidesmen, boatmen, waiters and others, and requir- ing the master to receive and lodge them under deck (without any authority to support it) is another cause of complaint—Some of those wretches are persons of such infamous characters that the mer- chants cannot possibly think their interest safe under their care—The liberty these fellows take of search- ing vessels before they are discharged, and sometimes before the master's have reported at the custom-house, is not only illegal, but *impudent*, and contrary to the practice in Great-Britain, where the officers never search the hold of any vessel till the master says she is discharged, and desires the waiter to certify the same to the custom-house. Another in- tolerable grievance is the appointment of officers of the customs on board the men of war, cutters and other armed vessels, the arbitrary, unlawful and wanton manner in which they have exercised this authority in this province is unprecedented in any other part of the British dominions.

Some of these officers by force of arms have enter'd vessels on the high seas, and in the harbours, insolently demanded of the masters their papers, broke open their hatches and search'd the hold with lighted candles, even ships from London, with hemp
.and

and powder on board, have been treated in this
manner, and both the lives and properties of his
Majesty's loyal subjects thereby greatly endanger'd
—Some vessels coming into this harbour before
the masters cou'd reach the custom-house to make
report, have been boarded by armed boats from
the Romney, commanded by Captain Corner ;
one vessel from the West-Indies had her hatches
open'd and twenty hogsheads molasses hoisted upon
deck to search the hold—Another vessel with lumber was carried along-side the Romney, her hold
unstowed, and the boards taken on board the king's
ship, before the master was permitted to go to the
custom-house to report.——A vessel from Lisbon
bound to Marblehead, was boarded on the high seas
by Mr. Panton, lieutenant of the Rose, (who was
likewise an officer of the customs) with a design
to impress the seamen, who concealed themselves in
the hold ; upon which Mr. Panton assumed the
custom-house officer, and pretended that he was going to search the vessel for uncustomed goods, and
under this pretence enter'd the hold and endeavor'd
to impress the seamen who stood upon their defence,
and told the officer upon his peril not to enter the
forehold, upon which they were fired upon,& one of
the seamen was shot thro' his arm,& another woun-
ded ; this brought on an engagement, in which the
Lieutenant was killed, and the vessel brought out
of her way to Boston by the man of war.—Several
other vessels have been seized in the bay,at the Vine-
yard and other ports, where they have been obliged
by contrary winds to make a harbour, sent into
ports

ports they were not bound for, and there detain'd at a great expence, on the trifling pretence that some article (not on cargo, but belonging to the mariners) was found on board, not specified in the cockets.

Upwards of 20 sail of men of war, cutters and other armed vessels, purchased by the board of Commissioners, have been employed this year to cruize on the trade of this province, without discovering one vessel in an illicit trade, tho' their expectations were raised in hopes of plunder, by the unjust and cruel representations made by wicked and designing men—Some of the commanders of the King's ships purchased small vessels on their own accounts, and sent them into the little harbors and coves where the men of war could not cruise; and some of these have been disguised as coasters, and every other method has been used to detect a supposed contraband trade; even the master of a little cutter purchased a fishing boat on his own account for the same purpose: But being disappointed of the advantages which were expected to be reaped from the condemnation of illicit traders, or the prizes as they call'd them; they have been induced to 'take advantage of the mistake and omissions of the masters of coasting vessels, several of whom have been seized by those guarda coastas, and two actually condemned for some trifles found on board without being in the clearance—They have indeed seized 23 other vessels upon some trifling pretences, all of which have been

been difmifs'd after being detain'd fome time at a
confiderable expence————The Fifhery has likewife
been greatly diftreffed by the guarda coaftas————
Many of our fifhermen cure their fifh at Canfo and
other places in Nova-Scotia, at a great diftance from
any cuftom-houfe; and when the fifhing feafon is
over, they take in the fifh, they have curred on
fhore, and return home; this has been the practice
ever fince the fifhery was carried on, till the paffing
of the late acts, and the appointment of officers of
the cuftoms on board the King's veffels, fince which
many of the fifhing veffels have been feiz'd by thefe
avaricious officers, and condemn'd in the court of
admiralty for taking in their dry fifh without firft
having a permit from the cuftom-houfe, and giving
the bond required for non-enumerated goods, and
the fkippers of thofe veffels are now obliged to make
two trips to Halifax or Louifbourg, firft to give
bond and take a permit to load, and when they
have taken in their fifh, to procure a clearance to
fcreen their veffels and fifh from the jaws of thefe
devouring monfters.

The Commiffioners themfelves (tho' by act of
parliament they are not intituled to any fhare of the
forfeitures) appear by the whole tenor of their
conduct, to have been more intent upon making
feizures, than upon promoting the revenue; nor have
they fhewn the leaft difpofition to ferve the trade,
but have taken every method in their power to embarrafs it, by their directions to the collectors and

other

other officers of the customs, * and by their employing persons of the most abandoned characters under them, some of whom have acted in open violation of the laws ; and one in particular, without the least provocation, fired upon the inhabitants, and by force of arms rescued a prisoner taken by the King's writ from the hand of justice.

The merchants and traders in the northern colonies, and more particularly in this province, have been greatly abused by the representations that have been made to Great-Britain, of their importing large quantities of the manufactures of France, Holland, Hambro'

---

* On the 27th of October 1768, John Hancock, Esq; Mr. Lewis Gray, Capt. Daniel Malcom, Capt. John Matchet, and others, were libell'd for £.9000 sterling each, and held to bail in £.3000 sterling each, to appear at the Court of Vice-Admiralty, no suspicion of their aiding and assisting at the landing a few pipes of wine imported in the sloop Liberty from Madera, more than was reported at the custom house ; the libel against Mr. Hancock came on the 7th of November, when a vast number of witnesses were examined upon interrogatories in the tedious method of the civil law, and no proof appearing against him, the court was adjourn'd to the next week, and a new sett of witnesses were produced and examined in the same manner, and to as little purpose ; after which the court was several times adjourn'd, and other witnesses summoned, even Mr. Hancock's most intimate friends and acquaintance, so that a great part of the winter was taken up in attending on the court of admiralty, and examining those witnesses ; and after every method had been tried, and no proof could be procured against him in the spring 1769, on the publication of the new judge of admiralty's commission, Mr. Hancock was discharg'd from this vexatious and unprecedented Libel.
The Libels against Mr. Gray, and others, on the same account, were dismiss'd at the same time, without examining any witnesses in the case.
About the same time Capt. Malcom, Capt. Dorrington, and others, were libell'd for £.2400 ster. each, & held to bail in £.800 ster. on suspicion of their assisting at the landing a few pipes of wine suppos'd to be imported in the schooner Friendship from the Western Islands ; and as no evidences could be produced to support the charge in these libels, they were all dismissed at the same time Mr. Hancock's was.
Other instances of the same kind of proceedings might be produc'd, but these will be sufficient to shew in what a cruel and vexatious manner the inhabitants of this province are treated by the Board of Commissioner'

Hambro' and other parts of Europe, in a clandestine manner, which are false and malicious; the merchants in this province carry on no trade with any part of France, except to their islands in the West-Indies; and no instance can be produced of any quantity of manufactures being bro't from thence. The goods imported from Holland and Hambro' are all enter'd in England, and the duties to a considerable amount, annually are paid there—When the duty upon molasses was 6d. sterling a gallon, as there was no appropriation made of that duty, it was well known in England the officers of the customs connived at the importation, and their conduct was not disapproved: How far this will justify such representations, is submitted to the impartial public—but since the duty on molasses has been reduced, the whole, tho' grievous, has been regularly paid.

The merchants do not desire liberty to import any kind of goods that are prejudicial to the manufactures of Great-Britain, nor have they ever yet complain'd of their trade being confin'd to Great-Britain for such goods as are manufactured there, so long as they might be imported duty free.

What the Colonists have a right to expect and hope for, is a repeal of all the acts imposing duties on any kind of goods imported into the British colonies for the purpose of raising a revenue in America, as being inconsistent with their rights as free subjects—the removal of every unnecessary burden upon trade, and that it be restor'd to the same footing it was upon before the act of the 6th of George the 2d, commonly call'd the sugar-act ——particularly,   That

That melasses so necessary to promote every branch of trade, and likewise sugars, be admitted free of duty.

That the importation of wines from Madera and the Azores may be permitted agreable to the act of the 15th of Charles the 2d.

And as the free importation of fruit, wine and oil direct from Spain and Portugal would be a great encouragement of the fishery, and will no ways interfere with the manufactures of Great-Britain, and the obliging all vessels with those articles on board to call at some port in Great-Britain, being attended with great expence and delay ; and as the acid of of lemmons and oranges is become almost necessary for the health and comfort of the inhabitants of North-America, and these fruits not being able to endure repeated transportation, it is hoped the direct importation of wine, oil and fruit of all kinds may also be permitted.

The taking off the duties on paper, glass and colours, will relieve the trade of the burdens it labours under——But should all the revenue acts be repealed, and the trade reliev'd from all unnecessary restrictions, and restor'd to the footing it was upon before the act of the 6th George 2d, and the indulgences now mentioned be granted, it would have a happy tendency to unite Great-Britain and her colonies on a lasting foundation—all clandestine trade would then cease—the great expence of men of war, cutters of the commissioners and other custom-house officers lately appointed to secure the revenue, might be saved— The trade, navigation and fishery would not only be revived, but greatly extended ;

extended; and in that cafe the growth of thefe colonies would be very rapid, and confequently the demand for Britifh manufactures proportionably increafed.

The foregoing Obfervations relate wholly to the revenue acts, and the conduct of the cuftom-houfe officers; but we cannot conclude without mentioning the great expence and needlefs trouble accruing to the trade by means of the *Naval-Office*.

Since the eftablifhment of Cuftom-Houfes, and the appointment of cuftom-houfe officers, this office is altogether unneceffary, and anfwers no valuable purpofe.

Upon this head it is proper to obferve, that foon after the fettlement of thefe colonies, the parliament thought it neceffary to take fome meafures for the regulation of the plantation trade. The act of the 12th of Charles the 2d for encouraging and increafing fhipping and navigation, ordains what qualifications fhall be nece ary for veffels trading to the colonies; and enjoins *the Governor, or perfons by him appointed*, to infpect and take care that the fame be obferved, and to take bonds for all veffels lading any of the commodities in faid act enumerated.

Three years after, by the act of the 15th of the fame reign, further regulations and reftrictions were made, and every perfon or perfons importing goods into the colonies obliged to deliver to *the Governor of fuch colony, or to fuch perfon or officer as fhall be by him thereunto authorized or appointed*, a true inventory of all fuch goods, &c. At this time and until ten years after, no duties were laid by act of parliament upon any commodities in the plantations, and of confequence no cuftom-houfes had been erected, or collectors or other cuftom-houfe officers appointed or thought of in the colonies, but the whole care and infpection of trade remained with *the Governor, or the perfon he appointed naval-officer* —Afterwards by the act of the 25th of the fame reign, chap. the 7th, fect. 3. duties being laid on fugars and fundry other articles, to be paid in the plantations, when carried from one plantation to another, the feveral duties fo impofed were to be levied and paid to fuch collector or other officer in faid plantations as fhould thereafter be appointed by the commiffioners of the cuftoms in England ; who did accordingly appoint collectors and fuch other officers as occafion required, for that purpofe, who ever fince their appointment, it is well known, have had the chief care and infpection of the trade.

From this account of the matter, it appears that as formerly there were no cuftom-houfes or cuftom-houfe officers in America, the government thought proper to devolve the care and infpection of the trade upon the *Governor of each colon ,or fuch perfons as they fhould appoint under them for that purpofe,* who have been called naval-officers ; that upon the eftablifhment of cuftom-houfes and cuftom-houfe officers, the eftablifhment of a naval-office, or the appointment of naval officers was rendered altogether needlefs. The original defign of government in the eftablifhment or appointment of either, was, that the trade might be duly taken care of and in-
                                                    fpected,

fpected, that frauds might be prevented, and that abufes in trade might be regulated : All thefe purpofes may be and are effectually anfwered by the appointment of collectors and other officers of the cuftoms ; therefore the naval office is altogether ufelefs. As it is a grievous burthen,and tends greatly to retard bufinefs,and is a needlefs expence, without any benefit to the government, or anfwering any one valuable purpofe, we have juft grounds of complaint, and cannot but hope this office will be difpenfed with.

Upon the whole, the trade of America is really the trade of Great-Britain herfelf: The profits thereof center there. It is one grand fource from whence money fo plentifully flows into the hands of the feveral manufacturers, and from thence into the coffers of landholders throughout the whole kingdom. It is in fhort the ftrongeft chain of connection between Britain and the Colonies, and the principal means whereby thofe fources of wealth and power have been and are fo ufeful and advantageous to her. The embarrafsments, difficulties and infupportable burdens under which *this trade* has laboured, have already made us prudent, frugal and induftrious; and fuch a fpirit in the Colonifts muft foon, very foon, enable them to fubfift without the manufactures of Great-Britain, the trade of which, as well as its naval power, has been greatly promoted and ftrengthened by the luxury of the colonies ; confequently any meafures that have a tendency to injure, obftruct and diminifh the American trade and navigation, muft have the fame effect upon that of Great-Britain, and in all probability PROVE HER RUIN.

A LETTER FROM A VIRGINIAN

Jonathan Boucher, *A Letter from a Virginian to the Members of the Congress to be held at Philadelphia, on The First of September, 1774* (reprinted in London, 1774), pp. 5–50.

Jonathan Boucher (1738–1804), born in England and trained as an Anglican clergyman, was a strong supporter of British rule in the colonies. In 1759 he immigrated to America and became a tutor to sons of the elite, including George Washington's stepson, John Parke Custis. He later served as the Rector of Annapolis, Maryland. Boucher became quite unpopular for using his religious position to preach against an American revolution and, by the end of his stay in America, had received so many threats that he took the precaution of carrying a pistol while he preached. He returned to England in 1775, where he became the Vicar of Epsom, Surrey, until his death.

In *A Letter from a Virginian*, Boucher urges the colonists to abandon their complaints and their incitement for a revolution against Great Britain. He also promotes the importance of authority in guiding society in order to prevent anarchy. However, the majority of the colonists did not accept his Anglican religious authoritarianism.

A
LETTER

FROM A

VIRGINIAN

TO THE

Members of the Congress

TO BE HELD AT

PHILADELPHIA,

ON

The Firſt of SEPTEMBER, 1774.

BOSTON, printed:

LONDON, reprinted; for J. WILKIE, No. 71,
in St. Paul's-Church-Yard, 1774.

[Price 1 s.]

A

LETTER, &c.

Gentlemen,

IN times of public danger, every man has a right to offer his advice; there are some men who think it their duty to do it, although on common occasions they may be naturally too diffident of their own opinions, or too indolent, to give themselves the trouble to obtrude them on the world. If such men happen to mistake their talents, not from vanity, but from an excefs of zeal, and meddle officioufly with matters above

their

their reach, they may be forgiven on the
fcore of their intention : Even a modeft
man is apt to over-rate his own judgment
where his affections and interefts are deeply
concerned.

My zeal therefore in the common caufe
muft ferve for my excufe, if in the courfe
of this letter I fhould give my opinion more
confidently than I ought to do, and feem to
think myfelf, which is a very common cafe,
much wifer than I am.

You are foon to meet on the moft ferious
occafion that ever prefented itfelf to this
country fince its exiftence.

The harmony which fubfifted, with little
or no interruption, between Great-Britain
and her Colonies, from their very infancy
until of late, is in danger of being deftroyed

for

for ever. The habits of kindnefs and affection, on one fide, and of refpect and obedience, on the other (which prevailed during fo long a period, were in the higheft degree conducive to the profperity of this country in particular, and are ftill neceffary to its fecurity and happinefs) are changed into murmurings, difcontents, and reproaches; and will foon end, without fome very extraordinary interpofition, in mutual and implacable hatred. Complaints of grievances, real or imaginary, are heard from one end of thefe Colonies to the other; the minds of the people appear to be agitated as at fome great crifis; they wifh, by a public confultation, to be affured of the general opinion, by a reprefentation of every province, to collect the calm, deliberate determination of all the provinces, to eftablifh fome public mark of mutual confidence, that they may hold it up to the parent country,

country, in all its weight and importance. For this purpose, Gentlemen, you are delegated to the Congress. An absolute, perfect representation of the people, never existed perhaps, but in theory. You, it is true, have not been summoned, or convened, by any formal constitutional authority, or invested with any legislative powers : But you have been chosen as freely as the circumstances of the times would admit ; with less cabal and intrigue than is usually employed for a seat in many of our legal provincial Assemblies, and without even the suspicion of venality, which is but too frequently and too generally practised among us for that purpose. Your persons, characters and principles, are familiarly known to your constituents ; you have been recommended by the most honourable of all interests, the general opinion of your knowledge, abilities and virtues. We look up to you as the oracles of our country ; your opinions will

have

have the effect of laws, on the minds of
the people, and your resolves may decide
the fate of America. All orders of men,
who enjoy the happiness of living under a
free government, may boldly assume the
character of politicians; they inherit a right
to it as much as the proudest Peer inherits
a right to his seat in Parliament, however
ridiculous the proportion may appear to the
conceit and arrogance of men who think
themselves born to domineer over their
fellow-creatures at pleasure. High birth
and fortune, when they are not abused, confer the solid and splendid advantages of education and accomplishments, extensive influence, and incitement to glory; but they
give no exclusive title to common sense,
wisdom, or integrity. The lowest orders of
men in such a country, have an unalienable
property in their industry, their liberty, and
their lives, and may be allowed to set some
value at least on the only property they can
boast

boaft of: Thefe may be all endangered, or loft, by the conduct of their Governors; they have therefore a right, as freemen, to examine their conduct, to cenfure, to condemn it; without this right the freeft government on earth would foon degenerate into the rankeft tyranny. The great outlines, the fundamental principles of our conftitution, are within the reach of almoft every man's capacity; they require little more than leifure to ftudy them, memory to retain them, and candour to form a a true judgment of them: unhappily for the order and peace of fociety, this ineftimable privilege is but too often abufed. Men in general are governed more by their temper than their judgment; they have little leifure and ftill lefs inclination, to inform themfelves exactly of the neceffary conftitutional powers of the fupreme Magiftrate, or of their own legal rights; they have been often told that liberty is a very great blefling;

bleffing; they talk inceffantly of it, they find fomething inchanting in the very found of the word; afk them the meaning of it, they think you defign to affront them; pufh them to a definition, they give you at once a defcription of the ftate of nature. Their ideas, of the nature, origin and conditions of civil fociety in general, are juft as confufed and inaccurate; they take their political as they do their religious opinions (upon truft) from the nurfery, the company they fall into, or the profeffions and fcenes in which they are accidentally engaged. They find the movement of the paffions a more eafy and agreeable exercife than the drudgery of fober and difpaffionate enquiry. Hand-bills, news-papers, party-pamphlets, are the fhallow and turbid fources from whence they derive their notions of government; thefe they pronounce as confidently and dogmatically, as if a political problem was to be folved as clearly as a mathematical

one;

one; and as if a bold affertion amounted to a demonftration.

Ambition and luft of power above the laws, are fuch predominant paffions in the breafts of moft men, even of men who efcape the infection of other vices, that liberty, legal liberty, would be in continual danger of encroachments, if it were not guarded by perpetual jealoufy. Crafty, defigning knaves, turbulent demagogues, quacks in politics, and impoftors in patriotifm, have in all free governments, and in all ages, availed themfelves of this neceffary fpirit of jealoufy; and by broaching doctrines unknown to the conftitution, under the name of conftitutional principles, by bold affertions, partial reprefentations, falfe colourings, wrefted conftructions, and tragical declamations, have frequently impofed on the credulity of the well-meaning, deluded multitude.   Thus the moft honourable

cauſe

caufe that wife and good men can engage in, the caufe of liberty, has been often difgraced ; nations once as free and as happy as ourfelves, have been frightened into anarchy, plunged into all the horrors of a civil war, and ended their miferable career in the moft humiliating and abject flavery, until the facred name of liberty has become a word of fcorn and mockery in the mouths of tyrants, and their abandoned minions and emiffaries.

Such are the calamities which have frequently arifen from an ardent miftaken zeal, and from the falfe refinments of fpeculative men, who amufe themfelves and the world, with vifionary ideas of perfection, which never were, nor ever will be found, either in public or in private life. You, Gentlemen, cannot even be fufpected of being under the influence of fuch delufions ; there are many among you who are eminently learned, not only in the laws of the
land,

land, but in the laws of nature and nations, in the general laws of reafon and
juftice, who know their authority and revere them, not as they have been fometimes
explained on the narrow illiberal principles
of party fpirit, but as they have been underftood
and acknowledged by the wife of all ages,
and have ferved for the bafis of the moft
perfect fyftems of legiflation. Thefe are
the only rules by which all political opinions ought to be tried and examined, by
which an honeft man and a good citizen
can form a true judgment of the duty he
owes to his King and his Country.

It would have been happy for the world
on many melancholy occafions, that the
revealed will of God, which ought to be
the fole rule of every man's conduct, the
only tranfcendent authority from which
there lies no appeal, had never received but
one general interpretation with regard to
the

the reciprocal duties of the Sovereign and the people: but even that facred and eternal ftandard of right and wrong, in private life has been alternately perverted and profaned in the political world, by the indif. creet zeal and wild paffions of mad enthufiafts, or flavifh bigots; has been equally abufed, to ferve the purpofes of a Charles or a Cromwell, of a Gregory or a Venner, to throw a veil over the horrors of anarchy and rebellion, or to fanctify the ridiculous and damnable doctrines of nonrefiftance and paffive-obedience, on a proper application of the general doctrines and principles I have mentioned. to the peculiar and local circumftances of this country; your proceedings and refolves ought to depend by a competent knowledge of the character of the times, when the Colony charters were granted; of the Kings, by whom they were granted; of the People, to whom they were granted;

of

of the purpofes for which they were afked and obtained; of the tenor and fpirit of the charters themfelves, how they were under-ftood, and conftrued by our Anceftors: by a knowledge in fhort of the hiftory of our country, we may difcover the general con-ftitution of the Colonies, and be able to judge whether the prefent difcontents are founded on truth or ignorance.

By a due and candid examination of this very interefting fubject, it may perhaps appear, that the character of the times, when moft of the charters were originally granted, bore very little refemblance to the prefent times; that the ineftimable privi-leges of a modern Englifhman, might in-deed be found, in fome degree, in the letter of the law, but had never been enjoyed, were generally very imperfectly underftood, and rarely claimed by our anceftors; that even thefe legal, conftitutional privileges were

were encumbered with a thoufand legal cuf-toms, which they patiently fubmitted to, although they would exceed the patience of a modern Frenchman; that they felt and difcovered infinitely more zeal for their re-ligious, than for their civil liberty, and would have been contented with half the privileges their pofterity enjoy for an act of toleration. It will appear, that the Kings, by whom the charters were granted, were not defpotic Kings; that they conftitution-ally poffeffed the executive, not the fu-preme legiflative power, of which they only made a part; that in all queftions of magnitude, they were under the control of the other parts of the legiflative power. That our anceftors were fubjects of the Kings of England, not as the inhabitants of Guyenne formerly were, or as thofe of the Electo-rate of Hanover are now, but fubjects of an Englifh parliamentary King; Englifh-men in the fulleft fenfe of the word, with the

the same habits and manners, speaking the same language, governed by the same maxims, customs, and laws, with scarce any distinction, but the latitude and longitude of their new residence.

That if their charters were granted without the concurrence of parliaments, it was not because a parliament had no right to interfere, but because they did not in those days appear of importance enough to be agitated in the great council of the nation.

That although by their charters, our ancestors were empowered to make by-laws for their own local convenience, they were neverthelefs expresfly and formally restrained from making laws repugnant to the laws of England; and were univerfally underftood, both there and here, to owe, in common with all

all Englishmen, an obedience to the laws, from which no King could release them, because no King could dispense with the laws. That from this parliamentary authority, they never wished, until of late, to be emancipated, but would rather have fled to it for protection, from the arbitrary encroachments of a James, or a Charles, armed with the usurpations, and abuses, of privy seals, benevolences, proclamations, star chambers and high commission courts, and from the enormities of the two succeeding reigns; that such were the practices of the times, when our early charters bear their dates, that if they were not granted by parliamentary Kings, they were granted by tyrants, and we shall gain nothing by recurring to first principles.

That no political society can subsist, unless there be an absolute supreme power lodged somewhere in the society, has been univer-

univerfally held as an uncontrolable maxim in theory, by all writers on government, from Ariftotle down to Sidney and Locke, and has been as univerfally adopted in prac-tice, from the defpotifm of Morocco, to the republic of St. Marino; as long as govern-ment fubfifts, fubjects owe an implicit obedience to the Laws of the fupreme power, from which there can be no appeal but to Heaven. We for fome years paft have been multiplying ineffectual refolves, petitions, and remonftrances, and advancing claims of rights, &c. our petitions have at laft been neglected, or rejected, or cen-fured; the principles on which we found our claims, have been formally denied. To what, or to whom, fhall we have recourfe? Shall we appeal to the King of Maffachu-fetts Bay, to the King of Connecticut, to the King of Rhode Ifland, againft the King of Great Britain, to refcind the acts of parliament of Great Britain, to difpenfe

with

with the Laws, to which as a neceſſary and efficient part of that body, he has ſo recently given his aſſent ? Ridiculous as theſe queſtions may appear, I am afraid they are but too much of a piece with doctrines which have been lately broached, inculcated every where, and almoſt every where received. The Colonies are conſtitutionally independent of each other : They formally acknowledge themſelves loyal and dutiful ſubjects of his Majeſty George the Third; but ſeverally claim an exemption from the authority of the Britiſh parliament. A doctrine ſo repugnant to the ideas of all our fellow-ſubjects in Great Britain, can, I truſt, have no place in your aſſembly. The buſineſs you have to tranſact, is too ſerious to be trifled with ; the confidence repoſed in you, too ſacred to be ſacrificed to idle ſophiſtry and viſionary diſtinctions; the fate of America, may depend on your reſolves; they ſhould be founded on prin-

ciples

ciples that are plain and intelligible, that are marked with the authority of univerfal opinions and truths.

The fupreme power of the Britifh parliament over her Colonies, was ever, till very lately, as univerfally acknowledged, by ourfelves, as by our fellow-fubjects in England. It ufurps no claim to infallibility in its opinions, but gives the fubject a legal right of petitioning, remonftrating, of propofing plans of reformation and redrefs. Neverthelefs, though it pretends not to infallibility, like all other governments, it requires an implicit obedience to its laws, and has a right to enforce it. A tribe of favages unreftrained by laws, human or divine, may live in fome harmony, and endure for ages, becaufe in the ftate of nature there are at the moft but two or three fubjects to contend about, and the individuals are reciprocally over-awed by the natural rights of private

vate revenge. But in civil fociety, compofed as it commonly is, of fuch an infinite
number of heterogeneous and difcordant
principles and interefts, in trade, in politics, and religion, where fubjects of con-
tention prefent themfelves by thoufands
every hour; no conftitution can fubfift a
moment, without a conftant refignation of
private judgment to the judgment of the
public.

What part then, Gentlemen, have you
left you to act, but to propofe, with
the modefty of fubjects, fome practicable
plan of accommodation, and to ob*y? Shall
the time of fo refpectable an affembly be
fquandered, in advancing claims of right,
that have been urged and rejected a thoufand times; that have been heard, confidered, folemnly debated, and decided by
the only power on earth, who has a right
to decide them? Shall the opinions and
                                    defires

defires of a fmall part of the community, prevail againft the opinions and defires of the majority of the community ? What new fpecies of eloquence can be invented to perfuade ? What new logic to convince the underftandings of our fellow-fubjects ? Shall the Britifh fenate be governed by the pernicious maxims of a Polifh diet, and the *veto* of a fingle member, or of a few members, however diftinguifhed by extraordinary wifdom and virtue, obftruct or fufpend, or annul the legiflation of a great nation ?

Thofe wife and virtuous citizens themfelves hold fuch doctrines in derifion. While a queftion is in agitation, they debate with freedom, but they claim no blind fubmiffion to their opinions, no authority, but the authority of their arguments. They arrogate not to themfelves, a monopoly of all the wifdom, and all the

virtue

virtue in the nation. When the queſtion is decided, they ſubmit their private ſpeculative opinions, to the opinion of the majority, to the law of the land. They revere the law, and make it the rule of their conduct.

You, therefore, Gentlemen, the delegates of a very numerous and reſpectable people, will ſurely think it below the dignity of your character, to aſſemble, with the paſſions and language of a common town-meeting, to ſit in judgment, like ſome foreign imperial power on the decrees of a Britiſh legiſlature; to arraign the conduct of adminiſtration, in the lofty emphatic tone of a manifeſto. Can ſuch proceedings anſwer any purpoſe, but the dangerous purpoſes of exaſperating and provoking the indignation and vengeance of all orders and degrees of men in the parent country? Of alienating the affections of the

the people here, feducing them from their allegiance, inflaming their paffions, and exciting them to popular tumults and infurrections? The order and tranquillity of government frequently depend more upon the manners and morals of the people, than upon their laws and inftitutions. For the honour of our native country, there are, I believe, few inftances on record of any people under a free government, who have paffed through the fame length of period, with fo few civil commotions, though the powers of government have never been vigilantly exerted, nor the laws held in any extraordinary veneration. But the manners and morals of our countrymen are undebauched and innocent, compared with thofe of the inhabitants of older countries, where the inftruments of corruption, and the incitements to vices and crimes are more general. The danger is neverthelefs the fame, or greater. There are no

people

people on earth more fecure from the humiliating effects of poverty, more fuperior to the fmiles or frowns of power, more unawed by the diftinctions of birth and fortune, more confident or tenacious of their own opinions, or more on a level with all the world in their converfation and behaviour. The paffions of fuch men, agitated by falfe principles, and miftaken zeal, are more dangerous to the repofe of the world, than the frenzy of the moft diffolute and abandoned flaves. You will furely beware how you inflame the minds of fuch honeft, deluded citizens, or the time may come, perhaps it is not very diftant, that you will wifh, when it will be too late, to calm the ftorm you have raifed, and will tremble every moment, left it burft on your own heads.

Upon the fubject of a non–importation and non-exportation agreement, I am at a

lofs

lofs what to fay; it has been fo often and
fo warmly recommended, as a fpecific remedy for all our complaints, has received
the fanction of fuch general authority, that
I am afraid it will look like an affront to
the underftandings of my fellow-citizens,
an apoftacy from my native country, to in-
finuate the leaft doubt of its efficacy. Yet
let me moft earneftly conjure you, by the
common love we bear to that country, by
the gratitude we owe to the parent country,
by the important truft repofed in you, as
you value your prefent and future peace,
and the interefts and happinefs of your
pofterity; beware how you adopt that
meafure, how you engage in that ftrange
conflict of fullennefs and obftinacy, till you
have given it the moft calm and ferious
deliberation.

The efficacy of the meafure, admitting
it to be a practicable one, depends, I prefume,

fume, upon the importance of our commerce with Great Britain; it is poffible that people in general here may have been much deceived in this matter, by partial and exaggerated calculations, made under particular circumftances, during particular periods, to ferve the purpofes of party. It would be difficult, if not impoffible, to afcertain the exact value of it. But if we may truft to the authority of men of eminence, who have treated this fubject as politicians at large, unbiaffed by partial, local, or temporary views, men who have traced it through the books of cuftomhoufes, merchants, brokers, manufacturers, &c. the beft fources of information; if we can depend on the opinions of the moft intelligent merchants of our own country; if we can believe our own eyes, every man of common obfervation, and reflection, muft be affured, that the amount of Britifh manufactures imported into this country,

is

is very inconfiderable, compared with the
opinions about it, that are fo induftrioufly
circulated through all the Colonies, and fo
generally received. Let us examine by the
fame rule, the amount of the inland and
coafting trade of Great-Britain, and her
foreign trade with all the nations on earth;
it will appear infinitely greater, than our
countrymen in general (accuftomed from
the vanity natural to all mankind to confider the little fcenes and tranfactions immediately under their eyes, as objects of
the greateft magnitude) can form any adequate idea of. The refources of her trade
are infinite, the combinations of it too various and complicated, the revolutions of
it too fudden and frequent, to be eafily explained or underftood. But we may judge
of it by the refult and effect of the whole,
whenever the aftonifhing power of the nation is called forth into exertion. Can we
ferioufly believe, that this wealth and
power

power is derived almoſt entirely from her North American Colonies? Can we (who by our own confeſſions do not yet enjoy even all the neceſſaries of life) can we reaſonably hope, to ſtarve into compliance, ſo great, and ſo powerful a nation? Shall we puniſh ourſelves, like froward children, who re-fuſe to eat, when they are hungry, that they may vex their indulgent mothers? Or like deſperate gameſters, ſtake at one throw, our ſmall, but competent and happy for-tunes, againſt the ſucceſſive ſtakes, the ac-cumulated wealth of ages? We may teaze the mother country, we cannot ruin her. Let us beware how we engage in ſuch an unequal conteſt, leſt while we are giving her a ſlight wound, we receive a mortal one.

If, notwithſtanding, we are confident, that the meaſure of a non-importation and non-exportation agreement, bids fair to be a ſuc-

a fuccefsful one, it certainly behoves us as men, and as chriftians, to be fure that it is a juft meafure. A combination to ruin, or to obftruct the trade of a fellow-citizen, who happens to differ from us in his religious or political opinions, adopted in paffion, profecuted by the intrigues of a cabal, by innuendoes, infinuations, threatenings, and publicly figned by large numbers of leading men, would, I prefume, be a manifeft violation of the laws of God and man, and would, on conviction, be feverely punifhed in every court of juftice in the univerfe. In what colours then will appear, the combinations of a large and refpectable body of fubjects, againft the fupreme power of the community; adopted from the fame motives, profecuted by the fame arts, and publicly figned, in the face of the whole world? Happily for us, by the generous and noble fpirit of the Britifh conftitution, our own conftitution, the crime of treafon, which in
almoft

almoſt every other country is vague and undefined, often in the breaſt of a venal and corrupt Judge, and made not to warn, but to enſnare the people, is exactly and circumſtantially aſcertained and defined.

Shall we abuſe the generoſity and beneficence of laws, made for our protection? Shall we ſkulk behind the letter of the law, while we wage war againſt the ſpirit of it? Becauſe our anceſtors had foreſeen the poſſibility of the ſubject's levying arms againſt the ſtate in paſſion and deſpair, but knew no inſtance on record, of their having meditated, in cold blood, its deſtruction, and had therefore made no regular proviſion againſt an enormity, which they preſumed could never happen.

It is, I believe, ſufficiently notorious, that there are great numbers of our countrymen, from one end of the continent to the other,
who

who are averfe from this meafure, fome of them from opinion, others from intereft, and many from downright neceffity.

For the fake of common humanity, Gentlemen, difdain to co-operate, with hand-bills, with news-papers, with the high menacing refolves of common town-meetings; do not confpire with them, to reduce, under the pains and penalties of difgrace and infamy, thoufands of your fellow-citizens, to the cruel alternative, of involving themfelves, their wives and children, in indigence and wretchednefs; or of being publicly branded and pointed out by the frantic multitude, as apoftates, and traitors to their country.

Let us, in the name of common fenfe and decency, be confiftent. Shall we, Proteus like, perpetually change our ground, affume every moment fome new and ftrange fhape, shape, to defend, to evade? Shall we establish distinctions between internal and external taxation one year, and laugh at them the next? Shall we confound duties with taxes, and regulations of trade with revenue laws? Shall we rave against the preamble of the law, while we are ready to admit the enacting part of it? Shall we refuse to obey the Tea-Act, not as an oppressive act, but as a dangerous, a sole precedent of taxation, when every post-day shews us a precedent, which our forefathers submitted to, and which we still submit to, without murmuring? Shall we move heaven and earth, against a trifling duty, on a luxury, unknown to nine tenths of the globe, unknown to our ancestors! despised by half the nations of Europe! which no authority, no necessity compels us to use? There are thousands of honest industrious families, who have no resources, but in the consequences of exportation and importation. Shall we levy a tax upon these innocent citizens, a tax unheard-of, of, difproportionate, a tax never fuggefted by the moft inhuman tyrant! A tax to the amount of their daily bread? Reflect one moment, on the terms, in which the re-folves of every town-meeting on this continent fpeak of the Bofton port-bill; although it is little more than a temporary fufpenfion of the trade of that city, until reftitution, which God and man calls aloud for, be made.   And although the ports, at a very fmall diftance from Bofton, and every other port on the continent, is as free as ever, fhall we multiply thefe calamities ten thou-fand fold? For fuch calamities muft be the inevitable confequences of a non-impor-tation and non-exportation agreement. You ought therefore to be conndent, that it will prove effectual before you adopt it.   Can any man ferioufly believe this, who is to-lerably acquainted with the hiftory and prefent flate of thefe Colonies; who has vifited our principal cities and towns, and

has

has obferved by what means they have rifen to their wealth and importance, how they daily increafe, and how their inhabitants fubfift? The horrid punifhments, inflicted by defpotic Princes, are commonly of little avail, againft a contraband trade, where any trifling extraordinary profit is an irrefiftible temptation. What can we expect from a loofe agreement, where the fole fubfiftence of thoufands is at ftake? In all trading na-tions, where there are duties or prohibitions, there are fmugglers; there ever were, and ever will be, until we find fome nation, where every individual is a patriot or a faint.

Such an agreement will have the defect and impotence of laws framed on monkifh ideas of purity, againft the indelible feel-ings and paffions of humanity. Can you hope, by promifes, by extorted promifes, to reftrain men from carrying on a clandef-tine

tine trade with Great Britain, who trade every day with our inveterate enemies, in defiance of all law, and who grow rich by the fpoils of the fair trader ? Will it not rather happen, as it has happened already, that province will fmuggle againſt province, citizen againſt citizen, till we are weary, and afhamed of being the dupes of each other, and become the laughing-ſtock of the whole world ?

Let us no longer deceive ourfelves with the vain hopes of a fpeedy repeal of the Tea Act, becaufe we triumphed in the repeal of the Stamp Act ; the Acts themfelves are totally different in their principles and their operation ; the occafion by no means fimilar. We have advanced from one extravagant claim to another, made fuch fudden turnings and windings, taken fuch wild and rapid flights, that the boldeſt of our

followers

followers can follow us no longer ; our moft zealous advocates are afhamed to plead a caufe, which all men, but ourfelves, condemn. Can we any longer doubt that our friends, on the other fide of the Atlantic, as well as our enemies, although they may differ in the mode of exercifing the authority of parliament over us, are almoft univerfally agreed in the principle ? Are we not convinced from a thoufand teftimonies, that the clamour againft us, is univerfal, and loud ? Is this, Gentlemen, a feafon to frighten the parent country into a repeal ? No man of fpirit in private life, even on the flighteft quarrel, will fubmit to be bullied, and expofed to the fcorn and derifion of the little circle he lives in. Can we ferioufly hope, that a great nation, a proud nation, will be infulted and degraded, with impunity, by her Colonies, in the face of every rival

king-

kingdom in Europe? Let us then, Gentlemen, relinquish for ever, a project fraught
with abfurdity and ruin. Let your con-
ftituents hope, that the occafion of fuch
an important affembly will not be wantonly
fquandered in opprobrious reproaches, in
bidding defiance to the mother country, but
in digefting and propofing fome new plan
of accommodation, worthy her notice and
acceptance.   Difputes are generally vain
and endlefs, where there are no arbitrators
to award, no judges to decree; where arguments, fufpected to be drawn from intereft
and paffion, are addreffed to intereft and
paffion, they produce no conviction. We
may ring eternal changes upon taxation
and reprefentation, upon actual, virtual,
and non-reprefentation. We may end as
we began, and difagree eternally: but
there is one propofition, a felf-evident propofition, to which all the world give their
                                    affent,

affent, and from which we cannot with-
hold ours; that whatever taxation and
reprefentation may be, taxation and government are infeparable. On the fubject of
taxation the authority of Mr. Locke is
generally quoted by our advocates, as par-
amount to all other authority whatever.
His Treatife on Government, as far as his
ideas are practicable with the corrupt materials of all governments, is undoubtedly
a moft beautiful theory, the nobleft affertion of the unalienable rights of mankind.
Let us refpect it as the opinion of a wife
and virtuous philofopher and patriot, but
let us likewife, as good fubjects, revere the
laws of the land, the collected wifdom of
ages, and make them the fole rule of our
political conduct. Let not Mr. Locke be
quoted partially by thofe who have read
him, to miflead thoufands who never read
him. When he is brought as an authority,
that

that no subject can be justly taxed without his own consent, why do not they add his own explanation of that consent? *i. e.* " The " consent of the majority, giving it either " by themselves, or their representatives " chosen by them." Do we compose the majority of the British community? Are we, or are we not of that community? If we are of that community, but are not represented, are we not in the same situation with the numerous body of copyholders, with the inhabitants of many wealthy and populous towns; in short, with a very great number of our fellow-subjects, who have no votes in elections? Shall we affirm that these are all virtually represented, but deny that we are so; and at the same time be too proud to solicit a representation? Or under the trite and popular pretences of venality and corruption, laugh at it as impracticable? Shall we plunge at once into

anar-

anarchy, and reject, all accommodation with a government, (by the confeſſion of the wiſeſt men in Europe, the freeſt and the nobleſt government on the records of hiſtory) becauſe there are imperfections in it, as there are in all things, and in all men ? Are we confederates, or allies, or ſubjects of Great-Britain ? In what code of laws, are we to ſearch for taxation, under the title and condition of requiſition, as we underſtand the word ? In what theory of government, ancient or modern ? Is it to be found any where on earth, but in modern harangues, modern pamphlets ? And in theſe only as temporary expedients. The ſupply of government muſt be conſtant, certain, and proportioned to the protection it affords ; the moment one is precarious, the other is ſo too ; the moment it fails, civil ſociety expires. We boaſt much of our bountiful compliance with the requiſitions made during

ring the laft war, and in many inftances with reafon; but let us remember and acknowledge, that there was even then more than one rich province that refufed to comply, although the war was in the very bowels of the country. Can Great-Britain then depend upon her requifitions in fome future war a thoufand leagues diftant from North-America, in which, as we may have no immediate local intereft, we may look perhaps with little concern.

From the infancy of our Colonies to this very hour, we have grown up and flourifhed under the mildnefs and wifdom of her excellent laws; our trade, our poffeffions, our perfons have been conftantly defended againft the whole world, by the fame of her power, or by the exertion of it. We have been very lately refcued by her from enemies, who threatened us with

flavery

flavery and destruction, at the expence of
much blood and treafure, and establifhed
after a long war (waged on our accounts,
at our moft earneft prayers) in a state of
fecurity, of which there is fcarce an example in hiftory. She is ever ready to
avenge the caufe of the meaneft individual
among us, with a power refpected by the
whole world. Let us then no longer difgrace ourfelves by illiberal, ungrateful reproaches, by meanly afcribing the moft generous conduct to the moft fordid motives :
we owe our birth, our progrefs, our deli-
very to her; we ftill depend on her for
protection; we are furely able to bear
fome part of the expence of it; let us
be willing to bear it. Employ then, Gentlemen, your united zeal and abilities in
fubftituting fome adequate, permanent, and
effectual fupply, (by fome mode of actual
reprefentation) in the place of uncertain,

ineffectual

ineffectual requifitions, or in devifing fome means of reconciling taxation, the indifpenfable obligation of every fubject, with your ideas of the peculiar and ineftimable rights of an Englifhman.

Thefe are objects worthy a Congrefs; meafures, that will confer lafting benefits on your country, and immortal honour on yourfelves.

If, on the contrary, like independent ftates, you arrogate to yourfelves the fole right of judging and deciding in your own caufe; if you perfift in denying the fupreme power of Parliament, which no Parliament will ever renounce, like independent ftates, we have no appeal but to the God of battles. Shall we dare lift up our eyes to that God, the fource of truth and juftice, and implore his affiftance in fuch such a caufe? There are caufes, where, in fpight of the ridiculous tenets of pious, deluded enthufiafts, or of the wicked and monftrous doctrines of flaves and tyrants; the very principles, the original principles on which civil fociety depends, require, where God and Nature call aloud for refiftance. Such caufes exifted in the horrid catalogue of oppreffions and crimes, under a Philip the Second, a Catherine of Medicis, and in the lift of grievances, during one period at leaft, of the reign of the ill-educated, the ill-advifed, the unhappy Charles; on fuch melancholy occafions, men of fentiment, fpirit, and virtue, the only genuine fons of liberty, engage in the honourable caufe of freedom, with God on their fide, and indignantly facrifice every advantage of fortune, every endearment of life, and life itfelf. Do fuch caufes exift now among us?

Did

Did they ever exift ? Are they likely to exift ?

Open, if it be not too late, the eyes of our infatuated countrymen; teach them to compare their happy fituation, with the wretchednefs of nine tenths of the globe; fhew them the general diffufion of the neceffaries, the conveniences and pleafures of life, among all orders of people here; the certain rewards of induftry, the innumerable avenues to wealth, the native, unfubdued freedom of their manners and converfation; the fpirit of equality, fo flattering to all generous minds, and fo effential to the enjoyment of private fociety, the entire fecurity of their fortunes, liberty, and lives; the equity and lenity of their civil and criminal juftice, the toleration of their religious opinions and worfhip.

Teach

·Teach them to compare thefe invaluable privileges and enjoyments with the abject and miferable ftate of men debafed by artificial manners, loft to all generous and manly fentiment; alternately crouching and infulting, from the vain and humiliating diftinctions of birth, place and precedence; trembling every moment for their liberty, their property, their confciences, and their lives; millions toiling, not for themfelves, but to pamper the luxury and riot of a few worthlefs, domineering individuals, and pining in indigence and wretchednefs: Save them from the madnefs of hazarding fuch ineftimable bleffings, in the uncertain events of a war, againft all odds, againft invafions from Canada, incurfions of favages, revolt of flaves, multiplied fleets and armies, a war which muft begin where wars commonly end, in the ruin of our trade, in the furrender of our ports and capitals, in the mifery

of

of thoufands. Teach them in mercy, to be-ware how they wantonly draw their fwords in defence of political problems, diftinctions, refinements, about which the beft and the wifeft men, the friends as well as the enemies of America, differ in their opinions, left while we deny the mother-country every mode, every right of taxation, we give her the rights of conqueft.

F I N I S.

EXCERPTS FROM
A VIEW OF THE CAUSES AND CONSEQUENCES OF THE AMERICAN REVOLUTION

Jonathan Boucher, *A View of the Causes and Consequences of the American Revolution; in Thirteen Discourses, Preached in North America between the Years 1763 and 1775: With an Historical Preface* (London, 1797), excerpts from 'Discourse I. On the Peace in 1763', pp. 8–45, and 'Discourse VII. On Fundamental Principles', pp. 307–24.

Whereas *A Letter from a Virginian* called on the colonists to stop agitating for independence, *A View of the Causes and Consequences of the American Revolution*, written more than twenty years later, looks back on the revolution. This text was incongruously dedicated to George Washington, for whom Boucher had the utmost respect. Despite their differences of opinion over American independence, Boucher and Washington corresponded over the years of transition in America. *Causes and Consequences* is difficult reading in many ways, particularly in its racist overtones. However, Boucher covers a number of interesting areas in these excerpts, including the Tory views on independence and agitators such as Arthur Lee. Boucher also makes clear his opinion of Adam Smith's *Theory of Moral Sentiments* (1759). This piece is also early evidence of the popularity of physiocracy in America.

A

VIEW

OF THE

CAUSES AND CONSEQUENCES

OF THE

AMERICAN REVOLUTION;

IN

THIRTEEN DISCOURSES,

Preached in NORTH AMERICA between the Years 1763 and 1775:

WITH AN HISTORICAL PREFACE.

BY

JONATHAN BOUCHER, A.M. AND F.A.S.

Vicar of EPSOM in the County of Surrey.

...... " At verò cùm a ſtrepitu tumultuque aures noſtræ paulu-
" lùm conquieverint, quid tandèm cauſæ eſt, cur de republicâ quid
" ſentiamus taciturnitate diuturniore celemus ?"

Præfat. ad Bellendenum de Statu, &c. p. xv.

LONDON:

PRINTED FOR G. G. AND J. ROBINSON, PATERNOSTER-ROW.

M.DCC.XCVII.

ON THE PEACE IN 1763.

One of the firſt duties of Chriſtianity there-fore is that, both as individuals and as communities, we ſhould all *follow after the things which make for peace*; and, *as far as it is poſſible, live peaceably with all men.* Viewed even in a political light only, war ſeems to be as incompatible with an improved ſtate of Society, as it certainly is with the doctrines of the Goſpel; and it is a circumſtance not a little to the credit of our religion, that it ſo decidedly diſcountenances it. War is a relict of barbariſm; and therefore ſtill to be conſidered as the virtue only of an uncultivated people *. And however offenſive it might ſound in the ears of ſome refined nations, who value themſelves on being alſo military nations, were we to go into the inveſtigation in any detail, there is reaſon to believe it would be found that the moſt ſavage people are in general the moſt warlike.+

When,

---

* The unnatural and ſhocking conſequences of war are ſummarily (but pathetically and ſtrongly) deſcribed in a ſpeech of Crœſus to Cyrus, in the Clio of Herodotus:

—— οὐδεὶς γὰρ οὕτω ἀνόητος ἐςι, ὃς τις πόλεμον πρὸ εἰρήνης αἱρέεται. ἐν μὲν γὰρ τῇ οἱ παῖδες τὲς πατέρας θάπτουσι, ἐν δὲ τῷ, οἱ πατέρες τὲς παῖδας.

A ſimilar paſſage occurs in Demades the orator, preſerved only in the rude verſes of Tzetzes, Chiliad. vi. 20.

And Polybius, in contraſting the bleſſings of peace with the miſeries of war, has adopted the remark, and almoſt the very words of Herodotus.

† This propoſition is far from implying, that the *leaſt* warlike nations are the *moſt* virtuous. Every friend to Chriſtianity muſt deprecate the wars in which Great Britain has ſo often been engaged: but,

When, therefore, a writer on Ethics lately called the various tribes of Indians around us *nations of heroes**, though the term was perhaps ftrictly juft and proper, it certainly conveyed no compliment to the Indians, as he no doubt intended it fhould. The words deſcribe Indians exactly as they are ; that is, as warriors and favages. As individuals, foldiers may be, and I fincerely believe generally are, diftinguifhed for their humanity, no lefs than for their courage ; but, as a body, they are the pefts and the fcourges of the world †.

It

---

but, at the fame time it muft be admitted, that we poffefs a tafte for the focial arts, a fpirit of manly fentiment, of induftry, and of integrity, which are rarely met with among fome of the more peaceable nations of the fouthern parts of Europe. In modern Greece, in Italy, and in Portugal, (which certainly are no longer military nations,) idlenefs, treachery, and cowardice are faid to be the predominant features of national character.

* Dr. Smith, in his Theory of Moral Sentiments.

† "In reality, were all his (Alexander's) actions duly eftimated, "he could deferve no other character than that of the great cut-"throat of the age in which he lived. But, the folly of mankind, "and the error of hiftorians, is fuch, that they ufually make the "actions of war, bloodſhed, and conqueft, the fubject of their higheft "encomiums ; and thofe their moft celebrated heroes that moft excel "therein. Whereas thofe only are true heroes, who moft benefit "the world, by promoting the peace, welfare, and good of man-"kind : but fuch as opprefs it with the flaughter of men, the de-"folation of countries, the burning of cities, and the other calami-"ties which attend war, are the fcourge of God, the Attilas of "the age in which they live, and the greateft plagues and calamities "that can happen to it ; and which are never fent into the world

" but

It is not one of the leaft objections to war that it occafions a perverfion and mifapplication of fine talents. How many men, with difpofitions naturally good, who, under a well-regulated fyftem, might and would have been the guardians and benefactors, have become the butchers and deftroyers, of their kind! Great parts are not fo common, that the world can afford to bear the lofs of them. When we fee a Julius Cæfar, with all his vaft natural and acquired powers, ftooping to be a mere warrior, we muft lament the wafte of fuch abilities. Compare, I pray you, any of the moft celebrated commanders, with whofe fame the world refounds; compare them, I fay, with a Socrates, a Fenelon, or a William Penn; and if good parts, directed to the attainment of good ends, be the criterion of a great character, fee how, on the comparifon, every mere hero will hide his diminifhed head. True greatnefs deferves all the honour that the world can pay to it: but, fields dyed with blood are not the fcenes in which true greatnefs is moft likely to be found. He who fimplifies a mechanical procefs, who fupplies us with a new convenience or comfort, or even he who contrives an elegant fuperfluity, is, in every proper fenfe of the phrafe, a more ufeful man than any of thofe mafters in the art of deftruction, who, to the fhame of the

" but for the punifhment of it, and therefore ought as fuch to be " prayed againft, and detefted by all mankind."———Prideaux's Connections, part i. book 7. vol. 2d, 8vo, p. 700.

world,

world, have hitherto monopolized almoſt all its honours.

It is at leaſt harmleſs, if it be not alſo rational, to indulge a fond hope, that the period cannot be very diſtant when, from the ſilent and unnoticed, but gradually prevailing, influence of Chriſtianity, France and Great Britain, (the two foremoſt nations of the world, which have juſt now ſheathed the ſword,) taught by long experience the better *arts of peace*, ſhall *learn war no more*. O that we might live to ſee the time when they ſhould give law to the world in peace, as they have long done in war! Such would be the great and bleſſed influence of ſuch an era in the world that he only would be the enthuſiaſt who ſhould not hail it as a milleanium.

It is no part of my purpoſe at preſent to enter into the queſtion how far war is, or is not, lawful to Chriſtians. Merely as a point of caſuiſtry, it might (perhaps) after all my pains, remain with you, (as I confeſs is the caſe as to myſelf,) undecided: but neither you nor I can for a moment entertain a doubt, that war is one of the ſevereſt calamities with which the Almighty has ever ſeen fit to chaſtiſe the ſons of men. As war in the elements deſolates the natural world, wars among men diſorder and deſtroy all the beauties of the moral world. Thunder and lightning, and hurricanes, and volcanos, are not more fatal in their reſpective ſpheres. It would not, I believe, be difficult to prove, from hiſtory, that no nation ever yet engaged in war, without being eventually a loſer by it.

it*. If any people can be thought an exception to this remark, it muſt be the Romans; who, owing their origin to war, ſeem to have purſued it, through their whole hiſtory, as a trade, and the means of their ſubſiſtence. And yet their greateſt orator, in a flouriſhing period of their empire, ſcrupled not to prefer an inadequate and unjuſt peace to the juſteſt war†.

Not much, if at all, more civilized than the bar-barous nations around us were the proud maſters of the world. Their hiſtory is compoſed of little elſe than a weariſome ſucceſſion of incurſions and in-vaſions, which, on the ſlighteſt pretenſions, they were for ever making on their more peaceful, but leſs powerful, neighbours. Theſe wars, however digni-fied by hiſtory, are, when philoſophically conſidered, in no point of view of more conſequence than thoſe of Creek, Catawba, or Cherokee Indians ; who want but a Thucydides, or a Livy, to render them as re-nowned as the Romans. Let but Indians be mea-ſured by Roman ideas, and they are not inferior to

---

* . . . . " nocitura petuntur
    " Militiâ."   Juvenal. Sat. x. l. 9.

† . . . . . " equidem pacem hortari non deſino ; quæ vel injuſta " utilior eſt quam juſtiſſimum bellum." Cicer. Epiſt. ad Atticum, lib. vii. epiſt. 14.

        . . . . " Pax optima rerum,
    " Quas homini noviſſe datum eſt ; pax una triumphis
    " Innumeris potior."
                                   Silius Italicus, lib. xi. l. 595.

                                   Romans :

Romans : the Romans were warriors, and fo are our North American Indians : the Romans were the fcourge and the terror of the neighbouring nations ; and fuch, we too well know, Indians alfo are. Wonderful are the ways of Providence! It was by the fword alone that the Romans became a people ; and by the fword they ceafed to be a people. A ftate of conftant war naturally rendered them irritable and quarrelfome. Hence, when they had, as they boafted, fubdued the world, and no foreign enemies were left for them to contend with, they quarrelled among themfelves, and fell the victims of civil war. And who does not fee, that thefe ill-fated nations, whom I have prefumed to compare with Romans, muft ere long, from their own natural propenfity to war, and from our illiberal and unchriftian fyftem of fomenting their inteftine quarrels and wars, be alfo totally deftroyed ? Already their numbers are greatly diminifhed ; and they will too furely continue to diminifh, unlefs, happily for ourfelves as well as for them, we fhall hereafter be fo wife and humane as to obferve a more juft and generous policy towards them. Would we but learn to regard them as human beings, capable of civilization, they might foon be brought to *break their bows,* and *knap their fpears afunder;* and *beat their fwords into plow-fhares.*

Our parent ftate, and the great and powerful kingdom, her neighbour, are, and long have been rival nations ; the Carthage and Rome of modern times. The comparifon hitherto has failed in one

refpect,

respect, indeed, that though they have had as many and as bloody wars as old Rome and old Carthage had, these wars have not yet effected the destruction of either. If it could be ascertained how much blood and how much treasure each of these two nations has, from age to age, expended in wars against each other; and contrasted with a similar enumeration of their respective conquests and acquisitions, it would enable both themselves and the world to form a fair estimate of the sum-total of their respective profit and loss. And I am much mistaken if the result would not be that all the territory, and all the advantages which, in all their wars, either has gained from the other, would be dearly paid for by the expenditure of a single year.

If the manifestos of the contending parties might be received as proofs, wars would always appear to be unavoidable and just. When, however, these appeals to the public contradict each other (as they necessarily must, and always do) it is impossible that both can be right. In the war now happily terminated we of this western world were immediately interested: and therefore our opinion of its justice may perhaps be suspected of partiality. As a counter-balance to this objection, it might be alledged, that, from our situation, we have had better means, and, from our more immediate interest, were stimulated by stronger motives, to obtain exact information respecting the true grounds of the quarrel, than the people either of France or England and, with
this

this advantage in forming our judgments, we have, both as a public and as individuals, again and again, declared the war to have been, on our parts, juſt. How far indeed any war is either juſt, or juſtifiable, we know not: happily we do know, that the one now ended has ended in our favour. Yet, beſides the enormous load of debt with which it has encumbered the mother country, (a ſhare of which it is highly reaſonable we ſhould bear,) and beſides all that we ſuffered during its continuance, (the recollection of which muſt ſtill be painful,) our joy muſt be not a little checked by the reflection, that we are ſtill left expoſed to many dangers, and ſubjected to many difficulties; which, though we may and do rejoice in a peace, afford us no ground of rejoicing that there has been a war.

Tempted by the imagery of my text, I cannot avoid here remarking, that, wherever war is ſpoken of by the ſacred writers, it is generally conſidered as a curſe, on account of the interruption it gives to the labours of the plow. Thus, in the prophet Joel, where the metaphor of the text is reverſed, war is ſtill viewed through the medium of its influence on huſbandry. *Prepare war; make up the mighty men; let all the mighty men draw near; let them come up: beat your plow-ſhares into ſwords, and your pruning-hooks into ſpears.* And the calamitous effects of war on huſbandry are thus pathetically deſcribed: *The field is waſted, the land mourneth; for the corn is waſted; the new wine is dried up, the oil languiſheth.*

Be

Be ye afhamed, O ye hufbandmen! Howl, O ye vine-dreffers, for the wheat and for the barley! becaufe the harveft of the field is perifhed. The feed is rotten under their clods, the garners are laid defolate, the barns are broken down, for the corn is withered. How do the beafts groan! The herds of cattle are perplexed becaufe they have no pafture; yea, the flocks of fheep are made defolate. War is the natural element of men of fierce and turbulent minds; who, like fome marine birds, which are never feen but in a ftorm, dwindle into infignificance in peace; becaufe they take no pleafure in rural quiet and domeftic enjoyments. They are *foldiers, and have to do with wars;* and, therefore, (to ufe the words, in the firft book of Efdras, of one of the young men, who contended for truth before king Darius,) *they do not ufe hufbandry* [*]. When the pofterity of Shimei fettled themfelves in *Gedor,* it is faid, they found *fat paftures and good.* The reafon follows: *the land was wide, and quiet, and peaceable.* God, in his Scriptures, every where fpeaks of war as one of the heavieft of his judgments, and the moft calamitous punifhment which fin can draw down on the fons of men. Accordingly, he

---

[*] In a book publifhed in 1790, intitled, Sketches of the Hindoos, &c. there is a ftriking paffage, perfectly analogous to this idea. " The Hindoos are the only cultivators of the land, and the only " manufacturers. The Mahometans, who came into India, were " foldiers, or followers of a camp; and even now are never to be " found employed in the labours of hufbandry or the loom."—See Sketch iv. p. 89.

who

who alone can make the creature his weapon, to correct and to controul the refractory and the difobedient, threatened his people, when *they walked contrary to him, and would not be reformed, to send a sword among them, and to bring their land into desolation.* On the other hand, he held out the bleffings which flow from agriculture to the obedient; thus speaking to the Ifraelites, *If ye will walk in my ftatutes, and keep my commandments to do them; then I will give you rain in due feafon, and the land fhall yield her increafe, and the trees of the field fhall yield their fruit. And your threfhing fhall reach unto the vintage, and the vintage fhall reach unto the fowing time: and ye fhall eat your bread to the full, and dwell in your land fafely. And I will give peace in the land: and ye fhall lie down, and none fhall make you afraid.*

Peace is welcome to us on ten thoufand accounts; and I do moft cordially congratulate you on the joyful occafion of the day. The ordinary occupations of lue are now refumed; and your fwarms of young men, heretofore fo frequently taken from you to go to war, now return to the common hive, to make and to eat the honey of peace. If fome have lefs glory all have more eafe: and even thofe who have only the neceffaries of life, now have them without peril. Thofe of our people who *go down to the fea in fhips and occupy their bufinefs in the deep waters* now no longer are terrified by a double danger: if they fall it is into the hands of God; they no longer have violent men alfo to fear.

Bear

Bear with me, I pray you, if (owing, perhaps, to my partiality to agriculture, which I have long regarded as the most pleasing of all employments) I congratulate you chiefly on the welcomeness of peace from the leisure it will afford you to attend to husbandry. With every encouragement of a genial climate, and a fertile soil, it is our great shame, and greater misfortune, instead of being the foremost people on the Continent, to be the most backward: though it might have been expected, as we were the first province of North America which was firmly settled, that we should by this time have attained a superior degree of improvement. Yet, if it be any excuse for demerit to have to alledge that there are others as faulty as ourselves, we are not singular in having incurred this reproach. A kind of fatality seems to attend some countries. In every place, where nature has been unusually bountiful, there human industry is proportionably remiss. In the Southern parts of Europe, which are naturally some of the richest kingdoms in the world, the farmers, even in this age of general improvement, pursue the most wretched system of husbandry *. Their inattention

---

* Spain, for instance, according to the accounts of a modern traveller, is most miserably cultivated.

"The husbandmen shovel up the stubble, weeds, and tops of "furrows into small heaps, which they burn; then spread them "out upon the ground, and work them in with a plough, which "is little better than a great knife fastened to a single stick, that "just *scratches* the surface."——Swinburne's Travels through Spain, 8vo edit. vol. i. p. 110.

10

to the most valuable of the arts may, perhaps, be fairly
aſcribed to the badneſs of their reſpective governments.

But we have no ſuch ſolid excuſe to offer for
our ſhameful neglect of agriculture. We not only
dwell in a land of liberty but in a land abundantly
ſtored with the gifts of nature. Like the moſt favoured
people of God we have been brought into *a good
land ; a land of brooks of water, of fountains and
depths that ſpring out of valleys and hills ; a land of
oil and honey, wherein we may eat bread without
ſcarceneſs.* To deſcribe Virginia the exacteſt geo-
grapher would be at a loſs to find terms more appo-
ſite or juſt. Yet, ſo far from being diſtinguiſhed
by having made a ſuitable improvement of ſuch
rare natural advantages, I fear we are diſtinguiſhed
only by our indolent neglect of them. Were
it not for the hope that, owing to many favourable
circumſtances now providentially thrown in your
way, this extreme ſupineneſs will not continue
to be characteriſtical of you, he would be far
from deſerving to be ſet down as your enemy, who,
ſeeing the ill uſe ye make of the rich ſavannahs,
and *pleaſant places,* in which *the lines are fallen*
to you, ſhould wiſh you removed to the bleak and
barren mountains of Acadia. There, neceſſity
would force you to a conduct which neither a ſenſe
of duty nor a ſenſe of intereſt have yet been able
to excite. You would become induſtrious; and
by

by being industrious you would of course also become
more worthy and more happy.

Indolence, it is probable, is every where the cha-
racteristic of the inhabitants of warm countries: I
have felt its influence, and therefore have less reserve
in owning that it is ours. As a proof of it permit
me to mention, what I have often observed, that most
of your inventions (in which, as far as mere natural
talents go, no people are more ingenious) are calculated, not immediately to improve either arts or sciences, but merely to lessen labour.

But, however freely I may allow myself to censure
you where you seem to deserve censure, it would be
unjust not to allow, as I do with great pleasure, that,
in many respects, you deserve praise. Your back-
wardness in husbandry is probably not altogether to
be ascribed to your indolence. The marked preference so long shewn to commerce is a strong indica-
tion that agriculture has never been much favoured
by the settlers of America. Far be it from me to suggest a sentiment, or to suffer an expression to escape
me, that is disparaging to trade. Continue to pursue it with ardour; pursue it with success: When
you were first planted here, it was, I believe, (at least
in the intention of the settlers,) almost for the single
purpose of trade. That you should be possessors of
immense tracts of landed property, as well as a great
trading people, that you should have, almost literally,
an unbounded territory; and (in that respect at least)
resemble

re.... le a great kingdom rather than a settlement of ... ters; could hardly be in the contemplation of our founders. And, indeed, unless every thing else had been made to correspond and keep pace with this very essential change of colonial system, it is by no means certain that we have done well in departing from the original *plan of the plantation.* Be this as it may, I charge this general preference shewn to trade, so injurious to agriculture, to this leading principle of colonization; which no subsequent change of circumstances has yet been able wholly to counteract.

It is high time that we should begin to adapt our conduct to our circumstances. By the fostering care of our parent-state, and by our own (oftentimes well-judged) co-operation; and, above all, by the blessing of Providence, we are become a considerable people. And whatever policy might be proper in the earlier periods of our settlement agriculture now claims our especial attention. We have few inducements to become artisans or manufacturers : our having much land, and but few people, proves that we may employ ourselves to better purpose as farmers. Besides, we can have manufactures from our fellow-subjects beyond the Atlantic better and cheaper than we can make them. But we have every inducement to follow the example of Uzziah, and to *love husbandry.* Every produce of the earth, from almost every spot on the globe, will with due culture, thrive and flourish in Virginia. Besides *wheat and barley*, we possess, almost

almost exclusively, that wonderful plant *, which I am at some loss how, with propriety, to call either a necessary of life or a luxury. A necessary it certainly is not, since it can neither be used as food or raiment; neither is it a luxury, at least in the sense of a gratification, being so nauseous and offensive, that long habit alone can reconcile any constitution to the use of it †. We also have not only the rich fruits of Persia and Asia Minor, but all the best plants and fruits of Europe; though, like the country from which we came, we can boast of but few indigenous productions. Our woods too are over-run with luxuriant vines and olives; a circumstance that shews with what certainty of great success they might be cultivated ‡. Thus, if from the vicissitudes of men's fancies the use of tobacco should cease, you still possess a never-failing resource of plenty, in possessing *a land*, like Palestine, *of corn, and wine, and oil:* and it is not unworthy your observation, that, in the three articles just enumerated, most of the necessaries, and most

* Tobacco.

† Mr. Locke says, bread or tobacco may be neglected; but reason at first recommends their trial, and custom makes them pleasant.

‡ The prophetic strains of the immortal Maro might be no less realized in America than in Italy :—

" Molli paulatim flavescet campus arista,
" Incultisque rubens pendebit sentibus uva :
" Et duræ quercus sudabunt roscida mella."

Eclog. iv. 1. 28.

of

of the luxuries of life are comprehended. *The principal things*, says the wise Son of Sirach, *for the whole use of man's life, are water, fire, iron, salt, flour of wheat, honey, milk, and the milk of the grape, and oil, and cloathing.* All these you do now actually possess, or soon may possess. And as by this happy termination of hostilities (blessed be God !) *every man may now fit under his own vine, and under his own fig-tree*, and securely cultivate and enjoy all the sweet arts of peace, ye are without excuse, if, hereafter, ye do not, like Noah, *begin to be husbandmen*, and to plant vineyards. Whilst you are duly grateful, as it highly becomes you to be, that *the lot is fallen to you in a fair ground, and that you have a goodly heritage*, forget not, I charge you, by what tenure you hold these great blessings ; nor forget how easily (as well as certainly) God can and will *make a fruitful land barren, for the wickedness of them that dwell therein* *.

Much

" * It was but a smal country, and a very littel plot of grownde,
" which the Israelites possessed in the land of Canaan ; which, as
" now is a very barren country : for that within fifteen miles of
" Jerusalem, the countrey is wholey barren, and ful of rockes and
" stoney ; and unles it be about the plaine of Jerico, I know not
" anie parte of the countrey, at this presente, that is fruitfulle.
" What it hath binne in tymes paste, I refer you to the declara-
" tion thereof, made in the Holie Scriptures. My opinion is, that
" when it was fruitfulle, and *a land that flowed with milk and honey,*
' —in those dayes God blessed it, and that as then they followed his
' commandements, but now, being inhabited by infidelles, that
' prophane the name of Christ, and live in all beastly and filthy
" manner,

Much has often been said, and much may still be said, in favour of husbandry: but its best recommendation is that it is favourable to happiness by being favourable to virtue*. This circumstance is beautifully illustrated by the author of my text; a man whose mind was well stored with all the learning of his age, and stored, in particular, with a knowledge of husbandry. This will appear from the parable I am about to quote; a parable well worth the attention of the curious, if it were only for the account contained in it of Jewish agriculture. *Doth the plowman plow all day to sow; doth he open and break the clods of his ground? When he hath made plain the face thereof, doth he not cast abroad the fitches, and scatter the cummin; and cast in the principal wheat, and the appointed barley, and the rye in their place? For,*

" manner, *God curseth it, and so is is made barren;* for it is so
" barren, that I coulde get no bread, when I came nere unto it,
" &c."——The Travayles of two Englyshe Pilgrimes to Jerusalem, Grand Cairo, Gaza, and Alexandria, &c. Printed for
Thomas Archer in 1608.

* " C'est dans l'agriculture principalement, que la France doit
" chercher les principaux moyens de subsistance pour son peuple.
" D'ailleurs, l'agriculture conserve les moeurs & la religion. Elle
" rend les mariages faciles, necessaires & heureux : elle fait naitre
" beaucoup d'enfans, &c."——Etudes de la Nature, par B. de St.
Pierre, Lond. edit. vol. i. p. 93.

See also Smith's Wealth of Nations, 8vo edit. vol. i. p. 197. and
vol. iii. p. 182. and The State of the Poor by Sir F. M. Eden,
Bart. vol. i. p. 440 and p. 443.

bis

his God doth inſtruct him to diſcretion, and doth teach him. For, the fitches are not threſhed with a threſhing inſtrument, neither is a cart-wheel turned about upon the cummin: but the fitches are beaten out with a ſtaff, and the cummin with a rod. Bread-corn is bruiſed; becauſe he will not ever be threſhing it, nor break it with the wheel of his cart, nor bruiſe it with his horſemen*.* The doctrinal inſtruction, or moral, couched under this parabolical imagery, not only intimates that, in the words of the Son of Sirach, *the Moſt High hath*

---

* In Virginia and Maryland, wheat, in general, is not thraſhed, but trodden out with horſes; very much in the manner deſcribed in the following account of this ancient practice. " They (the Euro-
" peans) do not thraſh out their corn, but have it trodden out with
" oxen or horſes; nor in a barn, or covered place, but in the open
" air, on a floor; which is made in the following manner. They
" take cow-dung, and a little ſtraw; and with water mix and work
" it together. When they have made a ſufficient quantity of this
" loam, they ſpread it pretty thick, in a circle of about ten yards
" diameter, and turn horſes upon it to tread it cloſe down. Then
" they leave it to harden in the ſun; and in a few days it becomes
" as hard as a ſtone.

" On the extremities of this floor they lay two rounds of ſheaves,
" ears to ears; and drive over them a team of eight horſes or oxen,
" round and round, now and then turning the ſheaves, till they judge
" the corn is all trodden out. This (Kolben adds) no doubt, will
" put the Scripture-reader in mind of the cuſtom of treading out corn
" by oxen among the children of Iſrael. But, for this purpoſe, I
" muſt needs prefer horſes to oxen. It is moſt certain, that corn is
" much more expeditiouſly got out of the ears by the tread of
" horſes and oxen, than by thraſhing."——Kolben's Cape of Good
Hope; tranſlated by Medley. Vol. ii. p. 73.

created

created husbandry * ; but that the process in carrying
on the work of grace, as well as the produce or fruit
of grace, bears a near analogy and resemblance to the
process of agriculture. The course of proceeding in
both cases seems to be accurately marked in the paffage now under confideration. The foil is firft broken
by the plough; it is then harrowed; then cleared of
weeds; and then fown. More precife or better
directions could not be given for the culture of
grace; the growth of which is alfo *God's husbandry*;
wherein we are directed, firft, to *break up the fallow
grounds of our hearts*; and then to *fow in righteoufnefs,*
that we may *reap in peace* †.

Some

* " Prima Ceres ferro mortales vertere terram
   " Inftituit."   Virg. Georg. lib. i. L 147.

† Since this paffage was written, I have noticed a fimilar comparifon in Latymer's Sermons: he fays,

" I lyken preaching to a ploughman's labour, and a prelate to a
" ploughman.—Firft, for their labour in all feafons of the yeare.
" For there is no time of the yeare in which the ploughman hath not
" fome fpeciall worke to do: as in my countrey in Lefterfhire, the
" plowman hath a time to fet forth, and to affay his plough, and
" other times, for other neceffary workes to be done. And then
" they alfo may be likened together for the diverfitie of workes, and
" varietie of offices that they have to do. For as the ploughman firft
" fetteth forth his plough, and then tilleth his land, and breaketh
" it in furrowes, and fometime ridgeth it up agayne, and at other
" times harroweth it, and clotteth it, and fometime dongeth and
" hedgeth it, diggeth it, and weedeth it, purgeth, and maketh it
" cleane: fo the prelate, the preacher——hath a bufie worke—to
" bring his flock to a right fayth, and then to confirme them in the
                                                    " fame

Some ancient, in drawing the picture of an happy people, says, it is necessary, peace and good laws should prevail; that *the ground should be well cultivated*; children well educated; and due homage paid to the Gods. And, among the Romans, to neglect the cultivation of one's farm was deemed a *probrum censorium*, a fault that merited the chastisement of the censor. No occupation, says Plutarch in his Life of Numa, implants so speedy and so effectual a love of peace as a country life. Accordingly, poets, who generally dwell with rapture on unsophisticated manners, speak of rural employments as comprehending all human virtue, and all human felicity. In every station and every sphere of life, men (if they be so disposed) may find cause to adore the wisdom and the goodness of God: but in none is it more conspicuous, or more striking, than in that occupation which requires us to be daily witnesses of the blessings of Providence so wonderfully manifested in *bringing forth grass for the cattle, and green herb for the service of man; wine to make glad the heart of man, oil to make him a chearful countenance, and bread to strengthen man's heart.* Blessed with health, the happy recompence of virtuous toil, with minds at ease, and un-

---

" same sayth. Now casting them downe with the law, and with
" threatninges of God for sinne. Now ridging them up agayne
" with the gospell and the promises of God's favour. Now weeding
" them, by telling them their faultes, and making them forsake sinne.
" Now clotting them by breaking their stony harts, &c."——
Latymer's Fourth Sermon——Of the plough.

agitated

agitated by all the mad contentions of a tumultuous world, farmers are generally contented to be quiet themselves, and to let others be quiet. And hence, the moſt virtuous and uſeful citizens are found neither in the higheſt nor loweſt departments of ſociety ; not among merchants and ſoldiers ; nor, perhaps, among artiſans, whoſe modes of living render them too prone to run into juntos, clubs, and cabals ; but in the middle conditions of life, among an induſtrious, peaceable, and contented peaſantry.

It is not without much undiſſembled regret that I ſee a ſingle cloud for a moment darkening our bright horizon. I ſhould be happy to congratulate you on the peace being as complete, as, no doubt, our rulers expected it would be, when they proclaimed this day of thankſgiving. But, the news from our frontiers is ſtill moſt alarming. Our ſavage neighbours, (who as ſavages alone are to be forgiven for delighting in war,) unſatiated with blood, have again taken up the hatchet, and are again ſpreading deſolation in our borders. There is, I truſt, little likelihood, that they will penetrate into the interior parts of the country. On the contrary, I hope my confidence is not ill-founded, that our young men, now gone out againſt them, (acquainted as they are with the Indian country and with Indian manners,) will, with little loſs of blood, though certainly not without much toil and danger, ſoon over-awe them into peace.

Let me not be deemed enthuſiaſtic, or romantic, when I avow that I expect much permanent good to

arise

arife from this tranfient evil.   Our rulers (both here and in Great Britain) will now have leifure to attend to every part of our American polity ; and, among other things, to the ftate of Indians : and, poffeffed of all the information which is now eafily to be had, there can be no doubt, they will adopt fome plan effectually to civilize thefe nations of barbarians.

If we may judge from any thing that has yet been attempted concerning them, they have been looked upon as untamed, and untameable monfters ; whom, like the devoted nations around Judea, it was a kind of religion with *white men* * to exterminate.   We have treated them with a rigour and feverity equally unfuitable to the genius of our government, and the mild fpirit of our religion.   I hope, indeed, Britons have never yet fo difgraced their national character as to have fhewn towards them fo much internecine fury as the Spaniards at firft fhewed towards the Aborigines of the Southern Continent. Yet, could the *poor Indian* be but his own hiftorian ; and, from his own experience, and his own feelings, relate all that has happened fince our arrival in America, it would appear (if I am not much miftaken) that he has not derived fo much benefit, as we are apt to flatter ourfelves, from being fubjected to Britons, rather than to Spaniards.

---

* I know not whether it may be thought of fufficient importance to remark that the North American Indians call Englifhmen, but Englifhmen only, *white men*: Frenchmen they call Frenchmen ; and Spaniards, Spaniards.   It fhews, however, that, in things which engage their attention, they are nice and accurate obfervers.

I own

I own to you, I have not feldom blufhed at their accounts of the treatment they have experienced from white men *: but, I truft, the period is not far diftant, when, for our own fakes, as well as for theirs, we

---

* I hope to be pardoned for recording here an inftance or.two (from many which occur to me) of favage heroifm and civilized barbarity. They were related to me on good authority; and, I believe, have never yet appeared in print.—"A gentleman in Maryland, well known for being the terror of Indians, having rambled into the woods with his fon (then very young) efpied an old Indian coming to his ftore (i. e. warehoufe) to trade, as was ufual in times of peace. The father, concealing himfelf and his boy behind a fallen tree, lay there, till the Indian, as far from fufpecting any danger as he was from intending any mifchief, got within reach of his gun. The boy was then directed to fire. He did fo; and killed his man: for no reafon whatever but that he might be able to fay he had killed his man." The perfon from whom I had this ftory, affured me it was related to him by one of the family as a meritorious fact.

" A party of white people, from one of the frontier fettlements of Virginia, once went out againft a body of Indians, who were in arms to oppofe a fmall colony of fettlers, who had taken poffeffion of fome lands, which the Indians alledged they had never fold. Indians remonftrate with their tomahawks; and therefore now declared war by driving off thofe whom they adjudged to be encroachers. The whites were not of a temper to be intimidated: they refolved, and were foon prepared, to attack the Indians, in their turns; who, being fallen upon when they were off their guard, and finding themfelves likely to be overpowered, fairly took to their heels. Among them was a young fquaw, with an infant in her arms. She was fuppofed to belong to a perfon of fome note, from her drefs being compofed almoft entirely of filk handkerchiefs. Checked in her fpeed by the burthen of her helplefs charge, fhe hoped to efcape by hiding herfelf and her child among the weeds of a marfh. The thought fhewed fhe poffeffed great prefence of mind; but, alas! it was of no avail. The

we shall endeavour to diffuse political security and happiness to the Indian nations with whom we have any intercourse; and to convert them into free men, useful subjects, and good Christians *.

When

The chieftain of the whites (whose name I forbear to mention) espied her; and took his aim. This she saw; and being sensible also that she must fall, (for, when rifle-men have a fair shot, they are rarely known to miss their object,) her last and only care was, if possible, to preserve her babe. With this hope, she instantly turned it from her back to her breast; that she alone might receive the ball. And even when she fell, by a kind instinct of nature (of the true force of which in such a case mothers only are, perhaps, the proper judges) she was anxious and careful so to fall as that her child might not be hurt.——I am shocked to relate, that both the mother and her babe were killed and scalped."

The admirers of Grecian or Roman story are challenged to produce, from their classic stores, any instance in which the force of nature is more forcibly displayed, than it is in this America-tramontane anecdote. It has been remarked of two illustrious Romans, Lucretia and Cæsar, that they regarded the το πρεπον even in the moment of death. Of the former Ovid says:

" Tunc quoque jam moriens, nè non procumbat honestè,
" Respicit: hæc etiam cura cadentis erat."—Ovid. Fasti, lib. ii. l. 833.

The same thing is mentioned of Julius Cæsar.

These are strong instances of the force of habit; whilst the ruling passion of the poor untutored Indian, in the same trying crisis, was the genuine dictate of nature. And, when it is considered, how many incidents of a similar nature must have occurred since our connexion with these Aboriginal nations, it is surprising that since the time of Capt. Smith (whose instructive and entertaining book is well worth reading, if it were only for the sake of the affecting story of Pocohontas) all such circumstances have failed to attract the attention of the writers of American history.

* Then, in the strong language of a great moral writer, " when " the woods of America shall have become pervious and safe, those
" who

When charters were granted to the firſt emigrants, two motives only were aſſigned; " the enlargement " of the Empire, and the farther propagation of Chri- " ſtianity*." The latter of theſe motives is not leſs juſt and proper now than it was then. Territory we do not want; having, it is probable, already more than we well know how to manage. Inſtead therefore of countenancing that vagrant and unſettled way of life which has become habitual to ſo many of our people; and that very general paſſion they have to be for ever running back in queſt of freſh lands; a practice not more unpropitious to all agricultural improvements, than likely to keep us involved in Indian wars; let us *enlarge our empire* by the civilization of the Indians; who already have a better title to any of our *un-located* † lands, than we can poſſibly give any new comers; and who, with little pains, might ſoon be made at leaſt as good ſubjects as thoſe whom we are likely to put in their place.

It is granted, that every attempt hitherto made to bring this fierce and intractable people within the pale of ſocial order has failed: but, happily, this does

---

" who are now reſtrained by fear, ſhall be attracted by reverence; " and multitudes who now range the woods for prey, and live at " the mercy of winds and ſeaſons, ſhall, by the paternal care of " our Sovereign, the father of all his people, enjoy the plenty of " cultivated lands, the pleaſures of ſociety, the ſecurity of law, and " the light of revelation."—Dr. Johnſon in his Preface to Adams's Treatiſe on the Globes, 1767.

* Maryland charter.

† An American term, denoting unoccupied lands.

not prove that therefore they are irreclaimable. The attempts hitherto made may have been made injudiciously; or they may not have been profecuted and perfevered in with fufficient earneftnefs. We found not thefe wretched tenants of the woods a whit more favage than our progenitors appeared to Julius Cæfar or Agricola. It is, moreover, well known, that in South America various wandering tribes of Indians, infinitely inferior both in bodily prowefs and in the endowments of the mind to North American Indians, have been collected and incorporated into a well-governed community *. Nay, the fingle influence

of

---

* " The cuftoms and cruelties of many American tribes ftill " difgrace human nature : but in Paraguay and Canada the natives " have been brought to relifh the bleffings of fociety, and the arts " of virtuous and civil life." Mickle's Introduction to his Tranfla-tion of the Lufiad, p. 6.—Dumouriez, in his account of Portugal, (fee Englifh tranflation, p. 183), beftows high praife on this go-vernment of Paraguay, which was founded by the Jefuits, " At the " end of fifty years, to the difgrace of the other colonies, the coun-" try of the miffionaries was filled with villages, the Catholic faith " was triumphant, and the favages civilized, happy, and fubject to " the wifeft of governments.——— The power of thefe reverend " fathers, by a fyftem of politics very different from the greater part " of human governments, was founded upon a perfect union of " public utility with individual happinefs."

This wonderful republic at length excited the jealoufy of the courts of Spain and Portugal ; who, with hardly any pretence of juftice, entered the country with arms in their hands, and, by the fuperior difcipline of European foldiers, fubjected to their yoke all who could not efcape it by flight : " the reft eftablifhed themfelves " further up the country, taking the fathers with them to confole

" them

of one fingle man among ourfelves has well nigh effected, in one tribe, all that is wifhed for with refpect to Indians in general; for, in comparifon with other Indians, the Mohawks are even now a civilized people. But Sir William Johnfon is another Peter the Great: and, by doing what he has done in this refpect, he has furnifhed the world with a practical proof of an important obfervation made by a diftinguifhed writer [*]. " The ftrongeft " political inftitutions may be formed on the favage " ftate of man. In this period the legiflator hath " few or no prior inftitutions to contend with; and " therefore can form a fyftem of legiflation confift-

---

" them in their diftrefs, and protefting againft the tyranny and in- " juftice of the barbarians of Europe."

In a very fenfible note (p. 187.) the tranflator remarks, that in France all their writers, except Dumouriez and fome others who were of Montefquieu's opinion, inveighed bitterly againft the re- public of Paraguay. The humane philofophers, who are now preaching the freedom as well as the political liberty of the African flaves, with Voltaire at their head, could not bear that civilization, equality, and a government purely evangelical, fhould be introduced among the free Americans of Paraguay. This inconfiftency of con- duct (he fays) it is not difficult to account for. The Jefuits, by their writings againft thefe philofophers, defended the Chriftian religion; and the ftate founded by them was a Chriftian common- wealth. The black flaves, on the contrary, have no religion but their *Fetifbifm*, which is the worfhip of any living or inanimate being *ad libitum*; and which, therefore, no doubt, agrees better with modern philofophy and indefinite liberty than any religious fyftem whatever.

[*] Dr. Brown on Civil Liberty, &c. p. 55.

ent

" ent with itfelf in all its parts: while the law-
" giver who reforms a ftate already modelled or cor-
" rupted muft content himfelf with fuch partial re-
" gulations as the force of prior eftablifhments and
" public habits will admit."

What elfe is the early hiftory of nations now the
moft polifhed, but the hiftory of Indians? The brief
character of uncultivated man is to *neglect agriculture,*
to *practife hunting,* and to *delight in war* *. From
Nimrod down to Atakullakulla † hunters have been
favage and bloody-minded. It would feem, then,
that we have only to wean Indians from the chafe, to
tame them. Every other effort to mollify and hu-
manize their ftubborn fpirits, without this preliminary
requifite, will continue to be made to little purpofe.
They may *make talks* ‡; they may *give ftrings of
wampum;* nay, they may even be baptized, and be
called Chriftians: but as long as they live by hunting
they will ftill be Indians. The putting an end to
hunting is the firft ftep in the progrefs of civilization.
And if this fingle expedient fhould be found fufficient
to remedy the many heavy evils arifing from their

---

* Such (we may recollect) were the Britons in ancient times:
" Agriculturæ non ftudent; vita omnis in venationibus atque in
" ftudiis rei militaris confiftit."——Cæf. de Bell. Gall. lib. vi.

† A noted chieftain of the Cherokee nation, commonly called
The Little Carpenter.

‡ A *talk* is an Indian term for a conference: and the *giving a
ftring of wampum,* (which is a fort of girdle decorated with beads
or fhells,) is a pledge of their peaceable difpofition.

being

being suffered to go on from age to age still in a savage state, it has the additional recommendation of being a simple one; a circumstance which, of it-self, is no mean proof of its being a good scheme. If gunpowder and the implements of war were either not sold to them, or sold only at an exorbitant price, and little or nothing given them for their furs and their pel-try; and if large and liberal bounties were granted for every thing they should raise or produce, either as farmers, shepherds, or manufacturers, it surely is fair to hope, that, as the first effects of such regulations would be the keeping of them at home, and gradually enuring them to the peaceful habits of pastoral and rural life, they would insensibly, like all the rest of the human race, when once they had learned a dis-tinction of property, learn also, for the sake of their own, to abstain from that of others *. As for the

---

* ——"The first thing, therefore, that we are to draw these "new men into, ought to be husbandry: first, because it is the "most easie to be learned, needing only the labour of the body: "next, because it is most general, and most needful: then, because "it is most natural: and lastly, because it is most enemy to war, "and most hateth unquietness, as the poet saith, ——bella "execrata colonis: for, husbandry being the nurse of thrift, and "the daughter of industry, detesteth all that may worke her scathe, "and destroy the travaile of her handes, whose hope is all her lives "comfort unto the plough: therefore are those kearne, stocaghes, "and horse-boys to be driven and made to imploy that ableness of "body, which they are wont to use to theft and villainy, henceforth "to labour and industry."——Spenser's View of the State of Ireland, p. 253.

Joſ

lofs of trade in fkins, which fuch a fyftem might occafion, it is beneath a nation's notice. According to the common courfe of things, it muft be loft in a very few years; as it is the trade, not of cultivated countries and civilized men, but of wildernefſes and favages.

This propofed reftriction from the blood of beafts is not only rational, but has, in fome degree, the authority of revelation. Among other reafons that might be affigned for the prohibition to eat blood; this was not the leaft, that mankind might thus be checked and reftrained from any propenfity to harſh-nefs, inhumanity, and blood-thirftinefs. The Jewifh ritual abounds with fuch moral and benevolent in-culcations.

Too much praife cannot be beftowed on thofe philanthropic and pious perfons who have laboured to convert thefe poor pagans to the pure faith of the gofpel. God forbid any thing here fuggefted fhould difcourage fuch laudable charity ! It is to be feared, however, that they have often, if not always, begun at the wrong end. With his hands perpetually im-brued in the blood of beafts and with appetites trained to thirft for human blood, taught from his earlieft infancy to liften with rapture to fongs of vindictive ferocity, can it be imagined that a favage will be perfuaded to liften to the precepts of that religion which is to teach him *good-will towards men ?* Se-conded, however, and fupported by the civil power, in fome fuch manner as has juft been intimated, the

fervices

fervices of the faithful miffionary will not be lefs useful to government in effecting their civilization, and *turning the fiercenefs of man to the praife of God*, than the co-operation of government will be to the miffionary : and I venture to pronounce, that it will be equally impolitic and impious ever to think of diffociating fuch fervices ; for, " the inviting and " winning the nations of that country to the know-" ledge of the only true God and the Chriftian faith, " is the principal end of this plantation *."

But Indians are by no means the fole or chief ob-jects of our prefent attention : the united motives of intereft and humanity call on us to beftow fome con-fideration on the cafe of thofe fad outcafts of fociety, our negro-flaves: for my heart would fmite me, were I not, in this hour of profperity, to entreat you (it being their unparallcled hard lot not to have the power of entreating for themfelves) to permit them to parti-cipate in the general joy.

Even thofe who are the fufferers can hardly be forry when they fee wrong meafures carrying their punifhment along with them. Were an impartial and competent obferver of the ftate of fociety in thefe middle colonies afked, whence it happens that Vir-ginia and Maryland (which were the firft planted, and which are fuperior to many colonies, and inferior to none, in point of natural advantage) are ftill fo exceedingly behind moft of the other Britifh tranf-

---

* Firft New England charter.

Atlantic

Atlantic poffeffions in all thofe improvements which bring credit and confequence to a country?—he would anfwer—They are fo, becaufe they are cultivated by flaves. I believe it is capable of demonftration that, except the immediate intereft which every man has in the property of his flaves, it would be for every man's intereft that there were no flaves: and for this plain reafon, becaufe the free labour of a free man, who is regularly hired and paid for the work which he does, and only for what he does, is, in the end, cheaper than the extorted eye-fervice of a flave. Some lofs and inconvenience would, no doubt, arife from the general abolition of flavery in thefe colonies: but were it done gradually, with judgement, and with good temper, I have never yet feen it fatisfactorily proved that fuch inconvenience would either be great or lafting. North American or Weft Indian planters might, poffibly, for a few years, make lefs tobacco, or lefs rice, or lefs fugar; the raifing of which might alfo coft them more; but, that difadvantage would probably foon be amply compenfated to them by an advanced price, or (what is the fame thing) by the reduced expence of cultivation.

With all my abhorrence of flavery, I feel in myfelf no difpofition to queftion either it's lawfulnefs, or it's humanity. It's lawfulnefs has again and again been clearly proved: and if it is fometimes cruel it is fo only from being abufed. But, if I am not much miftaken, more harm than good has been done by
fome

some late publications on the subject of slavery * ; a subject which, of all others, seems to be the least proper for a mere rhetorician. Thus much, however, I may be permitted to observe, that, in no other country was slavery so well regulated as it is in the British colonies. In some respects I hope it is on a better footing than it ever was, or is, any where else : but it is surely worse in this, that here, in one sense, it never can end. An African slave, even when made free, supposing him to be possessed even of talents and of virtue, can never, in these colonies, be quite on terms of equality with a free white man. Nature has placed insuperable barriers in his way. This is a circumstance of great moment ; though, I think, it has not often been adverted to by popular writers †.

If ever these colonies, now filled with slaves, be improved to their utmost capacity, an essential part of the improvement must be the abolition of slavery. Such a change would hardly be more to the advan-

---

* In the Virginia News-papers. By Mr. Arthur Lee.

† A convict, when purified by long service, and become industrious and honest, naturally coalesces with the people around him, and his former delinquencies and infamy are forgotten ; his children can never be upbraided with their having had a felon for their father: whereas the descendants of a white person, married to a black one, would, for many generations, by their complexion, proclaim their origin. Accordingly, though many mulattoes and people of colour have obtained wealth, I remember no instance, in any European colony, of their having obtained rank.

tage

tage of the flaves, than it would be to their owners.
An ingenious French writer * well obferves, that
" the ftate of flavery is, in it's own nature, bad: it is
" neither ufeful to the mafter, nor to the flave. Not
" to the flave, becaufe he can do nothing through a
" motive of virtue †; not to the mafter, becaufe, by
" having an *unlimited* authority over his flaves ‡, he
" infenfibly accuftoms himfelf to the want of all
" moral virtues, and from thence grows fierce, hafty,
" fevere, voluptuous, and cruel."

I do you no more than juftice in bearing witnefs,
that in no part of the world were flaves ever better

---

* Montefquieu.   Spirit of Laws, book xv. chap. 1.

† Surely the pofition that flaves have no motive to be virtuous,
is here laid down fomewhat too ftrongly: there are virtues growing
out of flavery, and peculiar to it, as there are in every other condition of life; fuch as attachment, fidelity, meeknefs, and humility,
which are the chief Chriftian virtues; and flavery is to be objected
to, not fo much from it's tendency to debafe and injure flaves,
(though I am fenfible it does this in a confiderable degree,) as
from it's being injurious to fociety at large. See fome juft obfervations on this point by Sir Frederic Morton Eden, Bart. in
" The State of the Poor," vol. i. p. 11.

‡ That *unlimited authority over flaves* is unfavourable to moral
virtue in the mafter, I readily admit; but in no European colony
has any fuch authority ever been exercifed. It is, however, remarkable, that the great champion of liberty, and advocate of
humanity, Mr. Locke, by the 10th article, or item, of the Conftitution which he drew up for the government of Carolina, gives
" every freeman of Carolina abfolute power and property over his
" flaves, of what opinion or religion foever.

treated than, in general, they are in thefe colonies. That there are exceptions, needs not to be concealed : in all countries there are bad men. And fhame be to thofe men who, though themfelves bleffed with freedom, have minds lefs liberal than the poor crea- tures over whom they fo meanly tyrannize ! Even your humanity, however, falls fhort of their exi- gencies. In one effential point, I fear, we are all de- ficient : they are nowhere fufficiently inftructed. I am far from recommending it to you, at once to fet them all free ; becaufe to do fo would be an heavy lofs to you, and probably no gain to them : but I do entreat you to make them fome amends for the drudgery of their bodies by cultivating their minds. By fuch means only can we hope to fulfil the ends, which, we may be permitted to believe, Providence had in view in fuffering them to be brought among us. You may unfetter them from *the chains of ignorance* ; you may emancipate them from *the bondage of fin,* the worft flavery to which they can be fubjected : and by thus *fetting at liberty thofe that are bruifed,* though they ftill continue to be your flaves, they fhall be *delivered from the bondage of corruption into the glorious liberty of the children of God.*

I come now, in the laft place, to exhort you not to difappoint the pious wifhes which our pious king had in thus publicly fummoning us to hail *the Lord of lords and King of kings with fongs of deliverance,* for having *given his people the bleffing of peace.* That a long and bloody war, unparalleled in all former hif-
tories

tories either for the variety of its operations, or the univerfality of its extent, is at length happily terminated, cannot but fill every benevolent heart with joy; even though men with fuch hearts were no otherwife interefted than as they take part in the general interefts of humanity. But, befides that near intereft which we cannot fail to feel in whatever materially concerns our mother country, on whom the chief burden of this general war has fallen; we muft not forget, that *for us and for our fakes* it was firft entered into; and that our welfare has been principally confulted in the terms on which it has been concluded. And, notwithftanding all that a difcontented party has faid, or has written, on the idea that the conditions of the peace are inadequate to our great fuccefs, fo far as they concern us we can have nothing to object to them. Our particular interefts, indeed, have been fo much attended to, that the happy fituation in which we are now placed has actually excited no little diffatisfaction among thofe who have long looked upon us with fufpicion and jealoufy: and our friends are told that the day may not be diftant when even they fhall forely rue that fo much has been done for the continental colonifts. Away with all fuch finiftrous furmifes! I join with you in refenting them, as equally ungenerous and unjuft. Your regard to your own interefts, your fenfe of duty, your feelings of gratitude, will all confpire to give the lie to thefe ill-omen'd prognoftications.

Inftead

Inftead of dwelling, as we are too apt to do, with a perverfe kind of gratification, on thefe now prevalent topics of difcuffion (which, like ephemeral infects, buzz around us awhile with a bufy kind of importance, and then are heard of no more), call to mind, I pray you, what your *fearchings of heart* were, when, not long fince, on the defeat of General **Braddock**, you faw (at leaft in your panic-ftruck imaginations you faw) your enemies at your very doors, ready *to fwallow you up*; when not only a folitary individual or two, but the whole land, with fafting and with prayer exclaimed: *Ob, thou fword of the Lord! how long will it be ere thou be quiet? Put up thyfelf into the fcabbard; reft and be ftill!* Let the ftrength of your fears, and the ardour of your wifhes at that time for a peace on almoft any terms, be fome meafure for your joy and thankfulnefs now; when you have obtained fuch a peace as, I believe, exceeded your moft fanguine expectations on the commencement of the war. And whatever praifes we beftow either on thofe who directed the war, or who negociated the peace; ftill the glory of all belongs unto God. He it was who infpired our ftatefmen with wifdom; and who covered the heads of our warriors in the day of battle. He it was who *turned the counfels of our enemies into foolifhnefs;* and who, in his mercy, has *lifted us up on high above them that rofe up againft us. God hath indeed done marvellous things for us; whereof we rejoice.*

But ftill, great as is the prefent occafion of our joy, it muft depend on ourfelves, whether peace, however

desirable

desirable at this moment, shall continue to be a blessing to us; or shall finally add to our condemnation. War is the just judgement which God inflicts on a sinful people. Had we not deserved it, so grievous a visitation would not have been our lot. But as peace has now once more been restored to us, let us humbly hope that we are become not altogether unworthy of so great a blessing. Let us, now that we are *made whole*, endeavour to *sin no more, left a worse thing come unto us.* Let us again turn our attention to cultivate the arts of peace, the only arts which, as Christians, we ought to be very solicitous to know; and so let us regulate our words and actions, so let us conduct ourselves towards God and our neighbours, that we may *lead quiet and peaceable lives in all godlines and honesty.*

" Grant, we beseech thee, O Lord, that the course
" of this world may be so peaceably ordered by thy
" governance, that thy Church may joyfully serve
" thee, in all godly quietness, through Jesus Christ
" our Lord!"

ON FUNDAMENTAL PRINCIPLES.

Happy in the eafier tafk of having left to our care the maintenance only of thofe excellent *foundations* which were laid for us by our progenitors, we are without excufe, if, either through heedleffnefs or through defign, we fuffer them to be *deftroyed*. Thofe great and good men, who, *like wife mafter-builders*, have from time to time fo *fitly framed together* our glorious Conftitution, well knew that *other fure found-ation no man could lay* than that already laid by *pro-phets and apoftles*, namely obedience, not only *for wrath*, but *for confcience fake*. Founded on this rock a fuperftructure of greatnefs and happinefs has been raifed, to which even fufpicion could apprehend no danger, were it not of the nature of human grandeur to totter and fink under it's own weight. Free go-vernments are moft endangered by falfe principles; juft as perfons brought up in healthy climates are moft apt to contract difeafes in unwholfome ones. *Except, therefore, the Lord keep*, as well as *build, the houfe, it is but loft labour* for us to think of having it propped up, not (in the language of the Apoftle) *with gold, filver, and precious ftones*, but with the feeble buttreffes of *wood, and hay, and ftubble**. It was founded in wifdom and in virtue; and on that foundation, if at all, it muft be maintained and preferved. *Righteouf-nefs* alone (which is the *foundation* or fundamental principle which it is the aim of this difcourfe to re-commend) *exalteth a nation*; whereas fin, or falfe

---

* 1 Cor. iii. ver. 12.

principles,

principles, are not only *the reproach*, but the *destruction of any people*. It is acknowledged, indeed, that, as in private life, *the way of the wicked* sometimes *prospereth, and those are* permitted to be *happy who deal* very *treacherously*; so virtuous States are sometimes, for a while, *oppressed and brought low*, whilst corrupt ones are *advanced to great power*. But, in general, the hand of God seldom continues to be long against a *righteous people*; nor does vengeance, though slow, ever fail, at last, to overtake either guilty individuals or guilty communities. States, as States, have no prescribed period of existence; yet they also may have *a time to die:* and to expect them to arrive at perpetuity without virtuous principles and manners in the people of whom they are composed, seems to be as vain as in the life of man it would be to hope for longevity without any regimen or without temperance.

I am not conscious that I am of a temper to rail indiscriminately against my own times. In many respects they merit much commendation; perhaps beyond all that have preceded them. Through a deference to public opinion, which abhors every thing that is monstrous in manners; through the influence of fashion and habit, our character as a people is not marked by any prevailing propensity to commit great and flagrant crimes: but, I own, I hardly know how far such negative kind of merit is entitled to praise; at most, it seems to be but the virtues of that particular class of bees which in autumn are called drones,

and

and which are innoxious only becaufe they are impotent. However commendable it is in the character of a people that they are not marked by any great and flagrant vices, we are entitled to this commendation, if at all, by accident rather than by defign, that is to fay, becaufe, fortunately for us, it is not fafhionable to be eminently vicious; whilft our equal deficiency in any great virtues is in no flight degree ftudied and deliberate. There never was a time when a whole people were fo little governed by fettled good principles. Nor is this unconcern about good principles confined to matters which relate to government. By a natural gradation in error, it pervades the whole compafs of our conduct. Wife and obferving perfons fee with forrow that it has gained a footing in, and materially injured, every department of fociety. Parents complain, and not without reafon, that children are no longer fo refpectful and dutiful as they ought to be, and as they ufed to be; whilft children might, with not lefs reafon, object to their parents ftill more culpable inftances of a failure of duty. Both employers and the employed, much to their mutual fhame and inconvenience, no longer live together with any thing like attachment and cordiality on either fide : and the labouring claffes, inftead of regarding the rich as their guardians, patrons, and benefactors, now look on them as fo many over-grown coloffufes whom it is no demerit in them to wrong. A ftill more general (and it is to be feared not lefs juft) topic of complaint is, that the lower claffes, inftead of

being

being induſtrious, frugal, and orderly, (virtues ſo pe-
culiarly becoming their ſtation in life,) are become
idle, improvident, and diſſolute.   And, however
much it is to be regretted by all ranks, it does not
admit of a doubt that this diſſolutenefs in the inferior
members of the community may be traced to ſome
correſponding profligacy in the higher orders.   The
manners of a community may be regarded as one
great chain, of which perſons in ſuperior ſpheres are
but the upper links.   The ſame cauſes which, in the
upper walks of life, lead men of active minds to engage in ſeditious and factious conſpiracies and rebellions, lead thoſe in lower ſpheres (when not attached
as ſatellites to powerful revolters) to become either
drunkards, and unmannerly, and abuſive; or elſe,
ſmugglers, gamblers, and cheats.

But theſe deviations from rectitude, though by no
means inconſiderable in themſelves, yet, when com-
prehenſibly conſidered, are but ſmall parts of a great
whole. It is in our character, as ſubjects, that our loſs
of good principles, and conſequent errors in practice,
are moſt manifeſt and moſt miſchievous.   The doctrine of *obedience for conſcience ſake* * is (as has juſt
been

---

* As the only remedy againſt ruinous confuſions in a State,
Ariſtotle, the great teacher of political wiſdom to the Heathen
world, recommends the laying the foundation of civil government in
religion : αρωτον η περι Θων επιμελεια. Ariſtot. Polit. lib. i. The
recommendation very clearly ſhews from what ſource he derived all
that he knew on theſe ſubjects.

Plutarch,

been obferved) the great *corner-ftone* of all good government; which, whenever any *builder* of conftitu-
tions fhall be fo unwife as to *refufe*, or, not refufing,
fhall afterwards fuffer to be *deftroyed*, what can he
expect but that the whole fabric fhould be overturned;
and that *on whomfoever it may fall it will grind them to
powder?* The importance of this principle of obedience cannot well be ftated in ftronger terms than it is
in an anfwer of a great man recorded by Plutarch.
When the Thebans praifed the government of Epa-
minondas, and gratefully acknowledged that they
were happy becaufe he governed fo well, that truly
great man replied: " Not fo; you, our country, and

Plutarch, alfo, compares a government without religion to caftles
built in the air: Αλλα πολις αν μοι δοκει μαλλον εδαφους χωρις, η πολιτεια
των περι Θεων δοξης αναιρεθεισης πανταπασι συσασιν λαβειν, η λαβουσα
τηρησαι.——Plut. adv. Colotem. Opera, vol. ii. folio edit. p. 1125.
   We who, bleffed be God! on the fubject of religion, have *a more
fure word of prophecy,* have alfo, on government, a furer *foundation.*
In Chriftian States religion and government reft on the fame bafis;
fuccefs in the latter being the neceffary and conftant refult of fin-
cerity in the former. The Church and the King do, and muft,
ftand or fall together: to pretend to approve of the one, whilft yet
we oppofe the other, is to approve of St. Peter when he drew the
fword, but to difapprove of him when he enjoins fubmiffion. It is
the peculiar boaft of the Church of England, that, amidft all *the
changes and chances* of our hiftory, fhe never, either in her doctrine
or her practice, has countenanced any principles tending to fedition,
faction, or treafon. Churchmen, as fuch, have often been fufferers
for, but never the oppofers of, lawful authority. This is fo well
known a fact, that, amidft all the contumelies with which her enemies have fo often loaded her, the refiftance of juft authority has
never been objected to her.

" WE

"we all are happy, not merely becaufe I govern well,
"but becaufe you obey well."

Yet who is there among us fo unobferving as not to
know how much it is the fafhion with the unhallowed
politicians of thefe unprincipled times to malign and
fcoff at this venerable doctrine? Or, who fo ill-
informed of the importance of this principle as not
to lament the fuccefs they have had in bringing it, at
length, into very general difrepute? I fincerely believe that the low eftimation in which this fundamental
principle is held is the great evil of our age. There
is, however, this confolation left to thofe who ftill
reverence it as the life and foul of all good government, that, however vilified it may be, it never can be
wholly abandoned and loft, till God, in refentment of
our fins, fhall fuffer the National Church to be *deftroyed*, and, along with it, our prefent glorious Conftitution. Men may debate as much and as long as ill-
judged policy and ill-regulated paffions fhall prompt
them; new theories may be invented, or old projects
under new names be revived and purfued; and what
is received as wifdom and truth in one age, and one
country, may, in others, be fcorned as folly, or reprobated as error: but the word of God *abideth faft for ever*;
and is no more affected by the agitation of human opinions, than a rock in the ocean can be moved or fhaken
by the winds and the waves that beat againft it * ?

* " Ille, velut pelagi rupes immota, refiftit;
" Quæ fefe, multis circumlatrantibus undis,
" Mole tenet: fcopuli nequicquam & fpumea circum
" Saxa fremunt——" Æneid. vii. 1. 586.

This

This great doctrine of the liturgy and of the homilies of our Church, as well as of the laws of the Land, we are now, alas, intemperately haftening with the moft deplorable ignorance to *deftroy !* and at the fame time encouraging a novel experiment in the world; an experiment by which it is propofed to keep fociety together, or, in other words, to build up a Conftitution without any *foundations.* So much perhaps has not in direct terms yet been avowed ; but all this, and even more than this, muft inevitably refult from that loofe notion refpecting government, which has long been diffeminated among the people at large with incredible induftry, namely, that all government is the mere creature of the people, and may therefore be tampered with, altered, new-modelled, fet up or pulled down, juft as tumultuous crowds of the moft diforderly perfons in the community (who on fuch occafions are always fo forward to call themfelves *the people*) may happen in fome giddy moments of over-heated ardour to determine.

By fomething like a fatality, thefe notions, fo well calculated for the loweft and moft ignorant of the people, do not appear now to have originated with them. To promote fome finifter ends, fome leading perfons (who, not being of that clafs of which mobs are moft generally formed, fhould therefore have been above the cherifhing of any mobbifh maxims) revived and propagated the ftale idea, (which it is probable they do not themfelves believe,) that government is a combination among a few to opprefs the many.

many, With having firſt broached this popular but dangerous ſlander, modern reformers however are not chargeable. This, as well as the principle of equality, is very faithfully copied from a ſimilar inſtance of it's adoption in an early period of the hiſtory of the Jews. *Now Korah the ſon of Izhar, the ſon of Kohath, the ſon of Levi; and Dathan, and Abiram, the ſons of Eliab; and On the ſon of Peleth, ſons of Reuben, took men. And they roſe up before Moſes, with certain of the children of Iſrael, two hundred and fifty princes of the aſſembly, famous in the congregation, men of renown. And they gathered themſelves together againſt Moſes and againſt Aaron, and ſaid unto them, Ye take too much upon you, ſeeing all the congregation are holy, every one of them, and the Lord is among them: wherefore then lift you up yourſelves above the congregation of the Lord?* Num. xvi. ver. 1, 2, 3. But wherever, or whenever, the poſition was firſt produced, it is ſo palpably abſurd, and has ſo often been ſhewn to be abſurd, that nothing could have given it any currency but the artifice of confounding government itſelf, or government in the abſtract, with the miniſters of government. In a certain ſenſe, and to a certain degree, government no doubt is the act of the executive power by it's miniſters; and therefore, to oppoſe, thwart, and embarraſs the miniſters of government, is to thwart and oppoſe government itſelf; and moſt generally, though not always, ſo far from being meritorious, that it is quite the contrary. Still the miniſters of government, and government

itſelf,

itfelf, however nearly connected, are diftinct : minifters may be unwife and unjuft, and, as fuch, may not
deferve fupport ; but the conftitution of government,
as long as it exifts, is to be regarded as infallible and
irrefiftible. Under this idea, that government even
in it's beft eftate is an evil, and that it's minifters muft
of courfe be corrupt, many conceive it to be meritorious to oppofe both the one and the other : for,
however poffible it may feem to be in theory to oppofe the minifters of government, and at the fame
time to fupport government, the hiftory both of the
mother country and her colonies fhews, that, in practice, it is always difficult, if not impoffible. To fyfte-
matical and indifcriminate oppofition it certainly is impoffible. It is not perhaps that any confiderable number of people ferioufly think, as it is here ftated they
do; but they certainly act as if they thought there
was great merit in oppofition, even when, in oppofing
minifters, government itfelf is alfo oppofed. The
principle, however, (if indeed it is to be regarded as a
principle,) is as indefenfible as when it is carried into
practice, it's effects are lamentable. In hardly any
fenfe of the word is it true that government is an evil :
but in this unqualified fenfe I cannot allow it to be an
evil ; that is to fay, what cafuifts call *malum in fe* ; even
admitting it to have originated from the wickednefs
of mankind. With equal reafon might we vote the
medicine to be an evil which cures us of a dangerous
difeafe ; or the furgeon our enemy, who faves our
lives by amputating a putrid limb. If, in fome inftances,

ftances, through abuſe, government does actually become (as no doubt it often does) an evil ; this, properly underſtood, is no more to be objected to good
government, than the fierce debates, the bitter quarrels, and the dreadful wars which have ſprung from
religion, are fairly to be charged to religion. Still,
however, it remains a queſtion, (and ſuch a one as I
think is incapable of being proved in the affirmative,)
how far an indiſcriminate oppoſition to the miniſters
of government, is the beſt way to correct even abuſes
in government : yet, as though there were no doubt
in the caſe, both in the mother country and in the
colonies, that ſpecies of parliamentary interference
uniformly exerted by a ſelf-created body of men, who
are generally known and deſcribed under the ſettled
title of the Oppoſition, is now ſuppoſed to be abſo-
lutely neceſſary to the preſervation of liberty. It is extraordinary that a poſition of ſuch moment has no where
(as far as I know) ever been fairly argued ; though I
cannot help ſtrongly ſuſpecting, that if ever the point
be carefully diſcuſſed, it will be found that, however
generally entertained and acted on, it is ill-founded.
If I am not miſtaken, it has thus been received as a
ruling principle in politics only ſince the Revolution ; ſince which time, men of all deſcriptions, and
of all parties, it is probable, have occaſionally ranked
under the banners of Oppoſition. And it is no mean
proof of the ſyſtem's being radically falſe and wrong,
that the ſame men have uniformly maintained opinions and principles diametrically oppoſite to each
other,

other, when in opposition, and when in places. Sir
Robert Walpole stands recorded as the most violent
patriot of his day, as well as the most corrupt minister: and such is the indulgence shewn by the public
to this glaring inconsistency, that men are rewarded
for their opposition by appointments to situations, in
which it is well known they must and will defend the
very measures they had before condemned.   The necessity or the advantage of a systematical opposition,
therefore, can, with any shew of consistency, be maintained by those persons alone, who think the interests of
those who govern, adverse to those of the governed:
whereas the fact is, that in no instance can the people
who are governed be so much injured by a weak or
wicked administration, as the constitution itself is injured.   Mal-administration, corruption, and tyranny,
in those who govern, sap the foundations of all good
government, if with less shew, yet with hardly less
reality, than they are sapped by sedition and rebellion
in those who are governed.   That it is of great moment
carefully to watch the conduct of all administrations,
is readily admitted; but it is of equal moment to attend
with equal care to every thing else which relates to
legislation and government. Such vigilance, however,
is the particular and exclusive duty of no individual
member or members of the community, whether in
a public or private capacity: it is the common duty
of every man in his sphere, and the especial duty of
our constitutional guardians, whom we elect for that
purpose, though not for that only.   This duty they
equally

equally difcharge, when, in cafes where the executive power requires and is entitled to fupport, they give it fupport ; as when, on a contrary fuppofition, they op= pofe and endeavour to counteract meafures of which they cannot confcientioufly approve. But this neither fuppofes nor juftifies a diftinct and united body of fyftematic opponents, nor indifcriminate oppofition : yet, both in the Britifh Parliament, and in our Colo= nial Affemblies, ever fince the fyftem began, there has never wanted a regular corps of members in oppo= fition ; as well known, and as clearly defignated as any of the officers of State. This body of men has far too often oppofed, not only particular meafures, (as every individual member is fuppofed to do when fchemes are patronized either by thofe entrufted with the adminiftration or others, which fuch mem= bers conceive to be unwife or unjuft,) but in general all meafures whatever which are fupported by the executive power, or by a minifter : and what is moft alarming is, that, in thus thwarting and oppofing the immediate fupporters of government, many inftances might be mentioned, in which the Members in Oppo= fition, as they are regularly denominated, have, indi= rectly at leaft, taken part with, encouraged, and affift= ed the avowed enemies of their country : one alfo of it's more certain and conftant effects is, that, in com= mon with it's minifters, government in the abftract is vilified and traduced.

That fome good has occafionally been effected by oppofitions (which now feem to be as regular appen=
dages

dages to our legiflatures, as if they actually were a conftitutional and effential part of them) I am far from denying ; but I much fear the good that is thus done bears no proportion to the evil : the former at beft is uncertain, but not fo the latter. As, however, it is no part of my purpofe to go into a full difcuffion of this important queftion, fuffice it for the prefent to obferve, (what perfectly correfponds with the aim of this difcourfe,) that one of it's certain effects is, (as has juft been obferved,) it's giving rife to a low and unworthy opinion of government. Hence men of ill-informed or mifdirected minds are naturally led, inftead of reverencing government, to do all they can to difhonour it. It was this general habit of *fpeaking evil of dignities, and defpifing dominion,* which in the laft century, more than any thing elfe, engendered and foftered infinite *confufion and every evil work* in the State ; and at length produced thofe *fecret, confpiracies and open attempts* againft the laws, the liberties, and the religion of the land ; fuch as now once more fill the minds of all obferving and thinking men with apprehenfion and awe.

This low opinion of government naturally produces another falfe and dangerous eftimate of things : in proportion as government is degraded, thofe who deprefs it exalt themfelves. Hence, to he the friend of government, fubjects a man to the mortifying fufpicion of being of an abject and fervile mind ; whilft popularity is fure to attach to thofe who oppofe government, or rather perhaps the minifters of government.

ment. And hence too, as flimfy oratory is always moft in vogue when found principles and found learning are leaft fo, our foreft committees, aping the members of our conventions and congreffes in their volubility of fpeech, as well as in their patriotifm, harangue not lefs vehemently on thofe unvarying topics, the abufes of government, the vilenefs of thofe whom they call the tools of government, the difintereftednefs of oppofition, and the genuine love of liberty which actuates thofe who conduct oppofition. Thefe feem always to have been the favourite topics of that " fwoln and turgid elocution *," which a Roman writer, diftinguifhed for his elegance, mentions as characteriftical of his countrymen in the decline of their empire +.

This is not all: as though there were fome irrefiftible charm in all extemporaneous fpeaking, however rude, the orators of our committees and fub-committees, like thofe in higher fpheres, *prevail with their*

---

* " Ventofa ifthæc et enormis loquacitas."—Petronius Arbiter.

+ " Eft magna et notabilis eloquentia alumna licentiæ, quam ftulti libertatem vocabant; comes feditionum; effrænati populi incitamentum; contumax; temeraria; arrogans; quæ in bene conftitutis civitatibus non oritur."——Tacit. Dialog. de Orator.

" The meek fpirit of obedience had given way to a turbulent impatience of legal reftraint, and to an overweening conceit of felf confidence. Every pert demagogue thought himfelf at liberty to difturb the decorum of popular affemblies by his feditious declamations: as if effrontery of face and volubility of tongue were the only neceffary accomplifhments of an orator and ftatefman."——Bever's Roman Polity, book ii. p. 85.

tongues.

*tongues**. To public speakers alone is the government of our country now completely committed : it is cantoned out into new districts, and subjected to the jurisdiction of these committees ; who, not only without any known law, but directly in the teeth of all law whatever, issue citations, sit in judgment, and inflict pains and penalties on all whom they are pleased to consider as delinquents : not only new crimes have been thus created, but also new punishments ; in comparison with which even the interdiction from fire and water among the Romans was mild and merciful. An empire is thus completely established within an empire ; and a new system of government of great power erected, even before the old one is formally abolished.

Now, could all this have happened had there not first been a great change in the public mind, and a total dereliction of all those fundamental maxims and principles by which the public has hitherto been happily influenced and governed ? If such a state of things does not prove a total *destruction of foundations* already to have taken place, it shews far too clearly that so aweful an event cannot be very distant.

I fear I might be thought to sport with your understandings, as well as with your humanity, if, notwithstanding all the testimonies of history, and notwithstanding all the fair deductions of argument, I were still to amuse you with hopes that what is yet to come

---

* Psal. xii. ver. 4.

will

will be better than what is paft, or is now paffing. It is true I do not pretend to bring any direct or pofitive proof, that it either is, or ever was, in the contemplation of any individuals among us, or even of any party, to kindle up a civil war, either in our Province, or on the Continent, for the purpofe of *deftroy-ing foundations*, and erecting on their ruins that better conftitution which we are told is fo much wanted. He who in fuch a cafe waits for proofs, refembles the man who, feeing that his houfe is on fire, fhould refolve not to fend for an engine till he faw the flames burfting out at the roof.

I feel I want fpirits to draw a picture of thofe miferable confufions which we may too furely look for, if for our fins the Almighty fhould fee fit to fuffer thefe unhallowed principles to produce all their natural effects. Good men are particularly interefted in praying to be fpared from fuch times of calamity. *If the foundations be deftroyed, what can the righteous do?* No queftion is made refpecting the unrighteous : the royal Pfalmift could be at no lofs to judge what they would do ; for he had been taught by experience, that a time of general diforder is to bad men what a fhipwreck is to barbarians. Like the willow, men of loofe principles bend and yield to the ftream ; whilft *the righteous*, in a deluge of iniquity, imitating the oak, are ufually torn up by the roots and fwept away by the torrent.

It can neither be concealed nor denied that the times are critical and aweful. *The foundations of the world*

world are out of courfe: the judgments of God are in the earth: much therefore doth it become the inhabitants thereof to learn righteoufnefs. In vain do even we, who profefs to fee and to own that our prefent confufions are not to be afcribed to any particular caufe or caufes which have operated juft at this particular juncture, but rather to a feries of accumulated caufes which feem at length to have arrived at their crifis; in vain, I fay, do we affect to lament bad principles, whilft we take fo little pains to promote good ones: in vain do we profefs with our lips to love our country and it's conftitution, whilft, by our lives, we difgrace the one and *deftroy* the other. It is only by found principles and a correfponding practice; by a deep and due fenfe of the duties of religion, evidenced by a fuitable purity of manners; it is, in fhort, only by *believing all the articles of the Chriftian faith*, manifefted by *keeping God's holy will and commandments*, that the peace of our Jerufalem can be reftored: and God forbid that on this folemn occafion we fhould afk pardon for fins which we do not intend to forfake, or faft for offences in which we refolve to perfift!

But, *that it may be well with us and our children for ever*, let us now at length, in good earneft, unite our hands, our hearts, and our prayers, againft thofe enemies (be they who they may) who meditate war, not only againft the Parent State, but againft every thing that is eftablifhed, venerable and good, whether in that country or in this: and more efpecially let us fet

ourfelves

ourfelves againſt thofe ſtill worfe enemies, our own fins. Thus, and thus only, may all things, by the bleffing of God, yet *be ordered and fettled on the beſt and fureſt foundations* ; *and truth and juſtice, peace and happinefs, religion and piety, may yet be eſtabliſhed among us, for all generations* !

EXCERPT FROM
THE ADMINISTRATION OF THE COLONIES

Thomas Pownall, *The Administration of the Colonies*, 2nd edition (London, 1765), pp. 89–140.

Although by 1760 Thomas Pownall had returned to England, he still maintained an active interest in colonial affairs, as *Administration of the Colonies* shows. He was a leading supporter of colonial unification and called for a redefinition of the union between the colonies and Great Britain. Pownall served as a Member of Parliament from 1767 to 1780, during which time he opposed Edmund Burke's 1775 bill for conciliation with the colonies. Pownall introduced a peace bill in 1780 that represented his opinion that the American colonies and Great Britain could never be reconciled, and that the only solution to this problem would be American independence.

Despite Pownall's views on colonial independence, *The Administration of the Colonies* shows support for the Navigation Acts, seeing them as a necessary ingredient in the continued success of the British commercial empire. Pownall believed that the economic role of the colonies was to provide raw materials for the finer manufacturing of goods in England, and then to provide a market for the completed goods. For this to be successful, restrictions on trade were necessary.

However, Pownall did question some mercantile ideas, such as the danger of a negative balance of trade. He argues here that an influx of settlers, who arrive in debt and acquire more debt as they begin farming or other businesses, generates a negative balance of trade for the colonies. However, this is not necessarily a problem as over the long run, debts are repaid and the settlers begin to produce goods and services for the colony in excess of the original debt. Pownall, like Benjamin Franklin, was a strong promoter of emigration to the colonies. He was clearly influenced by Franklin's *Observations Concerning the Increase of Mankind* (1760), which is also reproduced in this volume, and, in fact, Franklin and Pownall were partners in planning a settlement in the Ohio Valley. Although this scheme was eventually abandoned, the idea of expanding the boundaries of the colonies remained.

THE

ADMINISTRATION

OF THE

COLONIES.

By THOMAS POWNALL,

Late Governor and Commander in Chief of his Majefty's Provinces, Meffachufets-Bay and South-Carolina, and Lieutenant-Governor of New-Jerfey.

The SECOND EDITION,
Revifed, Corrected, and Enlarged.

Pulchrum eft benefacere reipublicæ, etiam bene dicere haud abfurdum eft. SALLUSTIUS.

LONDON:
Printed for J. DODSLEY, in Pall-Mall, and J. WALTER, at Charing-Crofs.
MDCCLXV.

As government, by thofe minifters whofe department it is to fuperintend and adminifter the public revenue, hath taken the colony revenue under confideration; and as the point of right, whether the fupreme legiflature of Great Britain (paffing by the fubordinate legiflatures of the colonies, wherein alone the Colonifts fay they are reprefented) can tax the colonies, is now brought forward as a matter of difpute; I do, as writing on this fubject, think it my duty not to conceal what has always been my idea of the matter. I do fuppofe that it will not bear a doubt, but that the fupreme legiflature of Great Britain is the true and perfect reprefentative of Great Britain, and all its dependencies: and as it is not in the power of the Houfe of Lords or Commons to exempt any community from the jurifdiction of the King, as fupreme magiftrate, fo that it is not, nor ever was, or could be in the power of the crown, to exempt any perfons or communities within the dominions of Great Britain, from being fubject and liable to be taxed by parliament. If the fettlers of the colonies were at their migration, prior to the grants of charter and commiffioned-conftitutions, liable to be taxed by parliament, no charters or powers
of

of any kind granted by the crown could
exempt them. When the doubt arifes on
expediency, whether parliament fhould exercife this right, where the colonies have legiflatures that do refpectively in each colony
lay taxes and raife revenues for the ufe of the
crown in that colony, I think it cannot but be
obferved, that as there are in each refpective
colony fervices which regard the fupport of
government, and the fpecial exigences of the
ftate and community of that colony, fo there
are general fervices which regard the fupport
of the crown, the rights and dominions of
Great Britain in general :—That as lands, te-
nements, and other improved property within
the colony, confidered as the private efpecial
property of that community, fhould be left
to the legiflatures of thofe colonies unincumbered by parliament, fhould, as the proper
object of taxes within the colony, be the
fpecial funds of thofe colonies; fo revenues
by impofts, excife, or a ftamp duty, become
the proper fund whereon the parliament of
Great Britain may, with the utmoft delicacy
and regard to the colonies power of taxing
themfelves, raife thofe taxes which are raifed
for the general fervice of the crown; becaufe
thefe kind of taxes are (if I may be permitted the expreffion) coincident with thofe
regulations which the laws of the realm pre-
fcribe to trade in general; to manufactures—
and

and to every legal act and deed;—becaufe they are duties which arife from the general rights and jurifdiction of the realm, rather than from the particular and fpecial concerns of any one colony.—Whenever therefore this point, now a queftion, fhall be decided, and government fhall find it expedient to extend to America, thofe duties under which trade, manufactures, and bufinefs, is carried on in Great Britain, the proper taxes, fo as not to interfere with the fpecial internal property and rights of the colonies, will arife from an impoft, excife, and ftamp duty.—The firft will arife from cuftoms paid by the exterior trade of the colonies, regulated as hereafter to be mentioned. *Secondly,* As the objects of manufactures, the product of the colonies, and all articles confumed by the manufacturers, ought not to be exempt from thofe duties which are paid on the like objects and articles by the manufacturers in England;—*As the manufacturers in America ought in this cafe to be under the fame predicament as they are in England,* the extenfion of the excife laws fo far as this rule of equality goes, can never be thought any matter of injuftice by the Colonifts: But in thefe laws one caution muft be carefully obferved, that no article bought by the Colonifts in England, wherein the excife duty already paid is part of the price which they give for it, ought to be
liable

liable to a fecond excife in the colonies. *Laftly*, As all matters of bufinefs between man and man, tranfacted either in proceedings or by the directions of law, all matters of bargain or fale done and performed, are done under the regulations and fanction of the laws of the realm, it can never be objected to, as to a point of injuftice, that thefe matters and things in America fhould be fubject, *mutatis mutandis*, to the fame duty as the like matters and things are in England. However one doubt will here arife that ought to be well attended to, namely, how far thefe colonies, who for the neceffity of government and the emergencies of fervice, have already by their proper powers laid thefe duties on the people, and granted the revenue arifing therefrom to the crown, by acts which have received the confent of the crown; how far thefe colonies may or may not be fuppofed to have precluded any act of adminiftration here on thefe heads.—I mention this matter as a point of doubt, which would unavoidably arife; but do not pretend to determine on it.

The rates at which the impoft duty fhould be laid, ought to be eftimated by the confideration of the reftraints and burthens already lying on the colony trade, by the act of navigation.

The

The rates of any excife, if ever it fhould be found proper to extend thofe laws to America, fhould be eftimated by an average made between the price of labour, the price of provifions, and expence of living in thofe countries, compared with the fame articles here in England, both which may eafily be known.

The rates of the ftamp duty ought to be much lower than thofe laid here in England ; becaufe the fame kind of tranfactions, acts, and deeds, paffed and done in America, as thofe here in England, are done for concerns of much lefs value ; but if that duty be laid *ad valorem,* it muft regulate itfelf to the ftricteft point of equity.

The Colonifts fay with great propriety, that before the mother country determines on the meafure of taxing them, it ought to be well informed of the abilities of the feveral colonies, as to the fpecies and extent of tax which each is refpectively able to bear ; that none but their reprefentatives can be *duly* informed of that, and therefore by the very fpirit of the Britifh conftitution, it hath been always hitherto left to the colonies " to judge by their reprefentatives of the ways and means by which internal taxes fhould be
raifed

raifed within the refpective governments, and of the ability of the inhabitants to pay them."

To which it may be anfwered,—that fo long as it is maintained by the government of Great Britain, and not difallowed by the colonies, that the mother country has a right not only to judge of, but to regulate by its laws, the trade, produce, and manufactures of its colonies; the mother country ought to be fuppofed to have the means of being *duly* informed of the ftate of thefe, and therefore to be the proper, and indeed the only proper judge of the whole of this fubject, as a mat-ter of police as well as revenue; in which perhaps the only true grounds and right of laying duties by impoft and excife may lie.

It is faid that the abilities of the colonies are not known, but it is a fhame that it fhould be fo faid; that ignorance fhould be thus imputed to thofe who ought to be fully informed of this fubject; or the art of con-cealing their circumftances, imputed to thofe who can have no juftifiable reafon for con-cealing them from government:—But this affertion arifes from a miftake. Govern-ment here in Britain does, or at leaft may at any time know,

1. The

1. The number of rateable polls.

2. The number of acres in each province or colony, both cultivated and lying in wafte.

3. The numbers and quantity of every other article of rateable property, according to the method ufed by the provinces themfelves, in rating eftates real and perfonal.

4. Government may know, and ought always officially to know it, what the annual amount of the feveral province taxes are, and by what rates they are raifed, and by what eftimates thefe rates are laid.

From whence, by comparing this eftimation with the value of each article, they may always collect nearly the real value of the property of fuch province or colony; all which compared with the prices of labour, provifions, and European goods imported, on one hand, and with the value of their exports, on the other, will as fully and precifely, as all the knowledge and juftice of their own reprefentatives could do, mark their abilities to bear, and the proportion which they fhould bear of taxes with the

mother

mother country. When this proportion fhall be once fettled for the feveral parts, by the fupreme legiflature which can alone extend to the whole; fo long as the arguments and reafoning of the Colonifts " that they fhould be permitted to judge by their reprefentatives of the ways and means of levying thefe *internal taxes* by rates on polls and eftates real and perfonal," go only to the matter of expediency and good policy ; whilft this privilege is not claimed as an exclufive right, and extends only to thefe *internal funds,* I own that I cannot but think that it would be expedient and of good policy, to continue to them thefe privileges exercifed on thefe objects, as their proper funds.

As it is my opinion that the polls and eftates real and perfonal are, as the fpecial internal private property of the province, the proper object of the province taxes, and that thefe ought to be left as the fpecial funds of the province unincumbered by parliament; my endeavouring here to give fome idea of the extent of thefe funds, and what they would produce annually, at one fhilling in the pound on the produce, cannot be mifconftrued to be a pointing out of thefe, as taxes proper to be laid on the colonies by Great Britain : Yet on the contrary, it may fhow what little reafon the Colonifts have to complain of
thofe

thofe moderate duties and impofts, which the mother country expects them to bear in aid to her, whilft government leaves to them untouched thefe internal funds, fo fully adequate to all the internal fervices of each province.

The following eftimates of the provinces, Maffachufett's-Bay to the northward, of South-Carolina to the fouthward, and of New Jerfey in the center, are founded in the tax-lifts of each province; which tax-lifts, being of ten Years ftanding, muft, in encreafing countries as the colonies are, fall fhort of the numbers and quantity which would be found on any tax-lift faithfully made out at this time. The eftimates which I have made thereon are in general at fuch an under-valuation, that I fhould think no man of candour in the provinces will object to them; although they be, in fome articles, higher than the valuation which the legiflatures directed fo long ago to be made, as the fund of the taxes that they order to be levied on them. This valuation of the eftates, real and perfonal, gives the grofs amount of the principal of the rateable property in the province. I think I may venture to affirm, that no man, who would be thought to underftand the eftimation of things, will object that I over-rate the produce of this property,

when

when I rate it at fix *per cent.* only of this moderate valuation; when he confiders that money, in none of thofe provinces, bears lefs than fix *per cent.* intereft; and that under loans of money, at five *per cent.* moft of the beft improvements of the country have been made.

The valuation of the provinces, New-York and Penfylvania, lying on each fide of New-Jerfey, are calculated in a different manner, by taking a medium between the fuppofed real value and the very loweft rate of valuation. Without troubling the reader, or encumbering the printer with the detail of thefe tax-lifts, and the calculations made thereon, I will infert only the refult of them, as follows.

The provinces under-mentioned could annually raife, by one fhilling in the pound on the produce of the rateable property, eftates real and perfonal in each province:

	£.	s.	d.
Province Maffachufett's-Bay,	13172	7	11
New-York, - -	8000	0	0
New-Jerfey, - -	5289	17	0
Penfylvania, - -	15761	10	0
South-Carolina, -	6971	1	11
Sterling, £.	49395	16	10

Suppofe now the reft of the colonies to be no more than able to double this fum:

The fum-total that the colonies will be able to raife, according to their old tax-lifts, and their own mode of valuation and of rating the produce of eftates, real and perfonal, will be, at one fhilling in the pound on the produce, *per annum*, - - - - - -

£. s. d.

98791 13 8

In juftice to the reft of the provinces, particularized above, I ought to obferve that, by the equalleft judgment which I can form, I think that the province of South-Carolina is the moft under-rated.

I fhould alfo point out to the American reader, that, as the calculations and lifts above referred to, are taken from the private collections of the writer of thefe papers, without any official communication of fuch papers as miniftry may be poffeffed of, I defire him to give no other credit to them, than fuch as, by referring to his own knowledge of the ftate of things in the colonies, he finds to be juft and near the truth. I fhould, on the other hand, inform the Englifh reader, that thefe were collected on the fpot, and communicated by perfons leading, and

and thoroughly converſant in the buſineſs of their reſpective provinces.

Another remark is neceſſary, That, except what relates to Penſylvania, theſe collections were made nine years ago ; ſo that, wherever any difference may áriſe, from the different proportion in which theſe provinces have encreaſed, that ought to be carried to account ; at the ſame time, that a certain addition may be made to the whole from the certain encreaſe of all of them.

If this moderate tax, raiſed by the above moderate valuation, be compared with the internal annual charge of government in the reſpective provinces, that charge will be found much below the ſupplies of this fund. The whole charge of the ordinary expence of government in the province Maſſachuſett's-Bay, which does, by much, more to the ſupport of government, and other public ſervices than any other province, is, in time of peace, ſterling 12937 *l.* 10 *s.* whereas that of New-York is not more than about, ſterling, 4000 *l.* annually.

When theſe points ſhall be ſettled, there cannot be a doubt but that the ſame zealous attention, which all parties ſee and confeſs to be applied in the adminiſtration of the Britiſh department to the public revenue, will be ap-

plied

plied to the establishing and reforming that of America.

A proper knowledge of, and real attention to, the Crown's quit-rents in America, by revising the *original defects*, by remedying the almost insurmountable difficulties that the due collection of them is attended with, may render that branch a real and effective revenue, which at the same time will be found to be no inconsiderable one.

By proper regulations for securing the Crown's rights in waifs and wrecks, in fines and forfeitures, and by proper appropriations of the same, that branch of revenue may be made effective: But, whenever it is taken up in earnest, whenever it shall be resolved upon to give a real official regard to the revenue in America, the office of *Auditor General of the plantations* must cease to be a mere sinecure benefice, and be really and effectively established with such powers as will carry the duty of it into execution, yet under such cautions and restrictions as shall secure the benefit of its service to the use of the crown.

Here it will be necessary to remark, that, while administration is taking measures to secure and establish those duties which the
subject

fubject ought to pay to government, it much behoves the wifdom of that adminiftration to have care that the fubject hath fome fpecies of money out of which to pay.

The Britifh American colonies have not, within themfelves, the means of making money or coin. They cannot acquire it from Great Britain, the balance of trade being againft them. The returns of thofe branches of commerce, in which they are permitted to trade to any other part of Europe, are but barely fufficient to pay this balance.— By the prefent act of navigation, they are prohibited from trading with the colonies of any other nations, fo that there remains nothing but a fmall branch of African trade, and the fcrambling profits of an undefcribed traffic, to fupply them with filver. However, the fact is, and matters have been fo managed, that the general currency of the colonies ufed to be in Spanifh and Portuguefe coin. This fupplied the internal circulation of their home bufinefs, and always finally came to England in payments for what the colonifts exported from thence. If the act of navigation fhould be carried into fuch rigorous execution as to cut off this fupply of a filver currency to the colonies, the thoughts of adminiftration fhould be turned to the devifing fome means of fupplying the colonies

colonies with money of some sort or other: and in this view, it may not be improper to take up here the consideration of some general principles, on which the business of money and a currency depends.

SILVER, *by the general consent of mankind, has become a* DEPOSITE, *which is,* THE COMMON MEASURE *of commerce.* This is a general effect of some general cause. The experience of its degree of scarceness compared with its common introduction amidst men, together with the facility of its being known by its visible and palpable properties, hath given this effect: Its degree of scarceness hath given it a value proportioned to the making it a DEPOSITE, and the certain quantity in which this is mixed with the possessions and transactions of man, together with the facility of its being known, makes it a COMMON MEASURE amongst those things. There are perhaps other things which might be better applied to commerce as a common measure, and there are perhaps other things which might better answer as a deposite; but there is nothing except silver known and acknowledged by the general experience of mankind, which is a deposite and common measure of commerce. Paper, leather, or, parchment, may, by the sanction of government, become a common measure to an extent beyond what silver could reach; yet all
the

the fanction and power of government never will make it an adequate depofite. Diamonds, pearls, or other jewels, may in many cafes be confidered as a more apt and fuitable depofite, and may be applied as fuch, to an extent to which filver will not reach; yet their fcarcity tends to throw them into a monopoly; they cannot be fubdivided, nor amaffed into one concrete, and the knowledge of them is more calculated for a myftery or trade, than for the forenfic ufes of man in common, and they will never therefore become a common meafure.

This truth eftablifhed and rightly underftood, it will be feen that that ftate of trade in the colonies is the beft, and that adminiftration of the colonies the wifeft, which tends to introduce this only true and real currency amongft them. And in this view I muft wifh to fee the Spanifh filver flowing into our colonies, with an ample and uninterrupted ftream, as I know that that ftream, after it hath watered and fupplyed the regions which it paffeth through, muft, like every other ftream, pay its tribute to its mother ocean : As this filver, to fpeak without a metaphor, after it hath paffed through the various ufes of it in the colonies, doth always come to, and center finally in Great Britain.
The

The proportion of this meafure, by the general application of it to feveral different commodities, in different places and circumftances, forms *its own fcale.* This fcale arifes from the effect of natural operations, and not from *artificial impofition:* If therefore filver was never ufed but by the merchant, as the general meafure of his commerce and exchange, coin would be (as it is in fuch cafe) of no ufe; it would be confidered as bullion only. Although bullion is thus fufficient for the meafure of general commerce, yet for the daily ufes of the market fomething more is wanted in the detail; fomething is wanted to mark to common judgment its proportion, and to give the fcale: Government therefore, here interpofes, and by forming it into coin *gives the fcale,* and makes it become to forenfic ufe AN INSTRUMENT in detail, as well as it is in bullion a MEASURE in general.

This *artificial marking* of this fcale on a *natural meafure,* is neither more nor lefs than marking on any other rule or meafure, the graduate proportions of it: And this artificial marking of the fcale, or graduating the meafure is of no ufe but in detail, and extends not beyond the market;—for exchange reftores it again in commerce. No artificial ftandard therefore can be impofed. Having

Having this idea of money and coin, I could never comprehend to what general ufes, or to what purpofes of government, the proclamation which Queen Ann iffued, and which was confirmed by ftatute in the fixth year of her reign, could be fuppofed to extend, while it endeavoured to rate the foreign coins current in the colonies by an artificial ftandard. It would feem to me juft as wife, and anfwering to juft as good purpofe, if government fhould now iffue a proclamation, directing, that for the future, all black horfes in the colonies fhould be called white, and all brindled cows called red. The making even a law to alter the names of things, will never alter the nature of thofe things; and will never have any other effect, than that of introducing confufion, and of giving an opportunity to bad men of profiting by that confufion.

The fafeft and wifeft meafure which government can take, is not to difcourage or obftruct that channel through which filver flows into the colonies,—nor to interfere with that value which it acquires there;—but only fo to regulate the colony trade, that that filver fhall finally come to, and center in Great Britain, whither it will moft certainly come in its true value;—but if through any fatality in things or meafures, a medium of trade,

a cura currency of money, fhould grow defective in the colonies, the wifdom of government will then interpofe, either to remedy the caufe which occafions fuch defect, or to contrive the means of fupplying the deficiency. The remedy lies in a certain addrefs in carrying into execution the act of navigation;—but if that remedy is neglected, the next recourfe muft lie in fome means of maintaining a currency fpecially appropriated to the colonies, and muft be partly fuch as will keep a certain quantity of filver coin in circulation there,—and partly fuch as fhall eftablifh *a paper currency*, holding a value nearly equal to filver.

On the firft view of thefe refources, it will be matter of ferious confideration, whether government fhould eftablifh a mint and coinage fpecially appropriated for the ufe of the colonies; and on what bafis this fhould be eftablifhed. If it be neceffary that filver, which in bullion is a common meafure of general commerce, fhould, that it may be inftrumental alfo to the common ufes of the market, be formed into coin, it fhould be fo formed, that while it was the duty of the public to form this coin, it may not be the intereft of the individual to melt it down again into bullion.

If a certain quantity of coin is neceffary for the forenfic ufes of the colonies, it fhould be fo formed as *in no ordinary courfe* of bufinefs to become the intereft of the merchant to export it from thence.

This coin fhould be graduated by alloy, fomewhat below the real fcale, fo as to bear a value in tale, fomewhat better than the filver it contains would fetch after the expence of melting down the coin into bullion,—fomewhat better *as an inftrument*, in common forenfic ufe, than the merchant *in ordinary cafes* could make of it, in applying it *as a meafure* by exporting it.

I have here inferted the caution againft ordinary cafes only, as I am not unaware that the lowering the intrinfic worth of the coin for America, will have in the end no other effect, than to raife the price of the European goods carried thither, while the coin will be exported to Great Britain the fame as if it were pure filver.

If fuch a neceffity of an artificial currency fhould ever exift in the colonies, and if fuch a coinage waseftablifhed, the Colonifts would, for the purpofes of their forenfic bufinefs, purchafe *this inftrument* either in gold or
filver

filver, in the fame manner as they do now, purchafe copper coin for the fame purpofes.

There are two ideas of *a paper currency*. The one adopts a meafure for eftablifhing a bank in the colonies, which is quite a new and untried meafure; the other turns the view to the regulating the prefent paper money currency, which the colonies have had experience of in all its deviations, and to the eftablifhing the fame on a fure and fufficient bafis.

I have feen this plan for *a provincial bank*, and think it juftice to the very knowing perfon who formed it, to fay, that it muft be becaufe I do not underftand it, that many objections arife in my mind to it. Whenever he fhall think fit to produce it, it will come forth clear of all objections, with that force of conviction with which truth always flows from a mind in full and perfect poffeffion of it.

In the mean while, I will recommend to the confideration of thofe who take a lead in bufinefs, a meafure devifed and adminiftered by an American affembly.—And I will venture to fay, that there never was a wifer or a better meafure, never one better calculated to ferve the ufes of an encreafing country, that

that there never was a meafure more fteadily purfued, or more faithfully executed, for forty years together, than the loan-office in Penfylvania; formed and adminiftered by the Affembly of that province.

An encreafing country of fettlers and traders muft alway have the balance of trade againft them, for this very reafon, becaufe they are encreafing and improving, becaufe they muft be continually wanting further fupplies which their prefent circumftances will neither furnifh nor pay for:—And for this very reafon alfo, they muft alway labour under a decreafing filver currency, though their circumftances require an encreafing one. In the common curfory view of things, our politicians, both theorifts and practitioners, are apt to think, that a country which has the balance of trade againft it, and is continually drained of its filver currency, muft be in a declining ftate; but here we may fee that the progreffive improvements of a commercial country of fettlers, muft neceffarily have the balance of trade againft them, and a decreafing filver currency; that their continual want of money and other materials to carry on their trade and bufinefs muft engage them in debt—But that thofe very things applied to their improvements, will in return not only pay thofe debts, but
create

create alfo a furplus to be ftill carried forward to further and further improvements.
In a country under fuch circumftances, money lent upon intereft to fettlers, creates
money. Paper money thus lent upon intereft
will create gold and filver in principal, *while
the intereft becomes a revenue that pays the
charges of government.* This currency is the
true Pactolian ftream which converts all into
gold that is wafhed by it. It is on this principle that the wifdom and virtue of the affembly of Penfilvania eftablifhed, under the
fanction of government, an office for the
emiffion of paper money by loan.

Some matters which were intended to
have been inferted here, are fufpended for
the prefent, for reafons which* I hope
may lead to more public benefit, than the
making them public in this work could do.
—I proceed therefore to the confideration of
the ordinary mode of making paper-money,
by the legiflatures of the colonies iffuing
government-notes, payable at a certain period
by a tax. It may be ufeful to give fome defcription of this, and to point out fuch regulations as will become neceffary in this cafe.

This paper-money confifts of promiffory
notes, iffued by the authority of the legiflature of each province, deriving its value from
being

being payable at a certain period, by monies arising from a tax proportioned to that payment at the time fixed. These notes pass as lawful money, and have been hitherto a legal tender in each respective province where they are issued.

As any limitation of the USES of these notes as a currency, must proportionably decrease its value; as any insecurity, insufficiency, or uncertainty in the FUND, which is to pay off these notes, must decrease their value; as any QUANTITY emitted more than the necessities of such province calls for as a medium, must also decrease its value; it is a direct and palpable injustice, that that medium or currency which has depreciated by any of these means from its *real value*, should continue *a legal tender at its nominal value*.

The outrageous abuses practised by some of those legislatures who have dealt in the manufacture of this depreciating currency, and the great injury which the merchant and fair dealer have suffered by this fraudulent medium, occasioned the interposition of parliament to become necessary :— Parliament very properly interposed, by applying the only adequate and efficient remedy, namely, by prohibiting these colony legislatures from being able to make the paper

cur-

currency *a legal tender*. And government has lately for the fame prudent reafons made this prohibition general to the whole of the colonies. For, *when this paper-money cannot be forced in payment as a legal tender*, this very circumftance will oblige that legiflature which creates it, to form it of fuch internal right conftitution, as fhall force its own way by its own intrinfic worth on a level nearly equal to filver. The legiflature muft fo frame and regulate it as to give it *a real value*.

Thefe regulations all turn upon *the fufficiency and certainty of the* FUND, *the extent of the* USES, and the proportioning the QUANTITY to the actual and real neceffities which require fuch a medium.

The FUND fhould at leaft be equal to the payment of the principal *in a limited time*; and that time fhould be certainly fo fixed, as that the legiflature itfelf could not alter it. Where the paper currency is treafurer's notes given for fpecie actually lent to government, the fund whereon it is borrowed fhould be alfo capable of paying, *ad interim*, a certain intereft, as is the cafe of treafurer's notes in the province Maffachufetts-Bay.

This medium ought to be applicable to all the equitable as well as legal USES of filver money

money within the colony or province, except that of being a legal tender.

The QUANTITY ought always to be proportioned to the neceffity of the medium wanted; which (the *fund and ufes* being fairly and abfolutely fixed) may always be judged of by the rife or fall of the *value* in its general currency or exchange: for where the quantity iffued is more than neceffity requires, the value will depreciate: and where the fund is good, and all proper ufes of the medium fecured, fo long as no more paper is iffued than neceffity does require, it will always hold a value near to, though fomewhat lefs than filver. On this fubject I here refer the reader to the following very judicious tract, written and given to me, feveral years ago, by *Tench Francis*, Efq; late attorney-general of the province of Penfylvania, converfant in thefe matters, both as a lawyer and a merchant. I print and publifh it by leave of a near relation, and fubjoin it as containing the moft exact and decifive fentiments on this fubject that I have any where met with. I entitle it, CONSIDERATIONS ON A PAPER-CURRENCY.

ALL value is given to things for their fitnefs or power to anfwer or procure the neceffary

ceffary conveniencies or pleafures of human life.

This value may be confidered as abfolute or relative. Abfolute value terminates in our efteem of any thing, without referring to any other; relative is that which it has compared with another. The latter only I fhall have occafion to treat of.

Men have power to difcover qualities in a thing, which fhall give it value. They can by laws, cuftoms, or fafhions, greatly increafe that value; yet, to know or fix its worth or price, compared with other things *à priori*, has always been found beyond their reach and capacity.

This is owing to an inability to forefee, eftimate, and govern exactly all the points and circumftances, on which the value of things turns, which are fuch as are in, or follow the nature and order of things in general, and then may be forefeen and judged of with fome certainty; or which confift of the paffions, prejudices, and mifapprehenfions of mankind, whofe number and influences we cannot rate or calculate.

From the *natural* ftate and order of things, I think it may be affirmed, that the worth

or

or price of any thing will always be, as the quantity and ufes amongft mankind; as the ufes directly, and as the quantity reciprocally or inverfely. Ufe is the fole caufe of value, and value the neceffary effect of ufe. Abating thefe diftinctions of caufe and effect, ufelefs and worthlefs, are fynonymous terms. Every man muft agree, that if you add to a caufe, you muft increafe the effect; fubftract from it, and the contrary effect muft follow. Let the quantity of any thing be as 20, and the ufes as 20, and let it have a value; let the ufes be increafed to 30, without inlarging the quantity; it is plain, the equal proportion that every man can enjoy will be as 20 divided by 30, $\frac{2}{3}$ds only. But this being lefs by $\frac{1}{3}$ than each man requires, the demand for it, and confequently the value muft rife. Subftract 10 from the ufes when 20, and then under an equal diftribution, each fhall have double the value he wants, which muft leffen the demand, and the value dependent upon it.

Governing the ufes is one of the rational powers, that men have over the value of things.

Experience teaches the meaneft underftanding, that price depends on quantity; and that they are to each other inverfely, or the
more

more of one the lefs the other. Water is as neceffary as any thing, and a diamond perhaps as little; yet the fuperfluous plenty of one has rendered it of no worth in moft places, and the fcarcity of the other has carried it to an extravagant price.

Limiting the quantity is another rational power men have over the value of things; and I do not know a third.

From hence it appears, that increafing the ufes, and leffening the quantity, and leffening the ufes, and increafing the quantity, muft always have the fame influence upon the rates and prices of things. Therefore, whenever I fhew the effect of one, for brevity's fake, let it be underftood, that I fuppofe the fame confequence will attend the other refpectively.

Although I affirm, that variation in quantity or ufe fhall caufe a change in the price of a thing, yet I do not fay, that this change fhall be in proportion equal to the variation in the quantity or ufe; for I think the contrary. To inftance in quantity, let it be in any thing as 30, and let the ufe be as 30, and it fhall then have a mean value. The ufe unchanged, let the quantity be at one time as 20, at another 40. Whoever confiders

fiders the prevalence of men's appetites for a scarce commodity, under the dreads and apprehensions of wanting it, with their different abilities to procure it, on one hand, and their great contempt of useless excess on the other, must agree it is more than probable, that the difference between the means and the extremes shall not be the same in the prices, as in the quantities. Merchants, by experience, have found the truth of what I advance. I think they have observed, that lessening a commodity one third from the mean quantity, *cæteris paribus*, nearly doubles the value ; adding a third, substracts one half from it ; and that by further increasing or diminishing the quantity, these disproportions between the quantity and prices vastly increase.

It is extremely difficult, if not impossible, to investigate these proportions mathematically ; but events springing from use and experience have equal certainty in them, and to all practical purposes are as much to be relied and depended upon.

It is further worth observation, that whatever fluctuates much in quantity, and consequently in worth, will sink beneath its mean value.

Suppose

Suppose the quantity of any thing produced in every 50 years be exactly the same: let the annual product be as *one* answerable to the necessities of mankind, then the value in each year shall be as one, and the whole equal to 50. But if the quantity of the annual product fluctuates, there will be annual fluctuations in the value; but as the proportions of the decrease of value, from experience above stated, will be greater than the proportions of the increase of value, this fluctuation will cause a deficiency in the mean value, which deficiency will always be in proportion to the greatness and quickness of the changes. This, I presume, is occasioned by the desire of mankind in general to rest on certainty, rather than rely on what is fluctuating and inconstant, though they should expect gain equal to the risque, and by the low circumstances of the majority of men, whose fortunes, in all prudence, direct to the first, rather than the latter. The case of insurances is an evident proof of this remark. If the insurers gain, which I think must be admitted, then they receive a premium beyond the value of the risque, and this gain the insured pay for *certainty* against *contingent losses.*

These few rules of estimating the value of things, well applied, will, I presume,
shew

ſhew when it is convenient to introduce paper-money into a country, and when it will prove hurtful; what are its advantages and inconveniencies, general and particular, when introduced; of what great importance it is to prevent an exceſs in quantity, and to extend the uſes; and nearly what its value will be in any given ſtate.

If a nation has a quantity of money equal to its commerce, the lands, commodities, and labour of the people ſhall bear a middle price. This ſtate is the beſt, and tends moſt to enrich the people, and make their happineſs laſting. If they ſhould mint paper to paſs for money, the increaſe of quantity in the former will leſſen the value of the latter, will raiſe the price of lands and rents, and make the labour of ſuch a people, and the commodities, be *rated* higher than in other places. Men's fortunes will riſe in *nominal, not real value*; from whence idleneſs, expence and poverty ſhall follow. Under theſe circumſtances, their *real money*, inſtead of their commodities, ſhall be exported from them. Here the paper will be their bane and deſtruction. But if their commerce, or uſes of money, exceed the quantity of it, their lands, labour, and commodities ſhall ſink beneath their worth in other countries. Few purchaſers of lands will be found

found in regard to the superior profit that must attend the use of money in trade: the *wealthy merchant shall be at the head of affairs,* with few competitions; he shall be able to grind down the farmer in the sale of his commodities, and, when those fail to support him, in the purchase of his lands. The artisan's labour shall be depreciated by the merchant who exports it, or the needy farmer that uses it. The wealthy only shall accumulate riches, the commonwealth shall decline, and in time farmers and artisans must desert the place for another, where their labour shall be better rewarded. Here the use of paper-money will shake off the fetters and clogs of the poor. Merchants will multiply; they will raise the price of labour, and of the fruits of the earth, and thereby the value of lands. An equal distribution of gain and profit shall succeed, and destroy the partial accumulations of wealth.

I think these marks, taken from the value of lands, labour, and commodities, compared with their worth in other countries, will be found the only infallible rules to judge of an equality, excess, or defect of money in any place wheresoever; and consequently will, at all times, unerringly shew the necessity of increasing coins, or the contrary. Had a neighbouring province well understood

ahd

and weighed thefe points, they had not created a paper credit far exceeding all their ufes for money, when they were able to fupply themfelves with gold equal to their trade, nor at the fame time have dammed up fo many ufes for it, which now cover them with clouds and confufion, that no man can fee his way through. The beft method they can ufe is to fink it as faft as poffible, and not let their fund lie in Britain at an intereft lefs than 4 *per cent.* when it is worth 6 in their own country, and their paper paffes 50 *per cent.* lefs than the nominal value. But to return : when it is found neceffary to add *paper-money* to the coin of any country, to fupport its value ought to be the main and principal view. This will turn upon the FUND, the USES, and the QUANTITY.

All value arifing from the ufe, I beg leave to call *extrinfick.*

Having fhewn that paper-money acquires its extrinfic value from the ufes, which ufes apparently may be encreafed or diminifhed; I think it would be needlefs and mifpending the reader's time, to demonftrate, that this value muft be in direct proportion to the ufes ; for it would really amount to no more than the proof of an axiom univerfally acknowledged, that the effect fhall always be

adequate

adequate to the caufe. Therefore, in all future arguments, I fhall take it for granted.

The fund ought to be as fatisfactory to mankind as human wifdom can devife and furnifh.

The community fhould become fecurity to anfwer all deficiencies in the FUND ; this is not only the higheft juftice, but the beft policy. It is juft, becaufe it is a creature of their own, calculated for their private utility and advantage, and is in the management of the country by their reprefentatives and officers. But when they receive an intereft from the money, the equity of it is unanfwerable : for it feems wholly inconfiftent with juftice, that one fhould receive the intereft, and another run the rifque of the principal. Policy requires it, becaufe the community will certainly receive more profit from its credit under their fupport, than, with due caution, they can probably lofe by accidents in the fund.

Our next confideration, with refpect to the value, turns on *what* the fund is to pay, and *when*. Thefe are arbitrary, being within the power of thofe by whofe authority the money is emitted. But for the prefent purpofe : let us fuppofe it is to pay filver money, according

according to the late Queen's proclamation, to the value of 1000 *l.* for fo much of the paper, as, according to the *nominal value,* amounts to that fum at the end of 15 years. In this ftate the 1000 *l.* paper, *with regard to the fund alone,* at the time of its emiffion, is worth no more proclamation money than what will produce 1000 *l.* of that money at the end of the term, at compound intereft, under as good fecurity.

For example, take a 1000 *l.* paper, and let it reprefent that the poffeffor fhall receive 1000 *l.* proclamation money for it at the end of 15 years, and let the ufe of money be worth 6 *per cent. per annum*; rebate 6 *per cent. per annum* with compound intereft for 15 years, and you have the value of the 1000 *l.* proclamation money in hand, which appears to be but 417 *l.* 5 *s.* 3½; more it cannot be worth, becaufe 417 *l.* 5 *s.* 3½, with 6 *per cent. per annum* compound intereft for 15 years added, will amount to 1000 *l.*

On this ftate it appears, that the longer the term, the lefs the value, with regard to the fund alone. From whence it follows, that by increafing the term, this value may be reduced to a degree beneath eftimation. But whatever the value thus proved be, I call it *intrinfick.*

The

The FUND eſtabliſhed, I proceed to the USES as they next require our attention in regard to the value of the paper-money.

If value, in reſpect to the uſes of things, ſhall always be in direct proportion to thoſe uſes, (which I preſume I have heretofore proved in general, and ſhall hereafter ſhew is true in relation to paper-money) and we deſign to raiſe the power, it follows clearly, that to bring this to paſs, we ought to give it all the uſes of money, or coined gold and ſilver in other countries. From theſe uſes alone it muſt derive all the worth it ſhall bear beyond what I called the *intrinſick* value. For the purpoſe *take the caſe ſtated* on the Fund only, that the poſſeſſor of 1000 *l.* paper ſhall receive 1000 *l.* proclamation money in exchange for it, at the end of 15 years. On this account the paper appeared to be worth but 417 *l.* 15 *s.* 3$\frac{1}{2}$. But ſuppoſe this 1000 *l.* paper may be immediately exchanged for 800 *l.* proclamation money, which is 382 *l.* 14 *s.* 8$\frac{1}{2}$ more than the intrinſick worth, how has it acquired this exceeding price or value? I think plainly from the uſes. To prove the truth of this, ſuppoſe all the uſes as money taken away; unqueſtionably then the worth of 1000 *l.* paper in proclamation money will be reduced to what I call the intrinſick value; becauſe, depending upon the

the fund alone, it will be exactly in the state of a fund to be paid at a future day; for in neither case can the creditor use it in the mean time. But if the creditor can by any contrivance use the sum in that time, as he may the paper when it passes for money, that use must be something worth. And when experience shews, that under this use the value advances from 417 *l.* 15*s.* 3¼ to 800 *l.* I apprehend it is evident to a demonstration, that the difference is derived from the use. To deny it must be as irrational and absurd, as if, upon adding and extracting an ingredient to and from a composition, we perceived properties in the composition appear and disappear, and yet were to deny that such ingredient was the cause of those properties. This leads me to attempt the solution of a question I have known frequently made. If we in Pensylvania, upon a sufficient fund answerable in silver, at a future day, mint a quantity of paper equal to the uses of the people for money, and they willingly and universally accept of the paper in all payments, why should it not, at all times, have *value* equal *to the nominal value,* or to the sum chargeable on the fund at the day to come. This reason, urged by many, to support the paper to this degree, is drawn from the nature of money in general. Money, say they, is but a ticket or counter, which represents to the mind of the possessor

a quana quantity or degree of power. No man, on the receipt of it, ever examines how, or from whence it acquired that power, but in order to difcover its reality and duration. For inftance, when an Englifh crown is received, does the acceptor regard any properties in the metal, or the figures of it, but thofe which are to convince him that it is what it appears to be? a crown. It muft be confeffed, he does not. If fo, then why may not a piece of paper, under diftinguifhing characters and impreffions, affixed by law and common confent, have the power of an Englifh crown annexed to it? It is to pafs in the fame manner as a crown does, and in the end will as certainly be a crown as the real one.

Therefore they conclude, that the paper may, and ought at all times, to be efteemed equal to the quantity of filver the fund is to yield for it at the end of the term.

I confefs I think this reafoning fair, and the conclufion juft and fatisfactory, if we do not ufe filver in our *commerce, foreign or domeftick:* otherwife not. The fact is, we do ufe filver *in our foreign commerce.* I prefume it will be eafily admitted, as the paper reprefents the filver in the fund, and from thence obtains its credit, that it fhall always
be

be at leaft of equal ufe with, or be as readily received as paper. Then if filver in hand has one power, *one ufe more* than the paper, to wit, that of procuring foreign commodities, it is impofiible we can efteem them equally. For that would be to controul the different virtues and influences of things over the mind of man, which neceffarily depending upon the things themfelves, no laws or confent can, by any means, vary or direct. Wherefore, in the cafe ftated, it feems to me certain and undeniable, that the paper muft have lefs worth than the filver.

Having faid, that the ufes of the paper fhould be as many as poffible, it may be proper for me to fpeak of fome of thofe ufes, the equity and advantage of which have been very much controverted. But here let it be underftood, that I proceed upon the cafe laft ftated, that the quantity of paper is to be equal to all the ufes of money *within* the country. For that ftate, and a partial fupply of paper credit, differing in principles, requiring different reafoning, and infer quite oppofite confequences.

Firft, then, it feems juft and reafonable to compel all perfons contracting for filver money, after the law that raifes the paper money to be paid in the country, to receive
                                                    the

the paper in lieu of it, and at the value ftruck, from the fund, although that be inferior to the real value. This perhaps may not be. ftrict equity *between the contracting parties,* but it is juft *from the community;* who have power from the confent of every member, by laws, to prohibit the exercife of a particular natural right inconfiftent with the welfare of the whole, and to inflict a penalty upon difobedience to the law. To ufe filver or gold with the paper, muft depreciate the latter. Therefore the law forbids it. This can't be unfair, becaufe every man has notice of what coin he is to be paid in, and *is not obliged to exchange more* for the, paper, than he thinks agreeable to the *real worth.* And if any fhould endeavour fuch ufe, the lofs of the difference between gold or filver and paper, is a kind of penalty for violating the law, which muft be as juft as any other penalty impofed on an act, *not evil in itfelf, but prohibited* only.

Again, upon breach of contracts for payment of money in foreign countries, I think it both convenient and right, that fatisfaction fhould be made in the paper. The convenience of it will appear, if we fuppofe the debtor a member of the fociety amongft whom the paper paffes; for as fuch, being reftrained by law from trafficking for gold

or silver, and thereby difabled from procuring them, he muft either pay paper in
compenfation, or lie in a goal, if the feverity
of his creditors requires it. In thefe circumftances, no man in his fenfes would dare to
contract a foreign debt, or transfer foreign
money in the ufual manner, by exchange;
the bad confequences of which are too numerous and obvious to admit of, or need
particular mention, and evidently prove the
convenience of allowing fatisfaction to be
made in paper.

The equity of this fatisfaction will be in-
difputable, if the debtor pays a fum of paper
really of equal value with the foreign money. It is the common cafe on breach of
fpecifick contract. If it cannot be performed, the moft exact juftice requires no more
than *an equivalent compenfation.*

Some perfons imagining the real worth of
the paper equal to the nominal, have affirmed, that it ought to difcharge thefe debts
at the nominal value; others confeffing a
difference between thefe values, under fome
political views, have afferted the fame. As
I fhall have occafion to fpeak on thefe opinions hereafter, upon a point fimilar to this
I fhall only add here, that if this mode of
payment fhould take place, it would as effectually

fectually deſtroy foreign credit and negoci-
ations by exchange, as if gold or ſilver were
to be inſiſted on here, to diſcharge a foreign debt. In one caſe, it would be the
higheſt imprudence to be the debtor, in
the other, it muſt be equally indiſcreet to
become a creditor.

Purſuing the uſes, I come to that of diſ-
charging by paper, the ſilver debts contracted antecedent to the law that raiſes the
paper.

To ſhew the neceſſity of admitting this,
I ſuppoſe it will be granted me, that there
muſt at all times be a very great number
of debtors who depend on their future labour and induſtry to pay their debts. This
dependence is reaſonable and juſt, founded
on the natural right of all fairly to purchaſe
ſilver, the then current money of the country. The debtor has the continuation of
this right in view and expectation at the time
of his contract; without it he cannot be ſuppoſed either prudent or honeſt to borrow.
If then, for the convenience and advantage
of the whole ſociety, this right muſt be taken away by a ſubſequent law which he
could not foreſee, it cannot be agreeable either to reaſon or good conſcience, to exact
a payment in ſpecie; for that would be requiring

quiring a performance when we had exprefsly taken away the means. Therefore I
think it clear in refpect to the debtor, that
the paper fhould have this ufe. But how
will this ftand with the right of the creditor,
who upon the contract as certainly expected
to be paid filver, as the debtor did the opportunity of acquiring it to pay.

I prefume, if he receives as much paper
as fhall be equal in power or value to the
filver, it will be juft in itfelf, and perfectly
fatisfactory to him. But can any man offer
fo high a degree of violence to his own
reafon, and the underftanding of others, as
to affirm, if he is forced to accept lefs, that
ftill he has juftice difpenfed him. If I borrow 100*l.* in filver before the law, under
agreement to repay it at the end of the en-
fuing year, and before the day of payment
the law takes place, commanding the lender
to receive 100*l.* paper for it, which fhall be
worth, or have power to procure 82*l.* filver
money only; with truth can this be called
a rational or upright law? Certainly no.
Nor fhall it be any juftification to me in
confcience to detain 18*l.* of my creditor's
money.

The rules of natural juftice flowing from
our fixed and unchangeable relations to each
other,

other, and the invariable nature and order
of things, inforced by the exprefs commands of God, are of eternal and indifpen-
fible obligation, No laws, no combinations of human power, cuftoms, ufages, or
practice, can controul or change them. We
may, by the confent of a majority, tie up
the compulfory hand of the civil magiftrate,
and thereby diffolve the power of coercive
laws, but can no more abfolve from the moral duty, than we can reverfe decrees in-
rolled in heaven. If my debtor fhould be
fo extremely weak, as to fuppofe this not
criminal becaufe it is legal, (which I think
next to impoffible to imagine of a rational
creature, and I make bold to affirm, never
was the cafe of a creditor of underftanding,
fufficient to know the meafure of his demand) his opinion perhaps may ferve for
an excufe, or extenuation of his crime, but
never can prove the rectitude of the act, and
ftill the guilt muft reft fomewhere. The law-
makers, the authors of his miftake, are culpable, unlefs they are under the fame delufion, which is yet more difficult to apprehend. Some, who gave up the juftice of the
law, defend their practice under it, by faying, they are creditors as well as debtors:
and as they are obliged to receive, fo they
fhould have liberty to pay. Alas! what
feeble arguments fatisfy, when they are caft
into

into the fcale of intereft, and gain is the confequence of conviction. If the actions of men towards us are to be the meafures of our dealing with others, then he that is cheated by any perfon, may juftly plunder the next he meets. And truly I can't fee why it fhould ftop here; for as we may be many times defrauded, and not know it, to be fecure, and keep the ballance on the right fide, we fhould pillage our neighbours as often as an opportunity offers. This may feem fevere reafoning, but really I think it fair from the firft pofition; that becaufe one keeps back part of another's due, therefore he may honeftly detain the right of a third innocent perfon.

Again, paying an equivalent cannot be injurious to the debtor. For fuppofe he pays 120 *l.* paper. If 100 pounds worth of coin'd filver, reduced to bullion, will then yield him fo much, what does he more than perform his contract to pay 100 *l.* of coin'd filver? feeing a compleat recompence is perfectly confiftent with the right of each contracting party. Any remaining objections muft arife from its being hurtful or injurious to the fociety in general. This has been afferted, and endeavours have been ufed to fupport the truth of it, by this kind of reafoning.

Firft,

First, if the law fhould oblige the debtor (for the purpofe) to pay 120 *l.* paper in lieu of 100 *l.* filver, the legiflature would thereby confefs the inferior worth of the paper, which will be attended with this ill confequence, that the general current value of the paper fhall be lefs than if the law had declared it equal to filver.

Secondly, That leffening the current value will be a lofs to the fociety in general. To the firft, That obliging to pay a larger fum of paper for a lefs of filver, acknowledges an inequality of value under the like denominations is felf-evident. But from thence to infer, that the paper fhall pafs in general, at lefs value than if they had been declared equal, with fubmiffion, I think miftaken, and inconclufive reafoning.

To be clearly underftood, permit me to examine this upon the fact. Suppofe the law, in the ftrongeft terms, enacts that the paper fhall be in value equal to filver money, according to their feveral denominations. Carry the paper from thence to ufe, by offering it in exchange or payment for fome commodity, and then I afk a fhort queftion, Who it is that really fets a value on the paper, the legiflature, or the perfon that has the commodity to fell? If it be anfwered, the firft, then I fay, this cannot be, unlefs they alfo

alſo limit the price of the commodity. For
if the ſeller can raiſe and proportion the price
of it to what he thinks the real worth of the
paper, the law-maker's declaration notwithſtanding, it is he that ſtrikes the value, and
not they. For inſtance, put the caſe ; a
farmer, juſt upon emitting the paper, has a
buſhel of wheat to ſell, which he rates at,
and will not part with, under three ſilver
ſhillings. The future current worth of the
paper being unknown to him, let him by
gueſs imagine theſe three ſhillings equal to
four ſhillings paper. A purchaſer then
preſſes him, under the influence of the law,
to accept of three paper ſhillings for this
wheat; but he, without regard to the law,
according to his own opinion, demands and
receives four ſhillings for it. Will any man
ſay, the legiſlature determined the value of
the paper here? Apparently the ſeller did.
For the legiſlature commanded, that the three
paper ſhillings ſhould be valued at three of
ſilver, but the farmer has made his eſtimate
at three fourths of that value only. Unqueſtionably the vender muſt always have
this power, unleſs, as I ſaid before, the
law-makers can limit the price of all commodities, which is not practicable, conſiſtent with the order of things, or the preſervation of men's properties. But it may be
alledged, although the receiver of the money

ney is not bound to obferve the legiflative command, yet ftill it may have fome weight. He may confider it to be the impartial opinion of the wifeft part of the fociety, what the future current value of the paper fhall be, and thereby add, in fome degree, to its worth.

In anfwer I muft obferve, firft, this gives up the point of power, and changes it to a matter of meer advice. Then, fuppofing that of any import, furely delivering it in a mandatory way, will be very little able to produce the defired effect. Imperative advice (pardon the expreffion) favours too much of felling the rabbit, to prevail or perfuade. In fhort, the words command and advife, convey two ideas fo widely different, and fo oppofite and repugnant to each other, that it is abfolutely impoffible we fhould take the firft for the laft. But granting it to be interpreted as a piece of cordial advice. Shall it be received implicitly, and pafs without any examination? I prefume not. When it comes to be examined, if the people fhould be informed, that, upon a nice examination, the legiflature had found a fourth, fifth, or fixth difference between filver and paper, as fuch calculations are generally out of the reach and comprehenfion of moft people, it feems not improbable that the paper might pafs at
firft,

firſt, agreeable to the given difference. *I
ſay at firſt*; for I contend, if the calcula-
tion ſhould be erroneous, (which the uſe of
the money in time will diſcover) this effect
ſhall not be laſting. But if, on the contrary,
they learn that the paper, without any cal-
culation, by gueſs, was pronounced equal to
ſilver, which every man's judgment, who
knows the ſuperior power of the laſt, muſt
diſapprove of, what influence can the legiſlative advice then have? Undoubtedly it
will be univerſally rejected, and each perſon
turned at large to make his eſtimate as well
as he can, without the leaſt regard to the
legiſlative opinion.

Once more, take it, that the quantity of
ſilver in 100 ſhillings proclamation money
is now worth 120 paper ſhillings in Penſylvania, and ſuppoſe this requiſite had hitherto been omitted in all laws relating to the
paper: let the ſupreme authority to-day
enact, that from henceforth all perſons ſhall
give as much for 100 ſhillings paper as they
do now for that quantity of ſilver, would this
make the leaſt alteration in the current value
of the paper? Might a man, with reaſon,
expect to buy more bread or wine to-mor-
row with 100 paper ſhillings, than he can
to-day? if the legiſlative power can bring
this to paſs, perhaps it may prove more than
ſome

some people desire ; for I conjecture it will shew, that we never had any occasion for paper. Whatever quantity of silver we had amongst us, when the paper was struck, might have been extended in value proportionable to our wants, and all the business of paper-money done at once. The absurdity of this lies open to the meanest capacity ; yet I aver, that to raise the value of paper by authoritative words or commands, is equally irrational and unfeasible.

I know no just means whereby mankind can give value to things, but increasing or lessening the *uses* or *quantity*. The paper derives its *intrinsick worth from* THE FUND which is stable and fixed. The *uses* give it further value, but that shall always be in inverse proportion to the quantity. The quantity is absolutely under the direction of the legislature, but the uses not. As they are raised, so they must be limitted, by our necessities, and the disposition and order of things. The utmost the legislature can do, or is needful to be done, is to make the paper answer *all those uses*. When they have ascertained the FUND, the *uses* and *quantity*, their power expires. And the current value, if the people receive it, flows from them by so unavoidable and a necessary consequence, that whatever the legislature or others will

will or do, (if it alters not the fund, ufes, or quantity) can work no change in it in general. For a time, as long as people are ignorant, I confefs it may ; but when experience, that excellent miftrefs, has difclofed what worth they give, all imaginary value fhall ceafe and vanifh, and on the three requifites, as on a folid and firm foundation, it fhall ultimately reft and fettle.

I conclude what I have to fay on this point with a fhort obfervation. That all the attempts of affemblies in America in this way even by penalties on difobedience, have proved fruitlefs and abortive. And it has been extremely remarkable, that although tranfgreffing the law, by making a difference between filver and paper, has been every day's practice, not in fecret, but openly, I have never heard, that any perfon has been fo much as queftioned publickly, or has loft any degree of reputation privately for doing it. So far do the dictates of juft and right reafon furpafs and tranfcend the force and power of any human device or inftitution, that oppofes or contradicts them.

A LETTER FROM GOVERNOR POWNALL TO ADAM SMITH

Thomas Pownall, *A Letter from Governor Pownall to Adam Smith, L. L. D. F. R. S. being an examination of several points of doctrine, laid down in his 'Inquiry into the Nature and Causes of the Wealth of Nations'* (London, 1776), pp. 1–48.

This text is one of Pownall's most intriguing writings, as it provides a timely review of Adam Smith's *Wealth of Nations* (1776). *A Letter from Governor Pownall to Adam Smith* follows a popular contemporary style in its open examination of a variety of Smith's economic ideas, including the labour theory of value, market versus natural price, not to mention his views on trade and the colonies. In particular, Pownall explains what he perceived to be Smith's conclusion: that the advantages of colonies arise from the monopolisation of trade with the colonies, rather than from the expansion of available natural resources and the growing population.

A

L E T T E R

FROM

GOVERNOR POWNALL

TO

A D A M   S M I T H, L. L. D. F. R. S.

BEING AN

EXAMINATION OF SEVERAL POINTS OF DOCTRINE,

LAID DOWN IN HIS

"INQUIRY INTO THE NATURE AND CAUSES OF

THE WEALTH OF NATIONS."

L O N D O N:

Printed for J. ALMON, oppofite Burlington-houfe, in Piccadilly.

M DCC LXXVI.

A

L E T T E R, &c.

S I R,

WHEN I firſt ſaw the plan and ſuperſtructure of your very ingenious and very learned Treatiſe on the Wealth of Nations, it gave me a compleat idea of that ſyſtem, which I had long wiſhed to ſee the publick in poſſeſſion of. A ſyſtem, that might fix ſome firſt principles in the moſt important of ſciences, the knowledge of the human community, and its operations. That might become *principia* to the knowledge of politick operations; as Mathematicks are to Mechanicks, Aſtronomy, and the other Sciences.

Early in my life I had begun an analyſis, of *thoſe laws of motion* (if I may ſo expreſs myſelf) which are the ſource of, and give direction to, the labour of man in the individual; which form that reciprocation of wants and intercommunion of mutual ſupply that becomes *the creating cauſe of community*; which give energy, motion, and *that organized form* to the compound labour and operations of that community, *which is government*; which give ſource to trade and commerce, and are the forming cauſes of the inſtrument of it, *money*; of the effect of it in operation, an *influx of riches*, and of the final effect, *wealth and power*. The fate of that life called me off from ſtudy. I have however at times (never totally loſing fight of it) endeavoured to reſume this inveſtigation; but fearing that the want of exerciſe and habit in thoſe intellectual exertions may have rendered me unequal to the attempt, I am extremely happy to find this executed by abilities ſuperior to what I can pretend to, and to a point beyond that which the utmoſt range of my ſhot could have attained. Not having any perſonal knowledge of the author, or of the port which I now underſtand he bears in the learned world, I read your book without prejudice.—I ſaw it deſerved a more cloſe and attentive application, than the ſeaſon of buſineſs would allow me to give to it; I have ſince in the retreat of ſummer ſtudied it: you have, I find, by a truly philoſophic and patient analyſis, endeavoured to inveſtigate *analitically* thoſe principles, by which nature firſt moves and then conducts the operations of man in the individual, and in community: And then, next, by application of theſe principles to fact, experience, and the inſtitutions of men, you have endeavoured to deduce *ſynthetically,*

tically, by the moſt precice and meaſured ſteps of demonſtration, thoſe important doctrines of practice, which your very ſcientifick and learned book offers to
the conſideration of the world of buſineſs.

Viewing your book in this light, yet ſeeing, as my reaſoning leads me to
conceive, ſome deviations which have miſled your analyſis, ſome aberrations
from the exact line of demonſtration in the deductive part; and conſidering
any errors in a work of that authority, which the learning and knowledge
that abounds in yours muſt always give, as the moſt dangerous, and the
more ſo, as they tend to mix themſelves in with the reaſoning and conduct of
men, not of ſpeculation, but of buſineſs—I have taken the liberty, by ſtating
my doubts to you in this Letter, to recommend a reviſion of thoſe parts which
I think exceptionable.

If theſe doubts ſhould appear to you to contain any matter of real objection, I ſhould hope thoſe parts might be corrected, or that the bad conſequences of thoſe poſitions, which I conceive to be dangerous, may be obvia-
ted. When I firſt wrote theſe obſervations, I meant to have ſent them to
you, by the interpoſition of a common friend, in a private letter; but, as I
think theſe ſubjects deſerve a fair, full, and publick diſcuſſion, and as there
are now in the world of buſineſs many very ingenious men, who have turned
their minds to theſe ſpeculations, the making this publick may perhaps excite their ingenuity, and thus become the means of eliciting truth in the moſt
important of all ſciences. It may animate even your ſpirit of inquiry, and
lead to further reſearches. It is not in the ſpirit of controverſy, which I both
deteſt and deſpiſe, but in that of fair diſcuſſion that I addreſs this to you.

When, in your inveſtigation of thoſe ſprings, which give motion, direction,
and diviſion to labour *—you ſtate " *a propenſity to barter;*" as the cauſe of
this diviſion: when you † ſay, " that it is that trucking buſineſs which *originally*
" gives occaſion to the diviſion of labour;" I think you have ſtopped ſhort in
your analyſis before you have arrived at the firſt natural cauſe and principle of
the diviſion of labour. You do indeed ‡ doubt, " whether this propenſity
" be one of thoſe *original principles* in human nature, of which no farther ac-
" count can be given; or whether, as ſeems more probable, it be the neceſ-
" ſary conſequence of the faculties of reaſon and ſpeech." Before a man can
have the propenſity to barter, he muſt have acquired ſomewhat, which he does
not want himſelf, and muſt feel, that there is ſomething which he does want,
that another perſon has in his way acquired; a man has not a propenſity to
acquire, eſpecially by labour, either the thing which he does not want, or
more than he wants, even of neceſſaries; and yet nature ſo works in him,
he is ſo made, that his labour, in the ordinary courſe of it, furniſhes him in
the line in which he labours, with more than he wants; but while his labour
is confined in that particular line, he is deprived of the opportunity to ſupply
himſelf

---

* B. I. C. II.   † P. 18.   ‡ P. 16.

himſelf with ſome other articles equally neceſſary to him, as that which he is in the act of acquiring. As it is with one man, ſo is it with the next, with every individual, and with all. Nature has ſo formed us, as that the labour of each muſt take one ſpecial direction, in preference to, and to the excluſion of ſome other equally neceſſary line of labour, by which direction of his labour, he will be but partially and imperfectly ſupplied. Yet while each take a different line of labour, the channels of all are abundantly ſupplied.

Man's wants and deſires require to be ſupplied through many channels; his labour will more than ſupply him in ſome one or more; but through the limitation and the defined direction of his capacities he cannot actuate them all. This limitation, however, of his capacities, and the extent of his wants, neceſſarily creates to each man an accumulation of ſome articles of ſupply, and a defect of others, and is the original principle of his nature, which creates, by a reciprocation of wants, the neceſſity of an intercommunion of mutual ſupplies; this is the forming cauſe, not only of the diviſion of labour, but the efficient cauſe of that community, which is the baſis and origin of civil government; for, by neceſſarily creating an inequality of accumulation, and a conſequential ſubordination of claſſes and orders of men, it puts the community under that form, and that organization of powers, which is government. It is this principle, which, operating by a reciprocation of wants in nature, as well as in man, becomes alſo the ſource to that intercommunion of ſupplies, which barter, trade, and general commerce, in the progreſs of ſociety, give. It is not in the voluntary deſires, much leſs in a capricious " *propenſity to barter*," that this firſt principle of community reſides; it is not a conſequence of reaſon and ſpeech actuating this propenſity, it is interwoven with the eſſence of our nature, and is there in the progreſs of, and as part of that nature, the creating and efficient cauſe of government; of government as *the true ſtate of nature* to man, not as an artificial ſuccedaneum to an imagined theoretic ſtate of nature.

The purſuing of the Analyſis up to this *firſt principle*, does not immediately, I agree with you, " belong to the ſubject of your inquiries;" for the doctrine contained in the ſecond chapter of your firſt book, ſeems only noted *en paſſant*, but is no where, either in the courſe of your Analyſis, uſed, nor applied in the ſubſequent explications. But as ſome thirty years ago, I had made this Analyſis of the * *Principles of Polity*; and as I have, in the practical adminiſtration of the powers of government, found, that thoſe powers on one hand do, as from the trueſt ſource, derive from theſe principles of nature, and

---

* A little Treatiſe which I wrote when I was very young, and which is very imperfect and incorrect in its manner and compoſition; but ſuch in the matter and reaſoning, as frequent reviſion and application of the principles to matters in fact, have confirmed me in the conviction of as true, although different from the common train of reaſoning in thoſe who follow Mr. Locke's phraſes rather than his arguments.

that

that the liberties of mankind are moſt ſafely eſtabliſhed on them: and as I think that great danger may ariſe to both, in deriving the ſource of community and government from paſſions or caprice, creating by will an artificial ſuccedaneum to nature, I could not but in the ſame manner, *en paſſant*, make this curſory remark.

Having eſtabliſhed and defined this firſt operation of man in community, that of *barter*, you proceed to conſider the *natural rules* by which this is conducted; what it is which gives *value*; what it is which *meaſures* the relative or *comparative value*, and hence the doctrine of *price*: and by the intervention of theſe, *the introduction of money and coin*. As in the former doctrine, I thought you had not purſued the analyſis to the real ſources of nature; ſo here, on the contrary, I think you have ſtretched your doctrine beyond the garb of nature. Some of your more refined doctrines have rather ſubtiliſed ideas, as they lie in your mind, than analiſed thoſe diſtinctions which lie in nature. On the firſt reading the eight firſt chapters of your firſt book, in which theſe matters are treated of, before I came to the uſe and application of your doctrines in the explication of practice and buſineſs, I began to apprehend, that ſome dangerous conſequences in practice might be deduced from theory, inſtead of thoſe ſound and beneficial doctrines which derive through experience, by a true analyſis of nature and her principles. I thought I ſaw, that many miſchievous impertinent meddlings might take riſe from a diſtinction between *a natural* and *a market price*. As I had been uſed to hold that only to be the meaſure of exchangeable value, which the world generally takes and uſes as ſuch, money formed of the precious metals; I could not but apprehend, that many extenſively dangerous practices might ariſe from your laying aſide, in your Analyſis of Money, the idea of its being A DEPOSIT. I ſaw, that that *theory in metaphyſicks*, led to a deſtructive *practice in phyſicks*; to the practice of creating a *circulation of paper*, and of calling ſuch circulation, money; and of introducing it as ſuch. In your doctrine, that " labour is the meaſure of " exchangeable value of all commodities," connected with your mode of explanation of the wages of labour, the profit of ſtock, the rent of land, and the effect of the progreſs of improvements, I thought I ſaw great danger, that Theory, in the pride of rectitude, might harden its heart againſt the real, though relative, diſtreſſes, which the labourer and the landed gentry of a country do ſuffer, and are oppreſſed by, *during the progreſs* of improvement, in conſequence of a *continuing influx of riches*; and might therefore depreciate, or even endeavour to obſtruct, all thoſe current remedies which give comfort and relief to theſe diſtreſſes, and alleviate even thoſe which cannot be remedied.

Although * the demand for thoſe who live by wages muſt naturally increaſe with the increaſe of national wealth; and conſequently the price of wages riſe in proportion to the riſe of every thing elſe; ſo as that the labourer will in the

end

* Pag. 85.

end partake of the general riches and happinefs of the publick. Although * the rife in the price of all produce is in the end no calamity, but the *forerunner* of every publick advantage : Yet as thofe prices do *forerun*, and muft, during the progrefs of improvement, *always forerun*; wages and rent muft always continue *at an under-value* in the comparifon. They will indeed rife alfo, but as this foreruns, they can only follow, *fed non paffibus æquis*. The labourer, and he who lives on rent, therefore, muft always, though improving, be unable to improve fo faft as to emerge from a continued diftrefs : if this diftinction, that a flowing encreafe of wealth, although it is the forerunner of every advantage to the publick in general, and *in the end* to every individual, yet is the continuing caufe to the continued diftrefs of the labourer, and of him who lives by rent, is not carefully attended to. If the ftate of the circumftances of diftrefs, which continues to opprefs thofe claffes of the community, are not conftantly adverted to with feeling, and with exertions of precaution and benevolence, we fhall, in the triumph of our general profperity, be the conftant oppreffors of thofe who have the beft title to fhare in this profperity.

Under thefe ideas and apprehenfions I did very carefully and repeatedly, before I proceeded to the applied doctrines contained in the latter book, revife the analytic part of the former. When I came to the doctrines applied to practice, and the bufineffes of the world, I found that my cautions had not been unneceffary, and that my apprehenfions, that fome fuch confequences might be drawn from it, were grounded : I found alfo what I did not from the principles expect (nor as yet do I fee how they derive from them, as any part of the chain of reafoning) that in the courfe of the doctrines you hold, you are led to difapprove the law giving a bounty on corn exported; and alfo to think, that the monopoly, which we claim in the American trade *, " like all other mean and malignant expedients of the mercantile fyftem," without in the leaft increafing, doth on the contrary diminifh the induftry of the country, in whofe favour it is eftablifhed ; and doth, although it may have the feducing afpect of a *relative advantage* †, fubject the nation, its trade and commerce, to an abfolute difadvantage. I hope you will not think, that I mifunderftand, or mean to mif-ftate, your pofition. You allow, and very fully explain the great advantages of the colony trade, but think that the monopoly is the reafon why, great as it is, we do not derive fo great advantages from it to the nation and to the landed intereft, and to the community in general, as we might have done, had it not been crampt and perverted by the monopoly.

In the many occafions which I have had to view this monopoly, I own, although I have feen fome errors in the extenfion of the *meafure*, further than is expedient or neceffary, yet I do not fee the malignancy of the principle of a monopoly ; nor while I have lived amidft the daily proofs of the *relative advantage* which it gives to the mother country, by its colonies, over all other foreign

* Pag. 286.   † B. IV. C. VII. P. 201.

foreign nations, I have not been able to difcover, nor have your arguments, although fo methodically and fo clearly drawn out, been able to explain to me, that abfolute difadvantage which you think it fubjects us to.

Although I agree entirely with you, having alfo previoufly read the fame opinion in Mr. Necker's Treatife, *fur la Legiflation & le Commerce des Graines*, that the bounty which our law gives to the exportation of corn, has not been the fole caufe which hath rendered corn cheaper than otherwife it would have been; but, on the contrary, hath, in each direct inftance, given it fome fmall advance in the general fcale of prices : Yet, confidering that fo far as it does this, and gives relief to the relative oppreffion which the landed intereft muft continue to feel under *a continued influx of riches*, and an advancing rife in the prices of every thing elfe; I think it one of the wifeft meafures for a country like England that could be devifed.

I think with you, that many of our laws and regulations of trade are practical errors, and mifchievous. I think that, while they feem to be founded on our navigation act, they miftake the fpirit of it, and no lefs miftake the real intereft of the nation : yet I cannot but hold thefe to be errors only, as they deviate from the true principle of the act of navigation, which is a different thing from the acts of trade.

Having prefaced thus much as to the feveral doctrines on which I have conceived fome doubts, I will now, following the order of your work, ftate thofe doubts. When I found you difcarding *metallic money*, that intervening commodity which having, by common confent, acquired a value of its own, hath been hitherto efteemed a common known meafure of the value of all other things, from being any longer fuch common meafure, and by a refinement of theory, endeavouring to eftablifh in its place " an abftract notion," *that labour was the common meafure of all value*; I did not only doubt the truth of the pofition, but, looking to the ufes that might be made of the doctrine, hefitated on the principle. If labour be the only real and ultimate meafure of value, money is but the inftrument, like the counters on the checkquer, which keeps the account; if this be all the ufe of money, then *circulation*, or even *an account opened with a banker* (according to a practice in Scotland, as defcribed by you) is to all ufes and ends as good as money. If it is not neceffary, that the common meafure fhould have fome known permanent value in itfelf, fo as to be a depofit of that abfent value which it reprefents, as well as meafures, fo as to convey to all who poffefs it an abfolute power of purchafe, then indeed the circulating inftrument, the machine that circulates, whether it be a paper or a leather one, or even an account, without any *depofit*, is equal to all the ufes and end of money, is that which we may fafely receive for the future. As I have been mixed in the bufinefs of a country, where the evils of this doctrine and practice have been feverely felt, and where it was my duty to watch, that nothing was impofed upon the publick as money, but what was either in itfelf

felf a depofit, or was eftablifhed on a fund equal to a depofit, and what had *all* the ufes of a permanent known meafure in all cafes of circulation; I could not but read this leading doctrine of your's with great caution and doubt. I muft doubt, whether it be labour fimply which creates and becomes the meafure of value, when I find other component parts mixed in the moft fimple idea of value: I cannot conceive, that equal quantities of labour are abfolutely of equal value, when I find the value of labour both in ufe and in exchange varying in all proportions, amidft the correlative values of thefe components parts; I cannot fuppofe labour to be the ultimate meafure, when I find labour itfelf meafured by fomething more remote.—You fay very properly in the major of your fyllogifm, that when the divifion of labour has once thoroughly taken place, it is but a very fmall part of the neceffaries and conveniencies of life, with which a man's own labour can fupply him. But when we come to the minor propofition of it, we muft confider alfo the objects on which labour is employed; for it is not fimply the *labour*, but the *labour mixed with thefe objects*, that is exchanged; it is *the compofite article, the laboured article*: Some part of the exchangeable value is derived from the object itfelf; and in this compofite value, which is the thing actually exchanged, the labour bears very different proportions of value, according to the different nature of the object on which it is employed. Labour, employed in *collecting* the *fpontaneous produce* of the earth, is very different in the compofite exchangeable value of the fruit collected, from that which is employed in raifing and collecting the *cultured fruits* of the earth. Labour, employed on a rich, cleared, fubdued and fruitful, or on a poor and unkindly foil, or on a wild uncleared wafte, has a very different value in the compofite object produced in the one, from what it bears in the compofite value of the other. As the object then makes part of the compofite value, we muft confider, in the exchangeable value, the object alfo, as a component part. Whofe then is the object? Who has acquired, and does poffefs, the object or objects on which the labour may be employed? Let us take up this confideration under thefe firft fcenes of man, which are ufually called a ftate of nature, fomewhat advanced in the divifion of labour and community. Previous to the employing of labour, there muft be fome acquifition of objects whereon to employ this labour; a ftrong and felfifh man, who will not labour, fits, we will fuppofe, idly under a tree, loaded with the fpontaneous fruits of nature; an induftrious, but weaker man, wants fome part of thofe to fupply his neceffity, the idler will not let him collect the fruit, unlefs that other collects alfo enough for both. Or if, ftill more churlifh and more felfifh, he will not let him who is willing, by his labour, to collect a fufficiency for *his* ufe, unlefs the labourer collects alfo more than fufficient for the idler's prefent ufe, fufficient for his future ufe alfo. Does the labourer here command or exchange, by his labour, any part of the labour of the idler? Certainly not. In this ftate *a divifion of*
the

the objects on which labour muft be employed, and with which it muft be mixed, as well as a divifion of labour hath taken place; and therefore the labourer muft be able, by his labour, to command in exchange a certain portion of thefe objects which another hath, as well as a certain part of that other's labour. It will not relieve this doubt by faying, as Mr. Locke (treating of right) fays, that there can be no *right of poffeffion*, but by a man's mixing his labour with any object; becaufe we are here not confidering the matter of right, but the matter of fact: nor will it anfwer to fay, that the acquifition itfelf is an act of labour, becaufe I have here ftated the cafe of a churlifh fluggard idler, ftrong enough to maintain himfelf in idlenefs, by commanding not only the actual labourer, but certain *greater or leffer quantity of that labour*, according as his felfifh churlifh temper leads him to prefs upon the neceffity of the weaker. Suppofe the fame idler, in this divifion of the objects of labour, to have got poffeffion of a fifhing lake, or a beaver-pond, or in a fandy defart of a fpring; or of a fpot of fruitful ground, amidft a barren country; or of a ford, or particular pofition, which commands a fine hunting-ground, fo as to exclude the labourer from the objects whereon his labour muft be employed, in order to form that laboured article which is to fupply his wants. You fee, that the means of commanding the *objects of labour, as well the labour* of another, make part of the fupply whereby a man muft live, whereby he may be faid to be rich or poor. Even you yourfelf (I hope you will excufe the expreffion under which I quote it) fay, with rather fome degree of confufion in terms, " that every thing is really *worth* to the man who has, *acquired it*, and who " wants to difpofe of it, or exchange it for fomething elfe; the toil and trouble " which it can fave to himfelf, and which it can impofe upon other people." This expreffes the conclufion which I draw from the cafe I have ftated, and not your pofition, that labour is the *meafure*, and that it is labour which is exchangeable for *value*: it is, on the contrary, the mixture of the labour, and the objects laboured upon, which produces the compofite value. The labour muft remain unproductive, unlefs it hath fome object whereon to exert itfelf, and the object is of no ufe unlefs laboured upon. The exchange therefore is made by A keeping a part of his labour mixed with a part of the object, and B ufing a part of his objects rendered, ufeful by the labour of A mixed with them. The confequence therefore in your fyllogifm cannot fairly conclude, that the value of any commodity to the perfon who poffeffes it, and who means not to ufe or to confume it himfelf, but to exchange it for other commodities, *is equal to the quantity of labour*, which it enables him to purchafe or command. On the contrary, it is a compofite value of the object and labour mixed, and takes part of its value from each of the component parts. It is not therefore labour (which is but one of the component parts of the exchangeable commodity) which gives the exchangeable value, but *the labour and the object mixed*, the compounded laboured article, in which the labour bears all
poffible

poffible proportions to the correlative value of the two component parts, according as the poffeffor of the object, or the exertor of the labour, or the common general courfe of the eftimation of mankind fhall fettle it. Real value, if any fuch thing there be different from market value, is *the mixed compofite laboured article*, not labour fimply.

You have, Sir, made a very proper diftinction of *value in ufe*, and *value in exchange*. That labour which varies in its productive power, according as it is differently applied, and according to the object it is employed upon, muft certainly vary in its ufe, and equal quantities of it muft be in fuch different circumftances of very unequal value to the labourer. *Labour in vain, loft labour—Labour which makes itfelf work*, (phrafes which, to a proverb, exprefs fome fpecies of labour,) *cannot be* faid to be *of any ufe* to the labourer. He who would fhave a block with razor, will labour in vain. He who fows on a rock, or on a barren fand, or in a drowned morafs, will lofe his labour. He who fheers his hogs, will have great cry and little wool, and only make himfelf work : but labour will ftill vary more in its *exchangeable value* ; equal quantities of labour will receive very variable degrees of eftimation and value. In the firft operation of barter of labour (the value of the objects being, for the fake of argument, laid afide) we will fuppofe A to fay to B, you fhall have as much of the furplus of my labour on the article o, as you will exchange for the furplus of your labour on the article ∆. By this, A " means to fave " as much of his toil and trouble to himfelf, and to impofe as much upon B, " as he can." B means the fame. What then is to be the real ftandard of meafure ? Not labour itfelf. What is to give the refpective eftimation in which each holds his labour ? Each alternately will be difpofed to eftimate his own moft valuable, and to each " the labour of the other will fometimes appear to " be of greater and fometimes of fmaller value *." This value cannot be fixed by and in the nature of the labour ; it will depend upon the nature of the feelings and the activity of the perfons eftimating it. A and B having, by equal quantities of labour, produced equal quantities of two of the moft neceffary articles of fupply, whofe values, in the general fcale of things, vary the leaft ; each having a furplus in the article which his labour has produced, and each likewife having an equal want of what the other has produced. This *quantity* of labour, although ftated as *equal*, will have very different *exchangeable values* in the hands of the one or the other, as A or B are *by nature* formed to make a good bargain in the common adjuftment of the barter. He who has not an impatience in his defire on one hand, or a foon-alarmed fear on the other of lofing his market ; who has a certain firmnefs, perfeverance and coldnefs in barter ; who has a certain *natural* felf-eftimation, will take the lead in fetting the price upon the meek and poor in fpirit ; upon the impatient and timid bargainer. The higher or lower value of thefe equal quantities of labour,

* Pag. 39.

labour, will follow the one or the other fpirit. The value is not equal, and is not fixed in, nor depends upon, the equal quantity of the labour; it is unequal and differs, and is fixed by, and derives from, the different *natures of the perfons* bargaining. The exchangeable value of equal quantities of labour, ftated equal in all circumftances, is not only not equal in this firft inftance, between that of A and B, but may, in other comparifons, vary both in A and in B individually. The exchangeable value of B, although inferior in barter with A, may acquire an afcendant value, and be fuperior in barter with C. This difference and this variation will run through every degree in the utmoft extent of the markets: nay, the fame perfon will, in different habits, relations and circumftances of life, eftimate that labour (which fhall be ftated to be abfolutely equal) as of very different value; he will, on different occafions, eftimate his " eafe, liberty, and defire of happinefs" differently. Equal quantities of labour, equal, I mean abfolutely, and in every refpect, will acquire and derive very different values both in ufe, and in exchange both in refpect of the perfon by whom fuch is exerted, as well as in refpect of the perfon who barters for it, from the objects with which it is mixed. Refpecting the perfon by whom it is exerted, if a day's labour always produces a day's fubfiftance, the value in ufe is always the fame; if it doth not, the value in ufe muft vary. In refpect of exchangeable value, labour will fometimes give value to things which, in themfelves, had little or no value: in others, it will derive value from the things with which it is mixed; it will itfelf have an exchangeable value from its compounded value; that is, from the proportion of value which it bears in the compofite laboured article.

What is thus varying in a relative value, muft require fome correlative, which, while this meafures other things, in return will meafure it; that which is itfelf meafured by fomething more remote, cannot be the final meafure or ftandard. It cannot * therefore be " alone the ultimate and real ftandard by " which the value of all commodities can, at all times and places, be efti- " mated and compared: it is not their *real price*." I muft therefore conclude, in a propofition which I quote from yourfelf, where I wifh you had let the bufinefs † reft; " That there can be no accurate meafure, but that exchange- " able value muft be fettled by the higgling and bargaining of the market, ac- " cording to that fort of rough equality, which, though not exact, is fuffici- " ent for the carrying on the bufinefs of life."

You confefs, that this propofition of your's, " *That labour is the meafure* " *of the value, and the real price of all commodities*," is " *an abftract notion*." As fuch I fhould not have taken any notice of it; but you endeavour to eftablifh it as a leading principle, whereby I think a *practical one*, which mankind hath univerfally and generally acted upon, may be in dangerous fpeculations diftinguifhed away. If the common forenfick idea, that money which,

in

* Pag. 39.   † Pag. 37.

in the common acceptation of it, hath actually been ufed to meafure, doth in ftrict truth meafure as " a common intervening commodity," both labour and all other things, and their relations, is to be confidered as a more practical notion, and we are in reafoning to look to fome abftract notion, as the real ftandard. What do we, but pervert our reafoning from diftinct notions in practice, to " abftract notions," and fubleties in theory: as I apprehend that thefe theories have been, and fear they may and will again be ufed, if admitted into the reafoning of the world, to very mifchievous and deftructive fchemes; as I think that they remove old bounds, and erafe old and folid foundations, and may be applied to the building paper caftles in the air; as they lead to fpeculations, which fwerve from the idea of *pledge and depofit in money matters,* and tend to create *an imaginary phantom of circulation,* erected on the foundation of credit and opinion of truft only, I have taken the liberty of ftating my doubts upon it.

While I have thus doubted, whether labour is the ultimate meafure and ftandard of the exchangeable value of all commodities, I fhould be willing with you to admit, that corn will not univerfally anfwer as fuch a meafure, had not you yourfelf *, in another part of your book feemed to think, that " the " nature of things has ftamped upon corn, *a real* value, which no human in- " ftitution can alter; and that *corn* is that regulating commodity, by which " the real value of all other commodities muft *be finally meafured* and deter- mined." Gold and filver, you fay, varying as it doth in its own value, can never be an accurate meafure of the value of other things. There is then, ac- cording to what I have always been ufed to think, and what from your Trea- tife I find myfelf confirmed in, no one commodity that will meafure all others, but that all are to one another in their reciprocal value *alternate meafures*; and that *gold and filver* is only the common and moft general, almoft the univerfal, meafure, fo found to be, and fo ufed by the general experience and confent of mankind, as *that intervening commodity* which will moft uniformly become *a common meafure,* at the fame that it doth (as being a depofit of value, which all mankind have agreed to receive) *give univerfal power of purchafe.*

As I think that there is no real meafure of value, fo I think there is no fix- ed natural rate of value, or real price diftinct from the market price. I think, that the doctrine which ftates the two definitions as an actual exifting truth, and as a practical diftinction formed for bufinefs, not true on one hand, but on the other a dangerous propofition.

You fay, † " That there is in every fociety or neighbourhood *an ordinary or* " *average rate* both of wages and profit, in every different employment of la- " bour and ftock;" thefe average rates you call " the *natural price,* at the " time and place in which they commonly prevail."

The

* B. IV. C. V. Vol. II. P. 101. † B. I. C. VII. P. 66.

The actual price at which any commodity is *commonly fold*, is called its market prince.

I clearly fee the diftinction in definition; but I do not learn how the ordinary average rates, or price paid for labour, or for the ufe of land or ftock, or for any commodity in the neighbourhood, where it comes from the firft hand, in the firft act of bargain and fale, is any more natural than the price which it finds and bears in any other fucceeding act of bargain and fale, at the time and place wherever it is fold. What is it, in the firft inftance, which fettles thefe average rates, which you call natural, but the competition of the effectual demand, compared with the fupply, and founded on fome proportion whereby the price paid for labour, ftock or land, will enable the feller to purchafe an equivalent quantity of thofe neceffaries and conveniences which his ftate of life requires? If, from this firft operation of bargain and fale, the commodity, by means of carriage, and the collection, ftorage, and diftribution of the middle man, goes to a fucceeding and more complicated value with thefe adventitious articles of expence added to it : Is not the price which is here, alfo the price at which it here commonly fells, and which is in like manner precifely determined equally, that ordinary average rate and *natural price* as the former ? Or rather, is not the price in the firft operation of bargain and fale *equally a market price* as the latter, fettled by that higgling and barter which doth and muft finally regulate it in all times and in all cafes ? The refinement which, ufing different expreffions, as in one cafe calling it " the ordinary average rate," and in the other, " that price at which it is com-" monly fold," is a diftinction of words without fcarce a difference in idea, certainly none in fact and truth. If there be any fuch thing as a natural price, both are natural; if not, which I rather think both are the artificial market price, fuch as the act of higgling and barter can fettle on the reciprocation of wants and mutual fupply. What elfe is it in *nature* which fettles the ordinary average rates, which you call the natural price? This price " *naturally* " *increafes*," as adventitious circumftances mix with the commodity brought to fale. The encreafed market price encreafes by the adventitious circumftances of labour in carriage, of rifque, ftorage, and the middle-man's profit. This encreafe is *naturally* regulated by the ordinary and average rates of thefe added circumftances in their time and place; and on thefe the competition, compared with the fupply, doth as naturally in one cafe as in the other create the market price; which may be called, if you choofe to call the former fo, a natural price ; but both are, in fact, equally in their time and place the market price. When therefore you fay, * " that the natural price is the *central* " *price*, to which the prices of all commodities are perpetually gravitating;" I muft own that I receive the metaphor of the propofition with great apprehenfions of the ufes in practice, which the doctrine may lead to. If any one, who

* B. I. C. VII. P. 70.

who has got a lead in bufinefs, fhould adopt your diftinction of *natural and market price*; and, following the delufion of your metaphor, fhould think, that, as in nature, all market prices do perpetually gravitate to the natural *central price*, fo the circuiting motion of all market prices fhould be made to take and keep this direction round their center; (perfectly fatisfying himfelf, that as he ought not, fo he does not, meddle with the *natural prices* of things:) he may, through a confufion and reverfe of all order, fo perplex the fupply of the community, as totally to ruin thofe who are concerned in it, and intirely to obftruct it. He may render trade almoft impracticable, and annihilate commerce. That the fucceeding prices of the fecondary operations of bargain and fale are regulated by the fame rules and laws of barter as the firft; and that the outfet of the firft will give direction of motion, as well as motion to all fucceeding operations, regulated by the fame laws of this motion, is certainly true; and that it will (while in the ordinary courfe of things) keep this motion equable by the refpective average rates in their time and place: that the violence and artifices of man will ever and anon try to warp and mifrate it, is certainly true; and a truth well worthy of conftant attention—not with a view to interfere and intermeddle with the *market prices*, under any theory of regulating them by fome fuppofed natural *central price*, but to obftruct and oppofe all interference and meddling whatfoever; and upon this truth to maintain in the market an univerfal freedom, choice and liberty.

Although, as I have ftated my opinion above, I think, that the general courfe of all prices, or that correlative value between commodities muft depend upon, and derive from the reciprocal higgling of bargain and fale, and are not meafured by labour: Yet fo far as they depend upon, or are mixed with labour, there is fome natural fcale below which they cannot go; which fcale takes its level from the quantity of fubfiftence which fuch labour will procure. The plain and home-fpun wifdom of our anceftors, therefore, did not attempt to meafure the prices of things by any *abftract notion of labour being that meafure*, but they meafured labour itfelf * "by the plenty or dearth of provifions," or the fubfiftance, according to the laboured productive effects of nature from time to time. Although therefore I agree with you, † " that the *common wages* of " labour *depends* every where *upon the contract* made between two parties, " whofe interefts are by no means the fame;" yet in that, ‡ " a man muft " always live by his work, and that his wages muft at leaft maintain him." There is a fcale of rate below which the price of labour cannot by any con-tract or bargain be lowered.

That the prices of wages do continually increafe with the advancing profperity of any community, and that they are the higheft in thofe communities, who are advancing with the moft rapid velocity, is a truth, a comfortable and an encouraging truth: yet as prices of wages follow but with flow and loaded

E

fteps,

* Vide the feveral ftatutes of labourers.　　　† B. I. C. VIII. P. 81.　　　‡ P. 83.

steps, in proportion to the quick motions of the rife of the prices of all other things, if fome care and attention is not given to aid the motion of the rife of wages, in fome meafure to keep it above the loweft fcale, which it can fubfift by; we may, in the triumph of profperity, and in the pride of rectitude, fee the poor labourer, of the lower claffes, under a continued ftate of helplefs oppreffion, amidft the profperity of the community in general; but of the nature, and of the manner of regulating thefe, I fhall have occafion to treat in another place, and on another occafion.

As value or price is not any fixed *natural* thing, but is merely the *actual* correlative proportion of exchange amongft all commodities; *fo that intervening commodity which* does in fact moft commonly, or on common refult, and by common confent, *exprefs this correlative proportion,* is *the common meafure* of this value: It is not an abftract notion of *labour,* " but *money* * (as " Mr. Hume fays) which is *by agreement* the common meafure." This common meafure does not barely exprefs the proportion of value between commodities when brought together in the act of exchange, but is that fomething, that moft common intervening commodity, which mankind hath generally and univerfally agreed fhall not only exprefs this act of exchange, and the relation of reciprocal value under which it is made, but which is in fact an univerfal equivalent depofit of value, which gives, in all places and at all times, with all perfons, a power of purchafe, and is in fact and truth that intervening commodity, which, as a common meafure, exchanges without actually bringing the things exchanged into barter. The thing which we thus exprefs in abftract reafoning by the word *money,* is *by ufe* univerfal, by general and common confent, *the precious metals applied as this practical common meafure,* the ufes which it hath, and the purpofes to which it is applied amongft the acts and things of the community, gives it *a value in its exchangeable operations.* This idea of money is fixed by *old bounds* of common confent and univerfal practice; and as I am not willing *to remove old bounds,* fixed in a real foundation, to follow an abftract notion † " on Dædalian wings through the air;" I will here next take the liberty to ftate the reafons which make me hefitate to follow you in thofe regions of theory. Although you tell me, that it is not the metallic money which is exchanged, it is the *money's worth;* that money may be the *actual* meafure of this exchange, but that it is the labour which the money reprefents and fells and purchafes, which is the *real meafure.* Yet when my ideas lead me in the very line of your analyfis to conceive, that labour is not, no more than any other commodity, the ultimate meafure, but is the thing meafured; that when meafured againft fubfiftance, it is actually meafured by that fubfiftance. When I confider, that although it is the money's worth which is exchanged, yet it is the money which meafures and exchanges it. I cannot but think it neareft even to abftract truth, and fafeft in practice,

to

---

* Effay on Money, P. 321.   † B. II. C. II. P. 289.

to abide by *the old bounds* of that idea which mankind hath generally and universally fixed, *that money* IS THE COMMON MEASURE, to be which adequately, and in all its *uses*, it must be a DEPOSIT also.

In your account * of the origin and use of money, you very properly state, that " every prudent man in every period of society (after the first establish-
" ment of the division of labour) must naturally have endeavoured to manage
" his affairs in such manner, as to have at all times by him, besides the pecu-
" liar produce of his own industry, a certain quantity of some one commo-
" dity or other, such as he imagined few people would be likely to refuse in
" exchange for the produce of their industry." If in the doing this, all, led
by any thing in the nature of any commodity itself, or by some coincidence
of reasoning and consent, should agree upon any one commodity in general,
which would be thus generally and universally received in exchange, *that*, in
the most refined strictness of abstract reasoning, as well as in decisive fact,
would become that † *intervening commodity* which would measure the exchangeable value, and be the real instrument of actual exchange in the market. It
would not only be that *measure*, but it would become a *real* as well as *actual*
deposit of value, and would convey to whomsoever possessed it, a general, universal and effective power of purchase.

When next then I inquire, what this intervening commodity is—I find,
‡ that metallic money, or rather " silver, is that which, by the general con-
" sent of mankind, has become that deposit, which is the common measure;
" this is a general effect of some general cause. The experience of its degree
" of scarceness, compared with its common introduction amidst men, toge-
" ther with the facility of its being known by its visible and palpable proper-
" ties, hath given this effect. Its degree of scarceness hath given it a value
" proportioned to the making it A DEPOSIT; and the certain quantity in
" which this is mixed with the possessions and transactions of men, together
" with the facility of its being known, has made it A COMMON MEASURE
" amongst those things. There are perhaps other things which might be bet-
" ter applied to commerce as *a common measure*, and there are perhaps other
" things which might better answer *as a deposit*; but there is nothing, except
" [the precious metals, or rather] silver, known and acknowledged by the
" general experience of mankind, which is *a deposit and a common measure*.
" Paper, leather, or parchment, may, by the sanction of government, be-
" come a common measure, to an extent beyond what silver could reach; yet
" all the sanction and power of government never will make it an *adequate* de-
" posit. Diamonds, pearls, or other jewels, may, in many cases, be consi-
" dered as a more apt and suitable deposit, and may be applied as such to an
" extant to which silver will not reach: yet their scarcity tends to throw them
" into

* B. I. C. IV. P. 28.   † C. V. P. 37.   ‡ Vide administration of the Colonies, C. V. Vol. I.

" into a monopoly; they cannot be fubdivided nor amaffed into one concrete;
" and the knowledge of them is more calculated for a myftery, or trade, than
" for the forenfic ufes of man in common, and they will never therefore be-
" come a common meafure.

" The quantity of this depofit, and the general application of it to feveral
" different commodities, in different places and circumftances, creates a cor-
" relative proportion between it and other objects, with which it ftands com-
" pared, and from this proportion forms *its own fcale*; this fcale derives from
" the effect of natural operations, and not from artificial impofition. If there-
" fore filver was never ufed but by the merchant, as the general meafure of
" his commerce and exchange, *coin* would be (as it is in fuch cafe) of no ufe;
" it would be confidered as bullion only. Although bullion is thus fufficient
" for the meafure of general commerce, yet for the daily ufes of the market
" fomething more is wanted in detail; fomething is wanted to mark to com-
" mon judgment its proportion, and to give the fcale: government therefore
" here interpofes, and by forming it into COIN gives the fcale, and makes it
" become to forenfic ufe AN INSTRUMENT in detail, as well as it is in bullion
" A MEASURE in general."

It is here, Sir, that I think your Analyfis, fubtilifed by too high refinement, deviates from the path in which the nature of things would have led you.
Quitting the idea of money being A COMMON MEASURE, and totally leaving
out all idea of its being a DEPOSIT, your Analyfis leads you to conceive no
other idea of it but as CIRCULATION, or, as you diftinctly exprefs it, a CIRCU-
LATING MACHINE; and of courfe, according to thefe principles, confidering it as an inftrument, you ftate it in your account *amongft thofe inftruments
which form the fixed capital of the community.* The refult of which in fair
reafoning is, that as thefe machines coft an expence (which muft be either
drawn from the circulating capital of the community, or from its revenue by
favings) both to erect them and to maintain them; fo every faving which
can be made in the erection or maintenance of fuch a machine, will be advantageous to the circulating capital, the fource of materials and wages, and
the fpring of induftry. In this line of deduction you come to the refult in
practice, and fay, * that " the fubftitution of paper, in the room of gold
" and filver money, replaces *a very expenfive inftrument* of commerce with one
" much lefs coftly, and *fometimes* equally convenient; *circulation* comes to be
" carried on by *a new wheel,* which it cofts lefs both to erect and to maintain
" than *the old one.*"

As my reafoning hath many years ago impreffed it ftrongly on my mind that
money is a COMMON MEASURE, and muft be a DEPOSIT, and *in coin an inftrument* of the market; and as many years experience in a country of paper
hath convinced me, that if any inftrument of the exchange of commodities,

other

* B. II. C. II. P. 350,

other than that which, while it meafures the correlative values in circulation, is founded on a DEPOSIT, equivalent at all times to the converfion of it into money, fhall be introduced, it will be a fource of fraud, which, leading by an unnatural influx of riches to luxury without bounds, and to enterprize without foundation, will derange all induftry, and inftead of fubftantial wealth end by bankruptcies in diftrefs and poverty.

So far as *circulation* can carry on the exchanges of commodities in the community, fo far paper bills of credit, or even accounts opened, may do in the room of the metallic money; but without a depofit, which is adequate and equivalent in all times and places, and with all perfons, to this converfion of it, I have no fure foundation, that I do poffefs, in all times and places, and with all perfons, *the power of purchafing or of accumulating as I like.* Although I have all the truft and confidence in the world in the credit of this circulating machine of paper, yet it has not the univerfal extent in, nor the operation of all the ufes of money, although therefore it may be "*fometimes* " *equally convenient;*" it is not that intervening commodity which hath *all the ufes of money,* univerfally and adequately. Circulation, even where no paper money or credit exifts, muft always much exceed in its total of exchange the fum total of the money depofit, how much that is, experience in the fact can alone determine: paper may certainly, without any danger, encreafe this power of circulation, if it does not exceed what the depofit will anfwer while it is in circulation, and is created *on fuch a fund, as will finally convert it into money.* So far as paper, by the extent of the ufes, and the abfolute fecurity and exchangeable converfion of it into metallic money, *can be and is made a depofit,* fo far it may fafely meafure as money, and become a convenient inftrument; but in that this fecurity is always more or lefs uncertain; in that it depends on the prudence and probity of the money-makers, it is always liable to exception, abufe and failure. So far forth as it is defective in its fund, the creation and ufe of it muft be always hazardous, and hath been generally ruinous; and however diftant and remote the end may be, *muft* be a fraud in the end. In a world of enterprize, where *truft and credit* is fubftituted *in the ftead of fund* and prompt change, paper money lofes the very effence of a depofit; unlefs I have *a depofit,* which gives me an abfolute actual power of purchafing, in all times and places, in all events, to all intents and ufes; or that which is abfolutely ready and immediate change for fuch depofit. The bill which I have, may or may not, here or there, now and then, *fometimes* not always, maintain in me *the power of purchafing,* or of real hoarding or banking as I like. General, univerfal, permanent confent of all mankind, has from *actual experience* of its ufes, given to *metallic money* a permanent and abfolute value: partial, local, temporary agreement, founded *in opinion of truft and credit,* can give to paper but a partial, local, temporary ideal value, which never will

 P. 359.

will be a real and univerfal depofit; it may become to certain local temporary purpofes a *circulating machine*, but money is fomething more : this paper is not that intervening commodity, which all mankind hath univerfally agreed to be *that common meafure which is a depofit*; fuch alone is money in the ftrict as well as common acceptation of the word and idea.

So far as paper money can be fo contrived as to have, while it is in circulation, *a l the ufes* of money; or is fo founded, that it can in all moments and in all places be taken out of circulation by converfion into metallic money at its nominal value, fo far it will be equal to money both as a meafure and as a depofit. But fo far as it is defective in any one ufe, however much it may excel in any other ufe, it will and muft depreciate below the real value of the metallic money, which it is fuppofed to reprefent; fo far as in any point of time or place the power of converting it into metallic money is remote, fo far is it ideal, unfubftantial, and no depofit. Although with a fund of 2c,000*l.* a banker, or the treafury of a government, may circulate 100,000*l.* yet as whenever, for any reafon, or by any event, it becomes neceffary to take that 100,000*l.* out of circulation, the banker or the treafury can but pay 20,000*l.* or four fhillings in the pound, that circulation muft end in a fraud.

Where, in the circulation of capital, paper money is fubftituted inftead of metallic money, you allow, that it will not anfwer in its ufes to foreign trade. I, for the fame reafon, add, it will not *pay taxes*, fo far as thofe taxes are to *fupply expences incurred or laid out abroad*. If great variety of *reabforbing glands* did not in Scotland take up, in the courfe of circulation, the amount of the taxes levied on that part of the kingdom, their paper money could not pay that amount.

Juft as much gold, as paper circulation becomes a fubftitute for, may be fpared from circulation, and will become, as you truly fay, a new fund for commerce, and will go abroad in foreign trade : if it is employed in a commerce of luxury or confumption, it is in every refpect hurtful to fociety; fo far as it purchafes raw and rude materials, or provifions or tools, and inftruments to work with, it may be beneficial. You think that, however individuals may run into the former, bodies and focieties are more likely to actuate the latter. Yet in countries where a fuperabundant quantity of paper money hath taken place, where the power of creating this money hath advanced fafter in its creation and emiffions than the labour, induftry and abilities of the inhabitants would have produced it. This *artificial plenty* hath always encouraged a commerce of luxury; an over-trading; a multitude and difproportionate number of fhop-keepers; extravagant expences in idle land-holders; more building than can be fupported; and all kinds of ambitious and dangerous projects. " * The commerce and induftry of a country, you muft ac-
" knowledge, and do candidly confefs, though they may be fomewhat augment-
" ed, cannot be altogether *fo fecure*, when they are thus, as it were, fufpend-
" ed

* B. II. C. II. P. 389.

" ed upon the *dædalian wings of paper money*, as when they travel *on the solid*
" *ground of gold and silver*. Over and above the accidents to which they are
" expofed from the unfkilfulnefs (*I would here add the fraud alfo*) of the con-
" ductors of this paper money, they are liable to feveral others, from which
" no prudence or fkill of the conductors can guard them."—You indeed reafon from the *abufe*, but all thefe arguments do equally derive from the *defect* of
this paper money. As it creates an *influx of riches*, which does not fpring from
induftry, which is not the effect and produce of ufeful labour; it creates, with
aggravated circumftances, all that diftrefs which the real ufeful labourer and
real man of property, the land-owner, muft feel, even under an influx of real
riches; it gives motion and velocity to this influx, without producing any real
depofit whereon the *riches*, which it pours in to circulation, *may be funded as*
WEALTH. The land-holder lives for a while under oppreffion and diftrefs;
he then, raifing his rents beyond what the real ftock will bear, lives in a delufive abundance of luxurious expence, but is finally ruined. The fucceffor,
who purchafes him out, fucceeds by the fame difeafe to the fame ruin. The
labourer, and all who live on fixed ftipend, are under a continued feries of oppreffion. The falfe wealth only of adventurers, jobbers, and cheats, become
the riches of the country; that real depofit, which would be a fund of real
wealth and real fupply in cafe of diftrefs, will be chaced away. The phantom
of circulation, which is fubftituted in its place, will, inftead of coming in
aid, fail, and vanifh on the firft alarm of diftrefs.

" * An unfuccefsful war, for example, in which the enemy got poffeffion
" of the capital (*who does not tremble as he reads?*) and confequently of that
" treafure which fupported the credit of paper money, would occafion *a much*
" *greater confufion* in a country where the whole circulation was carried on by
" paper, than in one where the greater part of it was carried on by gold and
" filver. The ufual inftrument of commerce *having loft its value*, no ex-
" changes could be made but by barter or upon credit. All taxes having been
" ufually paid in paper money, the prince would not have wherewithal either
" to pay his troops or to furnifh his magazines; and the ftate of the country
" would be much more irretrievable, than if the greater part of its circula-
" tion had confifted in gold and filver. A prince, anxious to maintain his
" dominions in a ftate in which he can moft eafily defend them, ought, upon
" this account (*and I add upon all others*) to guard not only againft the excef-
" five multiplication of paper money, which ruins the very banks that iffue
" it, but even againft that multiplication of it, which enables them to fill the
" greater part of the circulation with it."

I was willing to oppofe, in your own words, this fair defcription which you
give of the dangerous ftate of a country which abounds in *circulation of riches*,
inftead of a depofit, which is *wealth*, as an antidote againft the delufions of
this

* B. II. C. II. P. 389.

this powerful temptation : and as I think the dofe ought to be repeated, I will repeat it in the words of the very clear-minded and ingenious Mr. Hume *.

" He has entertained *(he fays from fimilar reafons as above ftated)* a great
" doubt concerning the benefit of banks and paper credit, which are fo gene-
" rally efteemed advantageous to every nation.   That provifions and labour
" fhould become dear, by the encreafe of trade and money, is, in many re-
" fpects, an inconvenience, but an inconvenience that is unavoidable, and the
" effect of that publick wealth and profperity, which is the end of all our
" wifhes.   It is compenfated, however, by the advantages which we reap,
" from the poffeffion of thofe *precious metals*, and the weight which they give
" the nation in all foreign wars and negotiations.   But there appears no rea-
" fon for the encreafing that inconvenience by *a counterfeit money*, which fo-
" reigners will not accept in any payment, and which *any great diforder in the*
" *ftate will reduce to* NOTHING."

It is for thefe reafons, becaufe I am not for *removing old bounds*, and that I wifh to preferve the old general eftablifhed opinion, that money is a *common meafure*; becaufe I am unwilling to receive that *new and delufive friend* CIRCULATION, inftead of *the old and fteady one*, MONEY, which being a DEPOSIT, will ftick by us in all times, that I have taken the liberty to examine this part of your Analyfis, and to wifh, if you fhould be perfuaded to revife it, that you would enquire, in the real track of nature, whether that commodity, by the inter- vention of which the exchanges of all commodities may in all times and cafes be actuated, muft not, *in truth as well as fact*, be that common meafure, in the ufe of which all mankind have univerfally agreed, and muft not be a depofit, which the metallic money alone is : and whether, where paper circu- lation is not fo proportioned to the depofit as that, that depofit is always ready to exchange it during its circulation ; is not eftablifhed on fuch a *fund* as will *abfolutely exchange it* ; whether, I fay, fuch paper circulation is not a delu- fion that muft finally, however remotely, lead to a fraud.

By what I have faid above I do not mean to fay, that paper is not ufeful ; I think, that under fuch due regulations refpecting the FUND, which is to ex- change it, the USES to which it is to be applied, and the QUANTITY in which it may be fafely iffued, as will make it a common meafure and a DEPOSIT, it is not only generally beneficial, but that the greateft advantages may be derived from it to the publick.

If now, Sir, by thefe principles, as I have ftated them, as they are found in the FUND and the USES, you examine all the fchemes of paper circulation from that of the bank of Amfterdam, founded on a real depofit, to that of the Scotch banks, founded on † truft and confidence, without any actual depofit; if you examine the paper money, and the operations of that wife and prudent inftitu- tion, the loan-office of Penfylvania, examine the foundation and the fucceed-

ing

---

* Hume's third Effay on Money.   † B. II. C. II. Vol. I. P. 351.

ing operations of the bank of England, you will find, that you have a fixed canon, by which you may precifely mark what are real, what delufive; what may be beneficial, what will be ruinous in the end. Whereas, if no other idea but that of *circulation* enters into our notion of money; if it be conceived to be nothing more than *a circulating machine*, under that conception every delufive fraudulent credit, which every adventurer can eftablifh *on a deceived and betrayed confidence*, may fet in motion a circulation, that may on every ground be juftified even in the moment of its bankruptcy. And even thofe juft and wife precautions, with which you have endeavoured to guard this circulation againft fraud, may tend to give an opinion of confidence to this circulation, when it fhall be fo guarded, which in any cafe it ought not to have, unlefs it can be fo framed as to have *all the ufe* of money in circulation, and be fo *funded* as in the end to be a real depofit.

It is impoffible to pafs over thofe parts of your learned work, wherein you treat of labour, ftock, and land; of wages, profit, and rent; of the monied prices of commodities, and efpecially your very curious and fcientifick Treatife on the Precious Metals applied as Money; it is impoffible to read thofe parts refpecting the effects of the progrefs of improvement in the community, of the nature, accumulation, and employment of ftock, without reiterating the idea and the wifh expreffed in the beginning of this letter, of feeing your book confidered as INSTITUTE OF THE PRINCIPIA *of thofe laws of motion*, by which the operations of the community are directed and regulated, and by which they fhould be examined. In that part, however, which explains the different effect of different employment of capital, wherein you feem rather to have engrafted fome foreign fhoots, than to have trained up, in the regular branchings of your Analyfis, to propofitions fully demonftrated, I will beg to arreft your fteps for a moment, while we examine the ground whereon we tread; and the more fo, as I find thefe propofitions ufed in the fecond part of your work as data; whence you endeavour to prove, that the monopoly of the colony trade is a difadvantageous commercial inftitution.

After having very juftly defcribed the four different ways in which capital ftock may be employed—firft, in drawing from the elements of earth and water the rude, the fpontaneous or cultured produce; next, in working thefe materials up for ufe; next, the general exchange or trade of thefe commodities, conveyed from place to place as they are wanted; and, laftly the retail diftribution of them to the confumer. After having divided by fair analyfis the general trade or commerce, defcribed under the third head, into three different operations—that is, the home trade; the foreign trade of confumption, and the carrying trade. After having fhewn the juft gradation of beneficial employ of capital, which thefe different operations produce, and how truly beneficial each in its refpective *natural* gradations is, * " When the courfe of " things,

* B. II. C. V. P. 453.

" things, without any conftraint or violence, naturally introduces it ;" you lay and prepare a ground of contraft, from whence in your fourth book to prove, that the eftablifhment of a monopoly in the colony trade, by perverting this *natural order and gradation of operations* in commerce, hath rendered the commerce of fuch colonies lefs beneficial than they might otherwife in general have been; I am here marking only the order of your argument, not trying the force of it. In the order of this argument, I think I difcover an effential mifconception of that branch and operation of commerce, which is in nature *circuitous*, and as fuch beneficial ; but which you conceive to be and call *a round-about commerce*, and as fuch of courfe, and in the nature of things, difadvantageous. Your argument goes to prove, that the monopoly, inftead of leaving the direct trade to its full and free operation, inftead of fuffering the round-about trade (as you call it) to take up the *furplus only* of capital which that produces, and next the carrying trade naturally to abforb what the others difgorge, doth force capital, which might have been more beneficially employed in a direct trade, into a round-about trade ; which is too commonly miftaken for the carrying trade of Great Britain.

I mean, in its place, to examine this your argument, in your application of it to the actual fubject. I will here, in the mean time, with your leave, make an affay of the truth of its combination ; for it appears to me, that in treating *a circuitous commerce* as a *round-about trade*, you confound two things the moft diftinct in their nature, and the moft different in their effect of any two that could have been put together.

A CIRCUITOUS TRADE or commerce is that by which receiving, *with the due profits of return of capital*, fome article of trade or fome commodity, *which is better to go to market with than money*, I go to market with that commodity fo received ; and perhaps again with fome other in like manner received ; and perhaps again with a third, making by each operation my due profits, annexed to each return of my capital ; and finally a greater fuperlucration of profit than I could have done by the fame number of direct trades ; and confequently either a greater revenue, or a greater accumulation of capital, that may again employ more productive labour.

A ROUND-ABOUT TRADE, on the contrary, with loft labour, with wafte of expence, and unprofitable detention of capital, fends to market fome commodity (as the proverb well expreffes it) *by Tom-Long the carrier*.

We will fuppofe, that the Britifh merchant or factor hath fold his Britifh manufactures in Virginia, in which he vefted his capital ; and that he has it in fpeculation, whether by taking money, a bill of exchange, or fome commodity, which is ready money's worth in the Britifh market, he fhall make a direct return of his capital, and its fimple accretion of profit ; or whether by taking fuch commodities, as by an intermediate operation in his way home, he

may

may derive an intermediate adventitious profit from, before the fame is again reinvefted in Britifh goods for the Virginian market.

In the firft cafe, his capital may be faid to return with its profit directly; in the fecond, although it may make a circuit, and be detained awhile in its way home, yet it is not detained, nor goes out of its way *unprofitably* to Great Britain; for by the fuperlucration, arifing from the intermediate operation, it gives proportionably either a greater revenue, or as an encreafed capital employs more productive labour.

We will fuppofe a fecond cafe taken up on this fpeculation, that he either receives corn by barter, or by purchafe invefts what he has received in that commodity, with which, inftead of coming directly home, he calls in his way at Cadiz or Lifbon; the fale of his corn there returns him his capital with a fecond accretion of profit. Here again he fpeculates in like manner, and determines to inveft this accumulated capital in wines, fruits, &c. which at the home market will again return his capital, with farther accretion of profit. Has not every movement of this circuitous trade been a different operation? Has not each operation made a diftinct return of capital? Has not each return given its peculiar profit? Has any expence been wafted? Any labour loft? Has there been any detention of capital unprofitably to Great Britain, while, at its return, it affords either more revenue, or, as capital, employs more productive labour than otherwife it would.

Let us in another line fuppofe, that this merchant or factor receives tobacco, rice, indigo, or peltry, which he brings directly home; with thefe commodities at the Britifh market he fpeculates, whether he fhall take ready money there for them, which, vefting in Britifh mannfactures, or foreign manufactures bought with Britifh produce, he will return directly to Virginia again with. Or whether thefe commodities, which reprefent his capital, with its accretion of profit, might not ftill more encreafe it, if he himfelf fent them to that market where they are purchafed for confumption. We will fuppofe, that his prudence directs him to the latter conduct. He fends them then to Ruffia or to Germany. They there return him his capital, with another accretion of profit. We will fuppofe, that he re-invefts his capital with hemp or flax for the Britifh, or in linnens for the American market. He is by this operation enabled to go back again to America, either with Ruffian or German manufactures, bought with Britifh commodities, or felling what he bought of Ruffia or Germany in the Britifh markets, with a ftill more increafed quantity of Britifh manufactures than what any direct trade between America and Great Britain could have purchafed. Here again the fame queftions may be afked, and muft receive the fame anfwers.

On the contrary, wherever there is a *round-about trade*, there the commercial operations are obftructed, and the advantages greatly defalcated, if not,

in

in many inftances, entirely loft. The obliging the merchant to bring rice from the foutheŗn latitudes northward to Great Britain, which rice muft go back again fouth to its market in the fouthern parts of Europe and the Streights, was a round-about trade, it was labour loft, it was a wafte of expence, an unprofitable detention of capital, and the commodity was fent by *Tom Long the carrier* to market. The monopoly therefore, in that cafe, where it created a round-about trade, hath been relaxed. Sugars are in the fame cafe; and a like relaxation, under peculiar regulations relating to that peculiar article, have been recommended, and might be fafely and beneficially given. There are fome parts of the tobacco crops, which, in the affortment, might be admitted to fomewhat a fimilar liberty without danger, but with benefit. Nay, *that intermediate operation of the circuitous trade,* mentioned above, which obliges the Virginian tobacco to come to England before it goes to Germany, and the German linnens alfo to come to England before they go to America, *is a round-about trade,* a needlefs and very difadvantageous operation, in which fome relaxation ought to be made. I can fee, that the Englifh merchant may lofe a commiffion, but labour and expence would be faved to the community. In like manner the obliging the Weft India fhips, which, fince the interruption of the American trade, load ftaves, lumber and corn in England, which articles are brought from foreign parts, is obliging them to take up thefe things by a round-about trade; whereas, if they were permitted to fhip, in Britifh fhipping only, thefe articles at the foreign markets directly for the Weft Indies, many inconveniencies, which the Britifh part of the community experiences, might be avoided, and both labour and expence faved to the community at large. If falt fifh, which is intended for the fouthern markets, was obliged to be brought northward firft to England, and fo go round about to the fouth, its proper market, it would create a round-about trade. If thefe fhips loading with falt for their back carriage were obliged to come round by England, it would create a round-about trade, and in either cafe would wafte labour, and might lofe all the profit of the capital employed. The monopoly therefore does not take place in this.

The permitting, in certain cafes ftated, and under certain regulations fpecified, the Americans who go with fifh directly to the Streight, Spain, or Portugal, to purchafe there, if purchafed of Britifh merchants, certain articles, and to carry the fame, fo purchafed, directly back to America, fo far as it would avoid the round-about trade, perfevering, and even extending at the fame time the Britifh market, has been for twelve or fourteen years fucceffively recommended.

I think in general on this fubject, that wherever the monopoly would create a round-about trade, it fhould not take place; and that wherever it hath occafioned any fuch round-about operation, it fhould be relaxed; al-

ways

ways however keeping in view this object and end, namely, that so far as our colonies are to be considered as an institution, established and directed to encrease the naval force of our marine empire, and so far as that force derives in any degree from the operations of their commercial powers, so far that monopoly, which engrafts them upon our internal establishment, is indispensible, and ought never to be departed from or relaxed. The sovereign power, which hath the care of the defence and strength of the empire, ought never to permit any the most flattering idea of commercial opulence to come in competition with the solid ground of strength and defence. In this way of reasoning I find myself joined by you, who reason in the same way, and almost in the same words, when speaking of the act of navigation you say, that, " although it be not favourable to foreign commerce, or to the growth " of that general opulence which might arise from it, yet, as defence " is of much more importance than opulence, it is the wisest of all the " commercial regulations of England". On the ground and deriving my reasoning from the same principle, I say, that the monoply is of the same spirit ; is not only wise, but is also necessary, and that it is not the monopoly, but the injudicious undistinguishing application of it, without that reason which alone can justify it, and in channels where it necessarily creates a round-about trade, which renders it disadvantageous, not only to the colonies, but to the general community of the empire.

As no round-about trade, unless where the obliging the colony trade to submit to such, is necessary to the system of defence, should be occasioned, but should even, where it has taken place, be relaxed, so, on the contrary, * I have always thought, that a circuitous operation in the colony trade, as the think which of all others tend most to increase and extend the American markets for British manufactures, should be allowed and encouraged, provided that trade in its circuition keeps its course *in an orbit that hath Great Britain for its center*.

Having thus shewn, simply to the point of stating the case, not arguing it, that a circuitous commerce and a round-about trade are two very different and distinct things, having very different operations and very different effects : having shewn that the circuitous trade is very advantageous, while a round-about trade is always detrimental, but that the circuitous commerce of the colonies is not that hurtful round-about trade which you treat as occasioned by the monopoly, I will now proceed to examine, under their several heads, your application of the principles which you lay down in your analysis, as what directs your synthetic reasonings on the commercial institutions which have taken place in the British œconomy.

---

* Vide Administ. of the British colonies, Vol. I. C. VIII.

Although

Although I perfectly agree with you, that the *reftraints on the importation* of fuch foreign goods as can be produced cheaper at home are ufelefs ; and that the laying reftraints on the importation of fuch as cannot be made fo cheap at home, anfwers no good end, but may be hurtful ; although I allow, that thefe meafures, as a kind of inftitution of monopoly in favour of in-ternal induftry in preference, or to the exclufion of the produce of foreign induftry coming to it, does not always tend to encourage the home induftry, but, on the contrary, gives a falfe turn to it, puts it on a falfe ground and profit, and may have the effect of forcing an unprofitable labour : yet I am unwilling to quit the principle of encouraging the firft efforts of home induf-try, if employed on home commodities in the home market, as I think the principle, applied only in cafes where it is wanted, may be very beneficial ; I had rather, in my notions of political œconomy, abide by the principle, and examine, upon each application of it, how it does or does not operate to en-courage a profitable induftry, fkill and habit in peculiar branches of labour, which the fociety has to learn, and which learnt will be profitable. If a fociety, which once ufed to fend abroad its rude produce to purchafe manufactures made of that very rude produce fo fent out, and which it knew not how to work up, had never been, by fome adventitious aid, over and above what the fources of the firft efforts of its induftry could have given, encouraged to be-gin in trials of its fkill ; if the individual is not, while he is learning his trade, and the fkill of working profitably in it, fupported in part, he can never at-tempt to learn it ; if the fociety does not pay for the learning, it can never have it ; although it be true at firft that the *apprentice* (for by that name I will ex-prefs the firft efforts of a manufacture) is not employed to the greateft advan-tage, becaufe he might buy the articles which he is learning to make, cheaper than he can make them ; although the community pays this difference ; al-though thefe efforts, thus artificially forced, are at firft difadvantageous and unprofitable to the community : yet by his induftry being fo directed to, and fo fupported in a line of labour, which he could not naturally have gone into, nor could have fupported himfelf by, thefe firft efforts, which the commu-nity pays for, do by repeated exercife produce fkill, which in time will work as well, and enable the home manufacturer (if his labour is *employed on na-tive home rude produce*) to fell as cheap, and foon cheaper, than the foreign workman and manufacturer ; his labour then will become profitable to him-felf, and advantageous to the community of which he is a part. It was thus our woollen and hardware manufactures were firft encouraged and fupported ; but the very fame principle, and the fame reafoning upon it, hath always led me to a perfuafion, that no aids of a monopoly in the home market, nor no bounties, can ever force a manufacture founded and *employed on foreign rude ma-terials*. It is an attempt, by robbing Peter to pay Paul, to eftablish a trade,

the

the natural profit of which cannot support the establishment, and the loss of which must be made up to it by payments from the society at large. Against such your principle, in the full force of its arguments, stands unanswerable. Such is the linnen manufacture wrought on foreign line and flax; such is the silk in some degree; this last, however, so far differs, as that rude material may be imported full as cheap as any rival country in Europe can raise it.

You think, the restraints upon the importation of live cattle and corn an unreasonable and ungenerous monopoly, for that the grazing and farming business of Great Britain could be but little affected by a free importation of these, and not in the least hurt. As, on the contrary, I think, any change in this part of our system might be attended with the most important consequences, especially to a class of people who bear the chief burthen of all the taxes, and are the support of the state of the community. I own, I tremble for the change, and should hope this matter may be a little more thoroughly explored, in all the effects of its operation, before any such idea becomes a leading doctrine.

You have with clear and profound reasoning * shewn, that in an improving state of the community, the prices of cattle and of butchers meat, and the lesser articles of the supply must start, and continue to rise until they come to such a rate, as shall make it worth the farmer's while to cultivate the land, which he rents, to the purposes of breeding and feeding such cattle, and to the raising these other articles for the market; this you properly call *the natural progress of improvement*, and these rising values *the natural course of prices*. If a free importation of cattle and of these lesser articles should be allowed, this *adventitious supply* coming from countries which have great wastes for breeding cattle, which do not pay such heavy taxes, and which are not arrived at that degree of improvement in which this country is found, such importation *must derange this scale of natural prices, and must arrest this progress of improvement in its course*. If such foreign country can breed and feed, and afford to import and bring to market cattle and these lesser articles cheaper than our grazer can, the grazing business at home must cease. Well—but say you, if under these circumstances grazing will not answer, the land will be broken up for tillage. But here again, if a free importation of corn, on a like plan, derived from such reasoning on these principles, is, as you recommend, permitted, that branch of business, not capable of farther extension, and met at market by such importation, will be at a stand, and finally become retrogade; we shall be obliged to give up all our improvements, and return to our wastes and commons. In order to obviate in some measure these objections, a kind of distinction is made between the importation of lean and fat cattle.

The

* B. I. C. II. Part III.

The importation of lean cattle would not, fays the argument, hurt, but he-néfit the feeding farms. The breeding farms, however, would be ruined; and there is a link of connection, which fo allies the whole progrefs of country bu-finefs in one chain of intercommunion, that all in the end would fuffer and be undone.

A fecond palliative ufed to obviate thefe objections, which naturally arife againft this idea of giving up our fyftem of reftraints on importation of cattle, * is, that the importation of *falt provifions* could never come in competition with the frefh provifions of the country. To try how this would operate, let us fuppofe that the Victualling-Office, as the law now ftands, is in the ordinary courfe of taking great quantities of cattle, and in the extraordinary demand which war occafions, takes off a proportionate encreafed number; this of courfe raifes the price of the grazers fales, and countervails, in fome meafure, with the landed intereft, the burthen of the encreafed taxes. But if a free im-portation of falt provifions is to take place as a fettled fyftem, the Englifh gra-zer, while the war encreafes his burthens, and raifes the price of every article which he purchafes, is himfelf met at the market by a competition brought againft him from a country that does not bear this encreafed burthen; and he cannot therefore find that *natural fcale of price,* which the maintenance of his bufinefs and relative ftate in the country requires; he muft be ruined, and the land foon rendered incapable of paying its rents, and of raifing thofe very taxes.

In the fame train of reafoning you think, that a free importation of corn could very little affect the intereft of the farmers of Great Britain, becaufe the quantity imported, even in times of the greateft fcarcity, bears fo incon-fiderable a proportion to the whole ftock raifed. From this argument, found-ed in fact, you think the farmers could have nothing to fear from the freeft importation; and you reproach them on the account of the fyftem of reftraint againft free importation of corn, as forgetting the generofity which is natural to their ftation, in demanding the exclufive privilege of fupplying their coun-trymen. If here, Sir, you had weighed well a diftinction which Monf. Necker † has, with exquifite precifion, explained, you would have fpared this reproach. It is not the ratio of the quantity of corn exported or imported, and the quantity of the whole ftock raifed, but the ratio between the *furplus* and this quantity exported or imported, which creates the effect; it is not a ratio of $\frac{1}{577}$, but a ratio of $\frac{1}{15}$, which acts and which operates on the market; it is not the $\frac{1}{577}$ part, but the $\frac{1}{15}$th part which would operate to the depreffion of the market and the oppreffion of the farmer.

Chearful under the burthen of the taxes, and fpiritedly willing to pay them in fupport of his country, he only wifhes to enable himfelf to do fo from his induftry, and the natural profits of it at his own market, without having that

market

---

* Vol. II. P. 41.   † Sur la Legiflation & le Commerce des Graines.

market loaded from an external supply, and depressed by a competition from countries which are not in that state of improvement, and do not pay those taxes, which he must add to his price, if he is to live and pay them; he does not desire the *exclusive* supply, but a fair and equal market on the natural scale of prices, which shall give vent to his supply; this surely he may do without reproach. On the contrary, were it possible to suppose that the country gentleman could be persuaded to change the system, and give up the security which the restraint on importation gives him in his interest, he would deservedly incur the real reproach of having lost that practical sense, which the country gentlemen have always hitherto been found to have, when they come to real business.

But I think you rather misrepresent our system of restraint on importation of corn; it does not absolutely prohibit corn from being brought into the country, and does not establish *an exclusive supply* in the country land-owner; it only restrains such an importation as may either in quantity or price injure the free and fair vent of our own supply in our own market, at such prices as the general state of the improvement of the community and the scale of prices, which is the natural consequence, require.

From the consideration of our restraints on importation of corn, whose operations act as a bounty, you proceed to the consideration of the direct BOUNTY which our system gives *on the exportation of corn*, to which you make the like, but stronger objections. As you seem on this subject to have adopted the reasoning which * Mr. Necker uses, and to have copied it closely; and as his book, as well as your's, will carry great authority with it, I will in this place examine both your objections *ensemble*.

Contrary to the common use made of the popular argument in favour of the measure, you both say, the measure has a direct tendency *in the instant* to raise the price of corn in the interior market, and to enable the merchant to introduce it into the foreign market at a lower price. What you say is fact, and the truth rightly understood; and yet while this measure encourages a plenty, overflowing with a constant succession of surplusses, it hath a tendency, *in a series of times taken together*, to lower the price. That our measure of the bounty has not been the sole cause of lowering the price of corn, Mr. Necker gives a decisive proof in fact, which you † copy. That the general lowering of the price of corn is not owing to the English measure of *the bounty on exportation*, is (he says) plain, because the same general lowering of the price has taken place in France in the same period, where a direct contrary system, *a total prohibition of exportation*, hath invariably prevailed till very lately. You add to his argument an assertion, " that it raises however *not the real but nominal price only*, " and is of no use to the landed interest." There is perhaps (you say) but one

set

* Sur la Legislation & le Commerce des Graines.   † Vol. I. P. 248.

set of men in the whole commonwealth to whom the bounty either was or could easily be serviceable, these are the corn-merchants; it loads (you add) the publick revenue with a very considerable expence, but does not in any respect encrease the real value of the landed man's commodity.

Mr. Necker has also said that the bounty is not necessary; for if there be a surplus, and the foreign market wants it, it will have it without the aid of the bounty. The difference only is, that if the merchant finds that he cannot export it at the price of the British market, so as to carry it to the foreign market, he must wait till it falls in price in England, or rises in the foreign market, as many shillings per quarter as the bounty would give: *then* he will be equally able to export it *without* as *before with* the bounty. In a corollary of which argument you join him in saying, as he had said, that if the surplus quantity may be, by the aid of the bounty, thus exported when corn is at a high price, the surplus of a plentiful year will always so go out, as not to come in aid to relieve the scarcity of a defective one.

After having (in a manner indeed which rather has reference to the effect it might have in France) reprobated the measure of granting a bounty on the exportation of corn, he gives an opinion, in which I own I was surprized to find you following him; that if an encouragement is necessary to agriculture, it should be given *not on the exportation, but on the production.*

I will first state what I think to be the real operations and end of the bounty on corn exported, and then consider the positions above, not by way of reply, but by comparison on fair examination, mark wherein they deviate and differ from the real state of the case.

Any country rising in that progressive state of improvement, by which England for near a century hath been rising, must have experienced *a continued influx of riches*; that continued influx must have and hath created *a continued progressive rise of prices*. If the continuation of the influx was arrested in its course, however great *the quantity of* riches which hath come in, however great the glut of money; yet, after it hath spread itself in all parts, and found its general level, *all* prices will be proportionably raised; the original proportions which they held, before the start of prices, will be restored; all therefore, however high, will be but *nominal*, and a greater or a less quantity of the precious metals will be totally indifferent; but the case is very different, while the influx is in continuance. During its operation it starts the prices of things, but of different things with very different velocity in the motion of the rise. Objects of fancy, caprice, luxurious use, and the lesser articles of food, which bore little or no price, while the necessaries must always have born a certain price, even what may be called a high price in a poor and unimproved state of the community, will, when the progression of improvement begins, start first in price, and with a velocity that will continue to *forerun* the velocity of rise in the price of

necessaries.

necessaries. The relative proportion of the scale of prices being changed, the difference of the prices is real, and corn will be always last and lowest in the scale. Although the price of corn may and will rise, yet not rising in proportion to other things, and the rents of land and the wages of labour depending on the price of corn, the price of every other thing must not only rise before rent and wages can start in price, but must continue *so to forerun* in their rise, that the landed man and labourer must be in a continued state of oppression and distress: that they are so in fact, the invariable and universal experience of all improving countries, actuating manufactures and trades, demonstrates. In the end all must equally partake of the general prosperity; corn must rise in price; rents must rise; wages must be encreased: but during the continuance of the influx there must be a partial distress, which, although relative, is not the less but the more aggravated from being relative, others being in the actual enjoyment of a prosperity which the landed man can but look up to and hope for in the end. If the operation was short, and if the influx soon spread itself into a level, it would not be of much moment in what order the scale of prices arose. In a country where the land-workers and owners are few, in proportion to those employed in trade and commerce, as in rich commercial countries of small extent, there this effect is soon produced; there the landed interest cannot suffer much from the disproportionate velocity of the rise of prices, however accelerated; but in a trading and commercial country, *of large extent*, the spreading and level of the inflowing riches must be an operation of so long time, and the effect so far removed from the first cause, that the land-worker and owner can never receive a proportionate relief, much less the benefit of an equable scale of prices, *while that cause is in operation*. If the influx be a continued encreasing operation, the scale will always be ascending. In a country circumstanced as thus described, if the legislator is ever to intermeddle, or can ever do any good by meddling in these matters, his interference should be directed to relieve this oppressed order and class of the community. The English measure of the bounty does this, by aiding in its first effect the relative, and therefore *real price* of the produce of the land *without obstructing the natural effects* of the advancing and improving state of the community. It relieves the relative distress, which the acceleration of the inflowing of riches occasions to the land-worker; it helps to accelerate the rising of the price of his commodity, and in some measure guards them from a greater distress, which they would otherwise feel: as it is, the traders and merchants eat out the landed man: they do suffer, but much less than they would do. In a country of this sort the velocity of the influx of riches (especially if *an artificial influx* by paper money is added to the real one) may have even too much acceleration, if care is not taken at the same time to accelerate also the distribution of these riches into every channel and duct. In such a country as England, but more especially in
France,

France, if commerce be encouraged by the force of any artificial fpring, if a difproportionate and * *more than natural* influx of riches comes in upon it, how much foever (when this influx may in the end have taken its whole effect and fpread itfelf into a level) the land and labourer muft necessarily fhare in the general profperity, yet if care is not taken to give acceleration to the motion of the landed intereft, in fome proportion to the motion of the advance of commerce, and the influx of riches, the landed intereft muft remain under a continued depreffion of circumftances. Under this relative depreffion the land-worker, while he is buying every thing he wants at an advanced price, requires fome adventitious force or fpring to aid the velocity of the rife of the price of his commodity which he hath to fell. The wifdom of our anceftors, men of bufinefs, acting not from felfifh and ungenerous motives, not from any jealoufy of commerce, but from feeling and experience, gave this very encouragement, and gave it, in the very way in which it could have the trueft effect; in which it could do the leaft harm, and the moft good. They encouraged the land-worker without checking the operations of commerce, or retarding the progrefs of improvement: and while in the direct inftant they effected by the bounty a rife of price to the faleable commodity of the land-worker, and gave that encouragement, which was thus become neceffary; yet they fo gave the bounty, as that in the remote effect it would prevent the enhancing of the general price, becaufe the bounty encouraged the raifing not only a furplus, but a fucceffion of furpluffes. They converted thefe furpluffes even of our food into an article of commerce, and encouraged, and made it the intereft of the corn merchant to trade with it in every part of the world.

Thus acted the homely underftanding of the country gentlemen *upon practice*; men of refined and great abilities, fpeculating in the clofet, *decide upon theory*, that it would have anfwered the fame ends better to have given the bounty *not on exportation, but on production.*

As the bounty on exportation goes only to the furplus exported, and as a bounty on production muft have gone to the whole quantity raifed, which meafure do you, who made the objection, think would load the publick revenue moft? But unlefs there was an affured conftant vent by exportation of any furplus that fhould be raifed, fuch a bounty as you and Mr. Necker recommend, would never encreafe the quantity, or raife a furplus, (for fay you, B. IV. C. V. P. 123) " unlefs the furplus can in all ordinary cafes be exported, the " grower will be careful never to grow any more than what the bare con-

---

* Either by an undue creation of paper motion, or by the bringing in great quantities of money amaffed by conqueft or by rapine, as was the cafe in Rome, by the money brought from Afia; as was the cafe in Britain, by the money brought from Indoftan.

fumption

" fumption of the home market requires, and that market will be very fel-
" dom overftocked, but will be generally underftocked." To what end, fay
I, fhould the farmer work; it would be only making to himfelf work, to
lofe profit, for the more he raifed, the lefs would be the price.

On the contrary, the bounty on the exportation, at the fame time that it
doth (as you and Mr. Necker juftly obferve) actually and directly raife the
price of the commodity, it raifes (I fay) *not the nominal* but the *real* price,
for it brings that price which was *relatively* too low, nearer to the level of the
general fcale of prices : At the fame time that it is (as you truly fay) ferviceable to the corn-merchant, it enables him, without lowering the price of corn
below the rate at which the farmer in the country can afford to produce it, to
throw it into the general circulation of the commerce of Europe at an average
rate which fuits that commerce. This tends to encreafe, and does encreafe the
quantity raifed, and yet preventing on one hand a difcouraging fall, or a difproportionate inhancement of price on the other, keeps that price equable ; and
by creating a fucceffion of furpluffes, obviates your fear, that the exportation
of the furplus of the plentiful year fhould prevent the ufe of a furplus, which
fhould relieve, and come in aid to the defects of a fcarce one; for it doth
actually, by the fucceffion of furpluffes, which the high prices of the home
market will always firft command, provide againft fuch fcarcity, which point
the regulations in the permanent corn law, of the 13th of G. III. on this
head do ftill more effectually fecure.

Let us now try how your's and Mr. Necker's objections to the Englifh meafure of granting a bounty on corn exported bear againft thefe operations.

Let us try Mr. Necker's firft objection, viz. that it is a meafure unneceffary, becaufe, fays he, if there be a furplus which the foreign market wants, it will take
it off, as foon as the home price falls, or the foreign prices rife, as many fhillings
in the quarter of corn as the amount of the bounty comes to. We fhall find, that
if no furplus of wheat, for inftance, can go out and flow in the channels of the
European market, at a higher price than 32 fhillings per quarter, (the general
average price of wheat in Europe) there will be no fuch furplus ; the farmer, in
the prefent improved ftate of England, loaded at the fame time as it is with taxes,
cannot afford to raife wheat at that price.: And if the Britifh merchant did
wait till the Englifh wheat did fink to that price, he might better never export it.; he would find, that the Dutch, Hambrough or Dantzic merchant
had got to market before him, and had foreftalled it. On the other hand
confidering that, at the very loweft eftimation, the farmer cannot raife wheat at a
lower average rate than 37 fhillings per quarter, the bounty adds the five fhillings,
per quarter, which is juft fufficient on one hand to enable the merchant to
give the farmer a living price, and on the other to carry it to the foreign market at the average rates of that market ; fo that if the encouragement of the
farmer, and of the fupply be proper, and if " the bufinefs of the corn-merchant

" chant be in reality that trade, (as you fay) which, if properly protected and
" encouraged, would contribute the moft to the raifing of corn."* This
meafure of a bounty on export is every way not only beneficial, but neceffary : although you have faid, in one place, that it is ferviceable to the corn
merchant *only*, yet in this view you yourfelf find, that this trade of the corn
merchant " will fupport the trade of the farmer, in the fame manner as the
" wholefale dealer fupports that of the manufacturer."

The next objection in which you and Mr. Necker join, is, that the doing
any thing to raife the price of *corn* (as you exprefs it, of *fubfiftance*, as Mr.
Necker rather more logically) in the home-market, muft of courfe raife the
expence of our manufactures, and give advantage to the rival manufactures
of every part of Europe againft us. This objection takes rife from a total
mif-ftating of the cafe.

If corn was the firft article which ftarted in price, fo that all other commodities followed it, then indeed both your pofitions would be true; firft,
that fo far as refpects the home market, we fhould only raife the *nominal*
price, for all rifing proportionably, there would be no alteration in the *ra-*
tios of the fcale : this would therefore be of no ufe to the farmer on one hand,
but by raifing *all the articles of fubfiftance and fupply*, our manufactures muft
become too dear for the average rates of the general market. But the contrary is the fact. Corn is the laft of all the articles of the market which
ftarts in its price, and rifes always with the floweft motion. It is only in
confequence of all other commodities having arifen, that a rife in this becomes neceffary, and when it does begin to rife, it follows with fuch unequal motion, that fome encouragement becomes neceffary, as a fpring to aid
the velocity of its rife in proportion to other things. It is not the rife of
the price of corn, but the general improved ftate of the country, raifing the
rates of all things, and the burthen of taxes fucceffively accumulated, which
raifes the price of our manufactures. On the contrary, encouraging the
raifing of corn by a good price in the direct inftant, creates a plenty : a
plenty, with a fucceffion of furpluffes, keeps down the price, taken in a general feries of times ; and in fome meafure it tends alfo to lower the price of
manufactures, by the number of hands which plenty of fubfiftance, if I
may fo exprefs myfelf, always creates.

Seeing then nothing narrow, invidious, felfifh, or ungenerous in our fyftem of reftraints and bounties on our corn trade, confidering it as a neceffary, wife and beneficial fyftem, interwoven into the general œconomy of
our agriculture, manufactures and commerce : perfuaded that a certain fober
conviction of experience, arifing from practice, firft fuggefted the truth, I
cannot but hope, that the fame wifdom which gave the bounty, will operate with the country gentlemen, to doubt every fpeculation of clofet doctrine,

* B. IV. C. V. P. 126.

trine, and to oppofe, on every occafion, every the moft diftant attempt to lower, or to confine within narrower limits this bounty.

You have made feveral obfervations on, fome objections to, and give rather a hafty and fummary judgment on the general fyftem of our corn laws; I have made fome remarks on thefe parts alfo, but I fhall referve thefe to another place, where I fhall have occafion to examine all the regulations relative to the fupply of the community with bread-corn, and to the manner in which the furplus of that fupply is converted into an article of commerce.

I will now proceed to the confideration of your opinions and doctrines refpecting the *monopoly of the colony trade.*

You allow, * " this colony-trade to be very advantageous, though not by " means, yet in fpight, of the monopoly, and that the natural good effects " of it more than counterbalance to Great Britain the bad effects of the mo- " nopoly; fo that, monopoly and all together, that trade, even as it is car- " ried on at prefent, is not only advantageous, but greatly advantageous." Although you allow this, yet while you confider our colonies " rather as a caufe of weaknefs than of ftrength", " as a fource of expence not revenue" ; while you fay, that + " the invidious and malignant project of excluding other nations from any fhare" in our colony-trade depreffes the induftry of all other countries, but chiefly that of the colonies, without in the leaft encreafing, but on the contrary diminifhing, that of the country in whofe favour it is eftablifhed; that, in order to obtain a relative advantage, that country not only gives up an abfolute one in this trade itfelf, but fubjects itfelf to both an abfolute and relative difadvantage in every other branch of trade wherein this monopoly does not operate. While you fay this, you conclude, ‡ " that " under the prefent fyftem of management, Great Britain derives nothing " but lofs from the dominion which fhe affumes over her colonies." In confequence of this doctrine, you are not only for breaking up the monopoly, but for a difmemberment of the empire, § by giving up the dominion over our colonies. This prompt and hafty conclufion is very unlike the author of " the Treatife on the wealth of nations," it favours more of the puzzled inexperience of an unpracticed furgeon, who is more ready with his amputation knife, than prepared in the fkill of healing medicines. If we lofe our colonies, we muft fubmit to our fate; but the idea of parting with them on the ground of fyftem, is much like the fyftem which an ironical proverb recommends, " *of dying to fave charges*". When fuperficial importants talk, write, or vend fuch their idle crudities, one is not furprized; unworthy of notice they are neglected: but when a man, who, like yourfelf, hath joined practical knowledge to the moft refined fpirit of fpeculation, can fuffer himfelf fo to be miflead, an examination of thofe fpeculations, or at leaft of their confequences, as they lead to practice, is due to him and to the world: I will therefore examine your objections to the monopoly, and

the

* B. IV. C. VII. P. 194.   + Ibid. P. 196.   ‡ Ibid. P. 224.   § Ibid. P. 224.

the reasoning whereon you found them, by the actual operations and effects of this colony-trade, acted upon by this monopoly.

But first I cannot but observe, that a round assertion, " that our colonies " have never yet furnished any military force for the defence of the mother " country, and that they have been a cause rather of weakness than of " strength", is such as should have followed only from a deduction of facts: and I will beg leave to suggest to you some facts that induce me, and may perhaps you also, to be of a very different opinion. That very naval force, which by their armed vessels they are now so destructively exerting against our West-India trade and transports, they did very effectively in the two late wars, especially in the last, exert to the ruin of the West Indian commerce of France and Spain, and to the almost total obstruction of all communication of those countries with their respective colonies. If you have not heard of what they did then, judge of it by what they are able to do now, against the whole undiverted power of their mother country.

The mother country, with her own immediate force, must always meet the immediate force of its enemies, wherever exerted. If therefore France sent its European forces to America, Great Britain, with her European force, must meet them in that field. If the strength of our colonies, exerted against the colonial strength of France or Spain was effective; or if it was ready to serve where it could best serve, and where most wanted; if it was not only equal to its own defence, but did act against the enemy offensively also, with effect, it did bring forth " a military force for the defence of the mother country." The military force of the province of Massachusett's Bay not only defended the dominions of the mother country in that province, but for many years exerted itself in defending Accadia or Nova Scotia. In the war which ended by the peace of Aix la Chapelle, the military force of that province took Louisburg and Cape Breton, an acquisition which purchased for the mother country that peace. So far as my assertion may go in proof, I will venture to assert, that had France during the last war effectuated a landing in Great Britain, and had been able to maintain themselves there until an account of it should have arrived in New England, I should have been able to have brought over, or sent from the province, Massachusett's Bay (perhaps joined by Connecticut also) " a military force " for the defence of the mother country".

On the point of revenue, I will also beg leave to repeat, because I have now still stronger reason for it, an assertion which I made in parliament, that before we went to decided war, a revenue might have been had upon compact, on terms which would have established the constitutional sovereignty of this country, regulating at the same time the trade and naval powers of the colonies, if those terms might have gone, at the same time, to the securing the rights of those colonies as granted by the government of that mother country,

country. As to the ways and means of coming at the *grounds of agreement*, and the nature of that revenue and compact, an explanation never will be withheld, if ever again events shall render them practical. The colonies did always raise a revenue in support of that establishment of internal government, which the mother country had set over them; I do not say that I approve the manner in which they applied it. As to their raising, while *under a state of minority*, farther taxes, *except port duties*, for the *external purposes of the empire at large*, I will give no opinion, but submit it to your judgment, who have thoroughly considered the different fructuation of surplus produce expended in revenue, or vested in circulating capital, for further improvements, which further extend the British market in America, to decide, which of the two were, in that state, most beneficial to the mother country. I reason here in the line in which you consider the subject, the line of political œconomy, not of administration of government.

Your objections to the monopoly endeavour to prove, that, in *the invidious and malignant project* (as you stile it) of excluding as much as possible all other nations from any share in the trade of our colonies, Great Britain sacrifices, in a great degree, an absolute advantage, to enjoy in a lesser degree a relative one : that if the trade had been free and open, the industry of the colonies would not only have been less cramped, but the source of all the advantages deriving to Europe, from the settlement of Europeans in America, would have been more abundant and more productive of advantage : and that, although Great Britain had sacrificed a relative advantage which she derived from the exclusive trade, she would yet have had a greater absolute advantage ; as an explanatory proof you instance in the monopoly of the article of tobacco. The market opened for this article would, you think, *probably* have lowered the profits of a tobacco-plantation nearer to the level of a corn-farm ; the price of the commodity would *probably* have been lowered, and an *equal quantity* of the commodities, either of England or of any other country, might have *purchased a greater quantity* of tobacco than it can at present. I will suppose with you, that by this new arrangement, and the consequential *new ratio in the scale* of prices betwixt Europe and America, that Great Britain as well as other coun-tries would have derived a great absolute advantage : yet as these other countries would have derived the same advantage from our colonies, this fancied absolute advantage could be but merely *nominal*; for although England thus got more tobacco for a less quantity of British commodities, yet as other countries also got the same on the same terms directly from Maryland or Virginia, what Great Britain thus got would not only be less in value, but would run the risque of being a drug upon her hands. In giving up therefore the relative advantage which she enjoyed by her exclusive trade, *while she gained a nominal*, she would lose every *real* advantage. Besides, there is surely some management to be observed in the culture of an article of produce, whose con-

sumption

fumption hath arifen from whim and caprice into an habitual, but not a ne-ceffary ufe: inftead of encouraging an unbounded produce of this, it were beft, *probably*, that it fhould be limited. I am fure it is an abfolute advan-tage to Great Britain, that Virginia and Maryland fhould find it moft to their advantage to cultivate tobacco, rice, indico, or any other exotick commodity, than that by bringing the profits of a tobacco-plantation nearer upon a level with thofe of a corn farm; they fhould find their advantage in raifing corn to the rivalling us at the European markets in our home commodity, and to the depreffion of our agriculture. So far therefore as this argument goes, it de-monftrates to me, at leaft, that by quitting the relative, *a real* advantage, we fhould not even gain a *nominal* advantage, but fhould run every rifque of lofing every advantage, both relative and abfolute, real and nominal, which is to be derived from this fource reftrained, and at the fame time of fetting up a rival culture againft our own agriculture. If you fee the matter in this light in which it appears to me, you will, I am fure, feel how dangerous it is to vend thefe novelties of fpeculation againft the fober conviction of experience.

Your argument goes on to ftate, that there are *very probable reafons for be-lieving*, that although we do facrifice this abfolute advantage (which would, *it is fuppofed*, probably be drawn from a free and open trade) for a narrow mean relative advantage; yet we do not poffefs even this relative advantage, without fubjecting ourfelves, at the fame time, both to an abfolute and to a relative difadvantage in almoft every other branch of trade of which we have not the monopoly.

It ftrikes me as material, and I am fure, therefore, you will excufe me making, in this place, one remark even *on the manner* of your argument, and how *you ftretch your reafoning nicely*. You in words advance upon the ground of *probable reafons for believing* only, you prove by probable fuppofitions only; yet moft people who read your book, will think you mean to fet up an abfo-lute proof, and your conclufion is drawn as though you had.

You proceed to defcribe thefe abfolute and relative difadvantages.

The monopoly of the colony trade, wherein the Englifh merchant was en-abled to fell dear and buy cheap, gave a rate of profit in that trade much above the level of profit in any other, and would therefore never fail of drawing ca-pital from thofe other branches into this, as faft as it could employ fuch. This double effect of drawing capital from all other branches of trade, and of raif-ing the rates of profit higher in our internal trades than it would otherwife have been, arofe at the firft eftablifhment of the monopoly, and hath conti-nued ever fince. Having thus ftated the effect, you proceed to prove them to be bad and difadvantageous.

By drawing, not through the natural effects of trade, but by the artificial ope-rations of the monopoly, capital from other trades, and other branches of trade in Europe, which were greatly advantageous both in a commercial and
in

in a political view, this monopoly, it is *probable* (you fay) may not have occafioned *fo much an addition* to the trade of Great Britain, *as a total change in
its direction.*

First, as to the affertion, that capital has been drawn from certain trades and
certain branches of trade in Europe, and turned by the monopoly into the colony trade, which without this would not have been fo diverted; that (I anfwer) is a matter of fact, which muft not be eftablifhed by an argument, *à
priori*—but on an actual deduction of facts. As I did not find the latter in
your book, I looked into the only records which we have of the progreffive
ftate of our commerce, in a * feries of returns of the imports and exports of
Great Britain, as made to parliament. I cannot afcertain in our European
trade that fact which your theory fuppofes. The tides and currents of commerce, like that of the ocean over which it paffes, are conftantly fhifting their
force and courfe, but this comes not up to your fact. I find no deprivation,
but an encreafed ftate of our European trade; and at the fame time an immenfe multiplied encreafe of our colony trade, and of every branch of commerce connected with it. Suppofing, however, that this fact was true, that
there hath been a *total change* in the direction of our trade, by drawing capital
from feveral of the European trades, and by employing more of our general
capital in the colony trade than would naturally have gone to it, had all trade
been free and open: yet that fuppofition will never, againft fact, prove, that
this monopoly, thus employing more capital in, and deriving more profits
from the colony-trade, hath occafioned a privation of advantage to the trade of
Great Britain in general—Fact contradicts that pofition. Well, but as Great
Britain cannot have fufficient capital to actuate all, it muft occafion a privation in fome of the branches of its trade; for, although there may not be an
abfolute decreafe in certain branches, there is a relative one, as they have not
increafed in the proportion in which they would have done. This is again
argument, *à priori*, in matters of fact, wherein it cannot act as proof; however, for the fake of your argument we will even fuppofe it, and afk the queftion, what then? To which, in my way of reafoning, I fhould anfwer, that
as in the divifion of labour no one man can actuate all the branches of it, fo
in the divifion of the commerce of the world, no nation nor no capital can
carry on all the branches of it in every channel in which it flows. That country then which, while it does lefs in thofe branches of trade wherein leaft is to
be gotten, but has the command in that which exceeds all others in profit,
doth furely draw the greateft poffible advantage from commerce. This part
then of your argument proves to me, affifted by the reafoning which you ufe
in other parts of your work, the very reverfe of the conclufion which you here
draw from it.

You

* A very ufeful collection, publifhed by Sir C. Whitworth, M. P.

You fay in the next place, that this monopoly has contributed to raife and keep up the rates of profit in all the different branches of the Britifh trade higher than they would naturally have been, or, which is the fame thing, to prevent them from falling fo low as they would otherwife have fallen ; and that this forced height of profit hath fubjeƈted the country, where it takes ef-feƈt, both to an abfolute and to relative difadvantage in every branch of trade, in which it has not the monopoly.   I could here anfwer in general by your own reafoning, as you ufe it in the cafe of the profits of grazing and corn land ; as when the ftate of the community is fuch, that it occafions a greater call for, and confequently a greater profit on the one than the other ; that other will foon be converted into the one which is in demand, and will give the greater profits, till both come to a level : fo in commerce, under whatever regulations, either thofe which the natural wants or the political inftitutions of men eftablifh, it is carried on, will always fhift about, and endeavour to flow in thofe channels wherein moft profit is to be had.   That country then which is under thofe fortunate and powerful circumftances, and has the wif-dom fo to profit of thofe circumftances, as to be able to maintain a monopoly of the moft profitable channels ; and be able to maintain, at the fame time, (notwithftanding the clog of its high rates of profits) a fhare of other branches of trade, even where it is underfold, has furely acquired *that afcendency in trad· and commerce*, which is always better underftood than explained.   But I will not reft within thefe entrenchments, I will meet your argument in your open field.

You fay *, that in confequence of thefe high rates of profit, under which our commodities and manufaƈtures muft be brought to market, we muft in our foreign trade " both buy dearer and fell dearer, muft both buy lefs and " fell lefs ;" but I deny the confequence, " that we muft profit lefs," † be-caufe, although thofe high rates may confine the extent, yet raifing the profit of the dealing, we enjoy as much, and produce in trade as much, as if we did more bufinefs of lefs profits : all is kept equal and level as to the foreign trade, and our colony trade goes on, the mean while, in a ftill more rapid profperity. Your conclufion therefore, " that it is in this manner that the capital of Great " Britain has partly been drawn, and partly driven from the greater part of the " different branches of trade, of which fhe has not the monopoly ; from the " trade of Europe in particular, and from that of the countries which lie " round the Mediterranean fea," is neither deducible from your argument, *à priori*, nor will you find it juftified by faƈt

Yet again that we, who think well of the monopoly, may not derive any fupport from thinking, that as the colony-trade is more advantageous to Great Britain than any other, fo the capital being forced into that channel, is of more advantage to the country than if employed any other way.   That we

may

* P. 201. Vol. II,   † P. 219. ibid.

may not avail ourfelves of this comfort, you proceed to fhew it to be " a na-
" tural effect of this monopoly; that it turns our capital from a foreign trade
" of confumption with a neighbouring into one with a more diftant country;
" in many cafes from a *direct trade* of confumption *into a round-about one*,
" and in fome cafes from all foreign trade of confumption into a carrying one."
And as in the analytick part of your work you have fhewn, that the direct
trade of confumption, efpecially that with a neighbouring country, main-
tains the greateft quantity of productive labour, by the direct and frequent returns of its capital; that a round about trade is always lefs advantageous, and
the carrying ftill leaft fo of all; you draw your conclufion, that therefore the
operation of the monopoly, thus acting, turns our capital into channels where
it employs lefs productive labour than it would naturally have done, if the
trade was left to its free and natural operations. By your firft pofition you
mean, that it hath turned the capital from the European trade to the North
American and Weft Indian trade, from whence the returns are lefs frequent,
both on account of the greater diftance, but more efpecially on account of the
peculiar circumftances of America. An improving country, always dealing
beyond their capital, muft wait to pay their debts by their improvements, by
which means, although the merchant may repay himfelf by the profit he puts
upon his goods, and by other means, yet the capital of Great Britain is detained and withheld; and, thus detained, prevented from maintaining fuch a quantity of productive labour as otherwife it would do. In anfwer to this ftate of
the argument (which I hope I have ftated fairly) I fay, that that part of our
capital, which is fome while withheld in America, and does not return directly, is not withheld unprofitably to Great Britain: like that portion of the
harveft which is detained for feed, it is the matrix of a fucceeding and encreafed production; by operating to advance ftill farther thefe improvements,
and confequently the population of thefe countries, it is *creating and extending
a new market*, whofe demands for our productive labour calls forth that labour
fafter and to more advantage, than the fame capital directly returned and
vefted in Britifh goods could do; as it encreafes this market in a conftant pro-
greffion, it calls forth more *manufacturers*; gives a fpring to *agriculture*; and
extends the *commerce* of Great Britain.

Well but, fay you, " fecondly, the monopoly of the colony-trade has, in
" many cafes, forced fome part of the capital of Great Britain from a direct
" foreign trade of confumption into a round-about one." Wherever it does fo,
that is an error in the fyftem, it fhould be corrected and amended, fo far as is
confiftent (as I faid above) with the eftablifhment of the unity of empire in all
its orders and fubordination of orders. I have in a former part of this letter,
and many years ago on other occafions, pointed out fome of thefe errors and
their remedy; but I muft beg here to apply thofe diftinctions, which, in my
remarks on the analytick part of your work, I fhewed to exift in nature and
fact, *between a circuitous and a round-about trade*; and to obferve, that where
your

your objections are pointed againſt the circuitous operations of our colony-trade, they do not act with effect; for theſe are always advantageous, and ſhould be even more encouraged than they are. Such a ſeries of ſuch circuitous operations as create and extend the market, accumulating by each operation a freſh profit, return home not only (by this accumulated capital) with the means of employing more manufacturers, but with having created * an encreaſing demand for more and more manufactures. The encreaſing market of our improving colonies, ſtill more and more rapidly improved by the circuitous trade, muſt, while we have the command of that market, multiply Britiſh manufacturers: theſe manufacturers thus multiplied, † " conſtitute (as " you ſtate it truly) a new market for the produce of the land, the moſt advantageous of all markets, the home market, for corn and cattle."

Another objection yet remains, that in many caſes the colony-trade becomes, by means of the regulations of the monopoly, merely a *carrying trade*. This carrying trade, which you deſcribe as a defect, would be ſo, if the carrying was the only part in which our capital was employed, and the hire of the carriage the only profit that we derive from it; but inſtead of that, joined as it is with the circuitous trade, it becomes, in a political as well as a commercial view, a beneficial part of the operations which employs our own ſhipping.

Having gone through your argument of objection, you cloſe with ſome corollary obſervations, as deriving from it. You think, that the unnatural ſpring applied to the colony-trade, has deſtroyed the natural ballance which would otherwiſe have taken place amongſt all the different branches of Britiſh induſtry, and that the direction of it is thus thrown too much into one channel. The idea then of a blood veſſel, artificially ſwelled beyond its natural dimenſions, ſtrikes your imagination, and you are brought under an apprehenſion of ſome terrible diſorder. As this diſorder did not ſeize Great Britain in the caſe you ſuppoſed, ‡ you then ſearch out five unforeſeen and unthought-of events (to which I could add another very perfectly foreſeen and thoroughly underſtood) which fortunately occurred to prevent it. As I am no *malade imiginair* in politicks, and have no fears of thoſe § " convulſions, apoplexy, or " death," which have been ſo often predicted, I know not how to go ſeriouſly, againſt fact, into reaſoning upon them. That our trade has felt, on a great and ſudden ſhock, no ſuch convulſions or apoplexy, but that its productive powers continue to be actuated, and its circulation to run *in ſome*

---

* This is what, in *the adminiſtration of the Britiſh colonies*, Vol. I. C. VIII. I call creating and ſecuring " an encreaſing nation of appropriated cuſtomers;" which idea you, from that ſuperiority that ſpeaking *è cathedra* always inſpires, treat with ſovereign contempt; " it is, you ſay, a " project fit only for a nation of ſhop-keepers, governed by ſhop-keepers." This idea, however, upon the cloſeſt and ſtricteſt analyſis is the only one I can find preciſely to define the relation which a commercial country bears to its colonies, and to expreſs that inſtitution of policy, in our act of navigation, which you rather too lightly and too contemptuouſly call (p. 222.) " a truly " ſhop-keeper propoſal."

† Ibid. 215. + P. 211. § P. 210.

other

other channels, though our American artery is obſtructed, proves, that this was not our principal, much leſs our ſole great channel of commerce; ſome part, perhaps great part, of our circulation paſſed through it into other remoter veſſels, which is now perhaps full as properly with more profit to the Britiſh merchant, poured through more direct channels. In ſhort, the whole ſtate of our trade, as it ſtands in fact, and is found in effect, is to me a proof in point againſt your caſe in theory.

" * The effect of the monopoly (you ſay) has been not to encreaſe the *quan-* " *tity*, but to alter *the quality* of the manufactures of Great Britain, ſuited to " a market from which the returns are flow," inſtead of keeping on in an old trade, " from which the returns are frequent."

If we conſider the effect which the opening a *new market under a monopoly*, or in *a free trade*, hath on a commercial country, we ſhall find, if it be a market which calls for ſome new aſſortment of manufactures of *a quality different* from the ordinary and accuſtomed ſort, in which that commercial country dealt before this new demand was opened, that *a free and open market*, into which the operations of a competition comes, *is more likely to alter the quality of the manufactures*, than where any commercial country poſſeſſes that market under a monopoly. In the former caſe they muſt watch and ſuit every call, every faſhion, and even caprice of their free cuſtomers; in the latter caſe they will oblige *their appropriated cuſtomers*, to take off ſuch goods as they pleaſe to ſend them, altho' the ſorts do not in quality entirely ſuit that market; they will under this monopoly, carry this ſo far as to drive the country, which is ſubject to the monopoly, into ſmuggling, not only on account of the price, *but merely to get goods of a quality which ſuits them*. Your great knowledge in the practick, as well as theoretick knowledge of our commerce, will be able to ſupply proofs of this fact from many revolutions of our manufactures in different periods of our commerce. It is not therefore *the effect of a monopoly*, ſo much as it would be *the effect of a free and open trade, to alter the quality* of the manufactures of Great Britain. We will then next enquire, *how this monopoly operates as to the increaſe or not of the quantity*. In the firſt ſtep we are agreed, that *this increaſing market of appropriated cuſtomers* doth at this one entrance *encreaſe the quantity* of manufactures demanded. Let us next enquire, how " the ſurplus produce " of the colonies, which (you juſtly ſay †) is the *ſource of all that encreaſe of* " *enjoyments and induſtry*, which Europe derives from the diſcovery and colo- " nization of America," operates under a monopoly, or would operate under a free and open trade to encreaſe the quantity of Britiſh induſtry and manufactures. The articles of this produce are (it is needleſs to enquire how) become of accuſtomed demand in the markets of Europe, not only for its more plea- ſurable enjoyment, but in the line of induſtry alſo. So far as Great Britain hath

* P. 216.   † P. 193.

hath the monopoly of thefe articles, fhe will become *a neceffary trader* in thefe markets. She will not go to fuch markets with thefe articles only; fhe will make up a cargo with affortments of her manufactures alfo; the one will neceffarily introduce the others; and if the firft cannot be had without the latter it will introduce thofe others, where, from the difadvantages of a high fcale of prices, they would not otherwife have been introduced; fo that *our monopoly* of thefe American fources of enjoyments and induftry to the Europeans, *doth not only tend to encreafe* the quantity of our induftry and manufactures *partially, but abfolutely*. As they are interwoven with our general commerce, they do actually tend to introduce and carry on our commerce in our manufactures, even under thofe difadvantages, which you have defcribed as the effects of the monopoly; this is one ground of that *afcendancy in commerce*, which I rather referred to, than defcribed as enjoyed by Great Britain.

As to the fact about the returns of capital, if you will compare notes between the merchant trading in Britifh manufactures to Germany, and the merchant trading with Britifh manufactures to America and the Weft Indies, you will find the returns of the latter upon the whole (if thefe goods go no farther than North America, or our Weft Indies) not flower than thofe from Germany. Credit has, even before the prefent war, been extended in Germany, and fhortened towards America: inquire after this fact in Norwich, London, and the other great manufacturing places, and you will find it fo.

That the productive labour of Great Britain is kept down by the monopoly; that this monopoly prevents its affording revenue fo much as it might; and that rent and wages are always lefs abundant than otherwife they would be, is a corollary of propofitions neither proved by reafoning nor eftablifhed by fact. That the monopoly, raifing the rates of mercantile profit, difcourages the improvement of land, is ftill more aberrant from the line of reafon, and more directly contrary to fact: the reafon you give is, that the fuperior profits made by trade will draw capital from improvements in land. It will fo in the firft inftance; but as this encreafing advanced intereft of trade "conftitutes a new " market for the produce of the land,' the rates of the price of the produce of the land will fo rife, and fo raife the profits made by improvements, that, although at firft, as I have fhewn above, it fuffers a relative depreffion, the application of capital to it will of courfe and neceffarily become a very advantageous employment of fuch: but the new and daily encreafing market of America, of which we have the monopoly, raifing the rates of profit in trade, draws after it the daily afcending rates of that land, which fupplies this market and the workmen in it; and is the very thing coincident with a general profperity, that hath given fuch a fpring to agriculture in this country.

When you fay in another wreath of this corollary, that the high rates of profit neceffarily keep up the high rate of intereft, which *è contra* muft lower the value of land. I anfwer, that the rate of intereft does not neceffarily depend

pend

pend on the rates of profit made by money, but on the proportion of demand for the ufe of it to the quantity which, and the velocity with which, the *influx* of riches, in confequence of an advancing mercantile profperity, brings it into circulation. High profits themfelves will occafion money to come in to the market which wants it; high profits, and an increafing demand, will open and give birth to a fecondary fource by paper circulation: fo that the major of your fyllogifm is not founded in reafon; nor is the con-clufion, that the natural encreafe of rent, and the rife in the value of land, is retarded by the effects of the monopoly, fact. I do here diftinguifh the effects of the monopoly from the effects of the trade itfelf: this, like all other advantageous applications of capital, where great mercantile profits are to be gotten, accelerates the rife of the profits of trade fafter than thofe of land; but thofe of land are in the effect raifed alfo by it; and although in a flower degree of velocity to that of the rife of mercantile profit, *yet not in a retarded but accelerated velocity alfo.*

Upon the whole, I fully and perfectly agree with you, that any regulation which gives a *confined courfe of direction*, and keeps in that line of direction any operation, muft check and deftroy part of the *vis motrix*; with which the body moving would fly off in a *direct courfe.* Juft as the central force, which confines any body to circulate round that center in any given orbit, doth check and diminifh part of the projectile force with which it would have flown off from that orbit: So the monopoly, which requires the colony-trade to obferve Great Britain as its center, doth certainly check and diminifh part of that *commercial activity with which it is at all points in exertion to fly off in a tangent.* Although I agree in this truth, yet being taught to think, that all feparate communities, until fome commercial millenium fhall melt down all into one, muft ever feek to give fuch a fpecifick direction to the operations of their own fpecifick powers, as fhall maintain the feparate and *relative ftate* of exiftence in which each community is placed; and knowing it to be an univerfal law of nature, that in any machine, part of the original *momentum* muft always find itfelf diminifhed in proportion as it becomes neceffary to give a *fpecifick direction* to its operation: So I confider the lofing or leffening part of the productive activity, which the culture and commerce of the colonies might give *in a direct line, that is, to the world at large,* but not to Great Britain efpecially, as analogous to that law of nature; as the very effence of that combination of force, and confequential fpecifick direction, which confines it circulating in an orbit round Great Britain as its center; and as the precife ftate of that theorem, which no politician in the one cafe, any more than any true mechanick in the other, would deny as untrue, or condemn as wrong.

I cannot therefore but remain, and do fancy, that every fober man of bufinefs will remain in the perfuafion and conviction, confirmed by experience,

that

that while the monopoly of our colony trade gives as fuch to Great Britain, in its *relative ftate* of existence in the world, a *relative advantage* in the commercial world; Great Britain doth not lofe unneceffarily any abfolute advantage, nor doth fubject itfelf to either abfolute or relative difadvantage, in all other branches of commerce in which it hath not the monopoly : That it employs our capital, upon the ballance of the whole, to the greateft advantage, and confpires in the means, together with other branches of trade, of drawing forth our utmoft productive induftry : And that under the true fyftem of a monopoly, Great Britain might derive from the dominion which fhe had in her colonies (of which dominion they were, in their due fubordination, part) *force, revenue, and every commercial advantage.*

These are the matters in which I think your book has erred. I have examined them with a view to fuch difcuffion, as may occafion a review of them; becaufe I do really think, that your book, if corrected on thefe points, planned and written as it is, might become an inftitute, containing the *principia* of thofe laws of motion, by which the fyftem of the human community is framed and doth act, AN INSTITUTE *of political œconomy*, fuch as I could heartily wifh, for the reafons given at the beginning of this letter, that fome underftanding Tutor in our Univerfities would take up, as a bafis of lectures on this fubject.

I fhould here have proceeded to the confideration of your plans of the fyftem, which you think Great Britain fhould adopt in her future conduct towards America; but the prefent ftate of events fufpends all political difcuffion on that head. If future events fhall ever lay a rational, found and true ground of colonial government, the propofing of fuch may then be proper, and fhall not be withheld. At prefent *jacta eft alea*, the fate of this country is now at the hazard of events, which force, and not reafon, is to decide. I am afraid we are reafoning here about things which once were, and were moft dear, but are no more.

I cannot conclude this letter without faying, that as I have impreffed upon my mind the higheft opinion of your abilities, learning, and knowledge, and think well of your fair intentions, I hope I have never deviated from the refpect which is due to fuch. I have taken pains to comprehend fully, and have meant to ftate fairly, your reafoning; and to propofe my own, as I ought, with diffidence. If any expreffion breaths the fpirit of controverfy, inftead of what I meant, fair difcuffion, I difavow it; for although perfonally unknown to you, yet from what I learn of you by your works, I find myfelf in every fentiment of refpect and efteem,

SIR,

Your moft obedient,

RICHMOND,
Sept. 25, 1776.

And moft humble Servant,

T. POWNALL.

F   I   N   I   S.

EXCERPT FROM
TYRANNY UNMASKED

John Taylor, *Tyranny Unmasked, an Answer to a Late Pamphlet, entitled Taxation No Tyranny* (London, 1775), pp. 1–19.

John Taylor (1753–1824), a staunch agrarian, was born in Virginia and was one of Thomas Jefferson's contingent. He served as a representative to the Virginia House of Delegates (1779–81 and 1783–5) and served in the US Senate (1792–4, 1803 and 1822–4). Taylor was also a political philosopher who wrote a number of tracts supporting individual and state rights. He was a primary supporter of the Virginia Resolutions of 1798, but opposed the Federal Constitution and permanent debt obligations. This was partly because the inhabitants of Virginia had made a concerted effort to pay off their debt from the War of Independence and so did not want to enter into any agreement that might make them liable for the debts of another state that did not pay in such a timely manner.

Tyranny Unmasked deals with issues of colonial taxation and trade, bringing this collection to the eve of the American Revolution. Taylor addresses the London catchphrase that 'taxation is not tyranny', with the argument that as long as the colonies are not represented in Parliament, taxation is unjust and tyrannical. Taylor claims that the Americans would not mind contributing a reasonable amount of taxes to such causes as public safety and defence, but the Navigation Acts and other duties are excessive and only enrich British merchants, rather than contributing to governmental actions that would benefit the colonies. Taylor concludes his analysis by citing John Locke's claim that a group retains the right to separate from the old society and form a new one that satisfies their own needs.

TYRANNY UNMASKED

AN

ANSWER

TO A

LATE PAMPHLET,

ENTITLED

TAXATION NO TYRANNY.

Profunt minus recte excogitata, cum alios incitent faltem ad
veritatis invectigationem.　　　*Fulb. A Bartel.*

Motos præstat componere fluctus.　　　*Virg.*

When Justice calls,
The noble mind feels honour in concession.
Thompson's Edward and Eleonora.

LONDON:
PRINTED FOR THE AUTHOR; AND SOLD BY W. FLEXNEY,
HOLBORN.
MDCCLXXV.

TYRANNY UNMASKED,

AN ANSWER TO A LATE PAMPHLET ENTITLED TAXATION NO TYRANNY

No subject has for a long time more generally engrossed the attention of the British nation, nor at any time with greater earnestness, than that of American Taxation. The press has now for many months, without intermission, teemed with the freest and fullest discussions of this matter. On all sides it has, for the main, been canvassed hitherto on the cool consideration of parliamentary power on the one hand, and the extent of popular privileges on the other: All seemed content to support or oppose the taxing of America in the British Parliament, as that measure should appear right or wrong, from the spirit of our free constitution. In deference to truth and fact, it must be observed, that reason and argument have for some time decided the matter in favour of American exemption. Without doors, the much boasted supremacy of Parliament, to tax an unrepresented and unrepresentable part of British subjects, hath hardly a single mouth left to echo it. Within the two great national assemblies, the *question* now decides, for government, those measures, which government no longer strives to discuss. It may still go on to adopt such as may promise success to it in its present struggle with America; but the generality are nevertheless unanimous, that America cannot constitutionally be taxed here.

In this state of the matter, when all men had hitherto weighed it by law and constitution, as applied to the specific circumstances of the American colonies, and when thus *put in the balance* it began to shew itself *wanting* on the side of government; steps forth a most redoubted ministerial champion, who tells us that *Taxation is no Tyranny*: thus shaking off at once all the shackles of local circumstances, specific rights, and constitutional liberties; cutting asunder the several knots, which all former combatants, finding themselves bound by them, had patiently tried to untie; and, with his own right arm, laying the Americans on their backs, stunned, silenced, crippled, defeated, at the mercy of the government.

Nothing indeed can be more decisive than the principle, which this advocate has chosen to convey the sense of his performance. It scorns exactness, as it scorns all fear. It scorns limitations, it scorns circumstances, rejecting all mesne views, it darts to an universal conclusion at once: *Taxation is no Tyranny*. We must consider this as an universal proposition. At least, it must be meant as a catch-word, to lay hold of those, who cannot reason; or to make those who can, and who think

America injured, distrust for a moment, at least, their reasonings. And truly, if men can be brought to swallow this proposition, it will prove an effectual *quietus* to silence the Americans, and to allay all the present serments, excited by American taxation, in the British Empire. But, was ever a more daring proposition offered to mankind? one more insulting to common understanding? 'Tis too absurd to deserve a confutation. To attempt to give it one by ever so little reasoning, would be an abuse and waste of sense. But to Englishmen the assertion is attended with double shame and effrontery: though it is entirely of a piece with what tyrants, and the tools of tyrants, even in this nation, have ever wished to establish; and therefore, though not new to Englishmen, yet the more unpardonable by them, who have ever shewn their indignation against it, and risen in fury to crush it. Methinks, therefore, the author might have chosen a more cautious and decent sentiment for the index to his pamphlet; one more near to truth, one less irritating to Englishmen. But these are times, perhaps, for ministerial advocates to try, what Tory-doctrines may be disseminated.

The pamphlet before us evidently fathers itself upon one of such principles. And here, before I proceed further in this thought, I cannot help remarking, that it is exceedingly odd to find, so early as in the third generation from the time that we put an absolute exclusion, as we thought, upon Toryism from the government of these realms, Toryism now again making its way upon us in open publications, countenanced even by an administration. This is indeed exceedingly grievous to all honest men; because, if government approves it, it teaches others the worst lesson against itself; as it insinuates, by a most odious implication, an injury done to those, who lost the Crown of England for their Tory principles.

If it should be found further, that the writer of the pamphlet abovementioned is so much distinguished by the immediate notice of government as to be *pensioned*; the remark I have just made will require other and stronger terms to be given to it, before it will adequately express my feelings. Fame strongly confirms this circumstance; and fixes that production on an eminent lexicographer, who has, on former occasions, drawn his pen to gloss over the bad measures of this very administration, and to save them, when gasping for life. If we may judge indeed from the internal marks of style and diction, I know not any writer to whom we should be more apt to ascribe so *operose a deduction*, than to that same person, whose very *operose* pen hath consummated more works of *operosity*, than that perhaps of any man existing; and now (if this same be true) is more *operose* than ever, having the defence of a minister added to its other *operosities* – the vindication of dark and difficult Machiavellian politics superadded to, perhaps superseding, the plain and pleasurable pursuit of science and the muses. Yet, notwithstanding these appearances, I can hardly concur in fixing this production on that gentleman: Because, on one hand, though he is pensioned, I have no doubt he would never convict himself out of his own mouth, nor invite the obloquy of the world, by becoming so very a pensioner, or (in his own words) so very *a slave of state,* as to be *hired by* his *stipend to obey his master* in all things: And yet, having once passed that definition, he must (if this production be his) inevitably have damned his own definition, or have damned himself for a slave. On another hand, when I consider with what singular virulence that gentleman has, all his life-long, written of the *Revolution* and the *House of Hanover*; I can as little believe that he would undertake the vindication of a minister in these days, as that a minister should employ him- reversing what rulers have ever shewn (I will not be so harsh as to say here to *traitors*, but) to *deserters*, and the *half-converted* of every kind, by *loving* and *trusting* the *deserter*, however they might *love* the *desertion*.

What effect the pamphlet hath had upon the public, I know not. But if it hath operated upon others, as it hath done upon myself, it must have rivetted all who have read it in an unalterable conviction, that America is unjustly dealt with. I understand however, that a great man in office hath thought proper to become the herald of its merits. He said there was *an abundance of wit* in it. Whether there be this or not, every one will judge for himself. But if there be no *argument*, or very little of it, I cannot see what all its *wit* can be worth. In my judgement, *wit* has no sort of business in the present question, nor can be employed in it, without bespeaking those who employ it to be, even in their own consciousness, on the worst side. I grant however, on recollection, that people may be *outwitted* of their *property*: and when that property cannot be otherwise fairly obtained, I know of no other mean but *wit*, by which it can be come at. I am one of the first to believe, that if the property of the Americans is wrested from them by British Taxation, it must be by *outwitting* them. In this view, therefore, I wonder not at all that the *wit* of that pamphlet should be so well spoken of. For if *that* be the ministerial battery against the property of the Americans, perhaps he that proclaimed the *wit*, and he that wrote it, may be equally dexterous in playing it off.

Whatever figure this gentleman may make in *wit*, he makes, I will venture to say, a very poor one in *argument*. If he be that Colossus of knowledge above hinted at, never could he have let himself down lower. Not even, when he attempted to palliate the wretched timidity, which sacrificed to our enemies the Falkland Islands and the honour of this nation together, was he more unfortunate, than when he vindicates the present blustering despotic measures against our fellow-subjects in America. But, in candor, I cannot lay the blame on the writer, but on his cause. *There is no making bricks without straw. Ex nihilo nihil fit.* Not all the wit, nor all the industry of man, not all the learning of *Johnson*, can strike abundance out of that which is barren, reason out of that which is absurd, nor make palpable wrong appear to be right. Accordingly, the writer of that pamphlet, whoever he is, hath left the ministerial cause very lamely defended. Whoever looks for argument from him, must be disappointed: Whoever is convinced by him, must be previously determined to be so convinced. No subject can be more loosely treated. There is an evident shyness in him at coming to the point. If ever he does so, he seems impatient in his situation, and eager to quit it. He dwells chiefly on the outlines of his subject, where his observations are seldom pertinent, oftner bold than exact. He seems to promise himself more from plausibility than truth; and to make invective, of which he is ever exceedingly profuse, supply the place of argument. Thus, notwithstanding the high-sounding title he has given to his book, we found it not in any degree proved: After all the expectations we were bid to form from that, and the name given to the writer, what has he told us? but that *the mountain labour'd, and brought forth a mouse.*

I might therefore comprise in very few pages what might be sufficient answer to all those parts of his book, which come at all close to the point. But as the most straggling thoughts, when they are supposed to come from able writers, are apt to have an influence on many, beyond their specific moment in the question; and as the ministerial party are rather industrious to puff that performance; I shall investigate it from the beginning to the end: Observing this, once for all, that where I find our author dealing in generals, and in detached arguments, I shall always bring them to their proper test in the main question; that being, as I conceive, the only way to know, in this or any other controversy, whether we advance towards the truth of it, or stand still; whether they who engage in it, throw any light upon it, or only intend to mislead us.

Our author sets out with a position, which he would have us to consider as an axiom. And it is right at all times to build upon a foundation. But then we must see that the foundation be a sure one; else, what we lay upon it will tumble upon our heads. Now this position, when it is to bear the weight of American taxation, happens to be a weak one; yet it is sophistical. Let us hear what it is.

The supreme power of every community has the right of requiring from all its subjects such contributions as are necessary to the public safety, or public prosperity.

I can have no objection to this position, where all the parts of a community are upon an equal footing, as to all the great advantages of society, and especially as to all the means of property, the source of contributions. If any particular parts of the community lie under any restraints in any of these circumstances more than others, then it evidently loosens the frame of the position; at least, it inevitably introduces an inequality in the contribution, proportioned to the inequality of their conditions. In order therefore to see what degree of decision this position can have in the present question, we must bring it to the touchstone of American circumstances.

In this view, the Americans immediately appear to us under very considerable restraints, not felt by the rest of the community, as to that which is now the greatest mean of property, and the most copious source of contribution, at least in the British empire – their trade and commerce. Tied down by the act of navigation, they can convey the produce of their own country to no other markets but those of the parent-state; nor can they supply themselves with what they want from other countries, but thro' this. Thus the advantages of their commerce are reduced to them, in proportion to the advanced terms on which they receive commodities from us, beyond what they could have them from others; which in most instances is not less that Ten Pounds per cent; while, on the other hand, those advantages are engrossed by their fellow-subjects in Britain, and absolutely taken out of their pockets: The manufacturer and merchant, enriching themselves, derive also supports to the nation, from sources shut up to the others: The land-holder, sharing in the local felicity, finds his lands from day to day swelling in their value: And both the labors of the one and the produce of the other, may be transmitted, without restraint, to any part of the world.

Now this, in my opinion, breaks in upon the terms of the above position very materially; and introduces a consideration, which renders those terms not sufficiently specific to be applied even as a medium for the decision of the main question. If an inequality in the participation of national advantages may fitly create an inequality in the national contributions; this certainly greatly reduces the original question itself. For by our authors own confession, page 14, *The Americans do not refuse to contribute at all to the exigences, whatever they may be, of the British empire*. And it also answers, for the present, the representation on which the minister some little time ago dwelt so strongly in the House of Commons, that "the people in America contribute to the exigences of Great Britain but as six-pence to every twenty-five shillings contributed by the people of England."

Comparing what our author hath said, in the place last quoted, with the terms of his position above, the observation we have just made on the proportionable measure of national contributions will appear the more seasonable and necessary; as it is obvious that he had in contemplation an equality of contribution, or something like it, from the several parts of a community. But as I will suppose that idea rather inconvenient to him by this time, I will imagine that he meant in his position only to lay a foundation for requiring from the Americans *some proper contributions.* We will therefore go on to apply his position, in this view, to the case of America; and enquire what complaints she is open to, on either of the two main grounds of obligation, suggested by the position, *viz.* the *public safety* and the *public prosperity* of the community. For if no just complaint can be made against her on those grounds, I see no use nor sense in the position, nor in the pamphlet itself.

How then is the fact? Did not America contribute to the *public safety,* in the last war, so largely, that parliament even refunded to her what she had advanced beyond her ability? And Governor Barnard himself declared, so late as the year 1765, that some years must pass, before even the forwardest of the provinces, with raising very large sums annually, could be able to discharge the debts they had contracted in the public defence. And in the more equal times of peace, I must again quote our author for the proof, that the *Americans do not refuse their contributions to the exigencies, whatever they may be, of the British Empire.*

Contributing then to the *public safety,* they must of course contribute to the *public prosperity* of the community. Yet, here I must beg a word; as the latter term, however proper in the general use of the position, becomes more fallacious than just, when it is applied as a ground to vindicate the present ministerial system of American taxation. It is indeed the colour, which is borrowed to tinge all the ministerial measures: it is the pretended sanction under which they are formed: it is the very catch-word for taxing the Americans: they must contribute to the *prosperity* of the community.

But is it then for the *prosperity* of the community, that they should maintain shoals of Excise and Custom-house officers? Is it for the *prosperity* of the community, that they should be taxed to establish other place-men and pensioners among themselves, or to multiply them among us? Is it for the *prosperity* of the community, that they should raise a revenue for corrupting more of the representatives of the people, making prerogative invincible, and establishing despotism here as well as in *Canada*? I would not be invidious, and the less so when I speak to the minister, who personally deserves well of all men. But let him say, how it comes to pass, that the finances of the government, now far greater than ever, leave the civil-lift more sunk in debt than ever; or, let his creatures forbear to tell us, that the Americans are to be taxed for the *prosperity* of the community.

Index

For Product Safety Concerns and Information please contact our EU
representative GPSR@taylorandfrancis.com Taylor & Francis Verlag GmbH,
Kaufingerstraße 24, 80331 München, Germany

Batch number: 08158389

Printed by Printforce, the Netherlands